## More Praise for *Total Integrated Marketing*

"Focusing on value creation rather than activity management, the book offers a clear mandate, a framework, and implementation tools for addressing modern marketing's critical shortcomings—ways of thinking that are foreign to most companies. Reminding us of often-overlooked strategic basics and dispelling marketing myths, the authors present specific, practical, proven alternatives to the disjointed 'silo-based' approaches. This book should be required reading for all managers."

> —Jerome Jewell
> President, Jewell Consulting Group

"Makes the best case yet for the demise of the dreaded 'Marketing Department' in today's competitive and information-intensive environment. As the authors argue forcefully and persuasively, the most successful firms integrate marketing with other aspects of the business. If you want to be a better practicing manager for the 21st century, with interdisciplinary, interfunctional marketing strategies, this is the book for you."

> —Russ Winer
> J. Gary Shansby Professor of Marketing Strategy,
> Haas School of Business, University of California at Berkeley

"Translates marketing gospel—focus on the customer—into practical steps that every organization can and should take to create organization-wide market-winning awareness, concern, and action."

> —Jefferson Freeman
> Partner, Vantage Point Associates LLC

"By linking economic forces and organizational objectives to marketing, the authors provide an outstanding systemic approach to the many facets of marketing in an engaging and easy-to-understand manuscript. The book is as much for the CEO and management of today's organizations as for their marketing departments. What's more, there is a moral to this book. I only wish that it had come out three years earlier, as it may have saved many an organization from forgetting its raison d'être."

> —Jon Peters
> President, Institute for Management Studies

"This is a must-read book for anyone responsible for their organizational survival and growth and enhancing shareholder value. *Total Integrated Marketing* gets at the essence of what it is all about. Hulbert, Capon, and Piercy are right on the mark."

> —Raymond B. White
> CEO, Watson Institute

Also by Noel Capon and James M. Hulbert:
*Marketing Management in the 21st Century*

Also by James M. Hulbert:
*Marketing: A Strategic Perspective*

Also by Noel Capon:
*Key Account Management and Planning*

Also by Nigel F. Piercy:
*Market-Led Strategic Change*
*Tales from the Marketplace*

# total
# integrated
# marketing

## breaking the bounds
## of the function

**James Mac Hulbert**

**Noel Capon**

**Nigel F Piercy**

**KOGAN
PAGE**

London and Sterling, VA

First published in the United States in 2003 by Free Press
A division of Simon & Schuster, Inc.,
1230 Avenue of the Americas,
New York, NY 10020,
U.S.A.

First published in Great Britain in 2003

Kogan Page Limited
120 Pentonville Road
London  N1 9JN
United Kingdom

www.kogan-page.co.uk

**British Library Cataloguing in Publication Data**

A CIP record for this book is available from the British Library.

ISBN 0 7494 4018 X

Printed and bound in Great Britain by Biddles Ltd, Guildford and King's Lynn
*www.biddles.co.uk*

To Patricia and Patrick Colagiuri
whose generosity has supported the R. C. Kopf Chair and
Fellowships that have permitted so many outstanding students
to benefit from a Columbia Business School education.

—Mac Hulbert and Noel Capon

To the memory of my mother, Helena G. Piercy (1911–2001).

—Nigel Piercy

# CONTENTS

# PREFACE

As we go to press with this book, the business world is roiled with concerns over inflated earnings and other accounting irregularities, creating the most turbulent capital markets we have seen in many years. It is, perhaps, worth reminding ourselves that a commitment to creating shareholder value should not translate into a desire to manipulate earnings by devious means, nor, indeed, misguided raids on the company pension plan. Some very genuine attempts to better align the interests of managers and shareholders have foundered on the rocks of avarice and greed. Yet, on a more optimistic note, we are convinced that the resulting investigations will rid us of the worst of these practices, and, with any luck, lead senior executives to get back to the basics of building enduring value, which is what this book is all about.

It is self-evident that the environment faced by companies today is becoming ever more turbulent and complex, and, in an increasingly networked world, traditional boundaries have become meaningless. In the face of these challenges, a narrow view of the marketing function can cause severe problems. Yet, so often, a limiting perspective is actually encouraged and rewarded by higher levels in the organization. Overwhelmed by the turbulence of their markets and an endless flow of consultants' ideas on how they should change, it is not surprising that managers sometimes lose sight of the customer imperative. Collectively, we have spent many years studying the practice of marketing, and we remain committed to the importance of marketing for the well being of the organization. But we have frequently been distressed and dismayed by the way in which marketing is practiced.

Despite the firm's commitment to shareholders and other stakeholders, it remains as true as ever that without customers there are no revenues and therefore there is no business. After all, the basic sources of corporate cash flow are customers and investors and, as the dot-coms discovered, even investors eventually want returns based on cash flows from customers! As many have discovered the hard way, there remains much truth in the old comment that "profit is a matter of accounting opinion—only cash is real." This simple yet essential message has been ignored far far too often.

In this book, we seek to redress this imbalance. We want to convince you that the only way to achieve competitive success in the twenty-first century is to orchestrate the entire set of firm capabilities into a seamless system designed to deliver exemplary satisfaction, if not delight, to customers. Those who create superior customer value, will build superior shareholder value.

As a marketing executive, you have to look in two directions: (1) You must focus externally—you must undertake information-gathering and analysis on customers, competitors, and the environment in general. Out of this data-filled complexity, you must forge market strategies and design implementation plans. This is the classic view of marketing that hopefully, over the years, is being increasingly adopted by corporations. (2) You must also focus internally. As a marketing executive, you must reach across internal organizational boundaries to ensure that your colleagues in sales, customer service, human resources, finance and accounting, operations and research and development are as involved with, and as committed to, the market strategy as you are.

If your organization is defined by functional silos, it will never be able to rally and place the full set of firm resources in support of that strategy. Increasingly, those same integration skills will be essential to reach out across conventional organizational boundaries to work with partner organizations in the supply chain. Ensuring a seamless offer to customers will be vital in the years ahead.

Embracing the responsibility to ensure that the totality of organizational resources are committed to satisfying and delighting customers, and defeating competitors, is what we call *Total Integrated Marketing*. In an era of total competition, commitment to customers must also be total; that is why Total Integrated Marketing is such a critical value for long-run organizational survival and growth, and enhancing shareholder value.[1]

# ACKNOWLEDGMENTS

Our approach has been shaped by working with many companies and management students in different countries, who are too numerous to mention individually by name. Nonetheless, we are grateful to them for what they have helped us learn about the reality of marketing, and the imperative for Total Integrated Marketing.

So many people have generously contributed their efforts and insights to this book that we apologize in advance for any we have forgotten. However, for his sustained support for our efforts, despite missed deadlines, we owe a great deal to our editor at the Free Press, Bob Wallace. The editorial support of Ron Roth was likewise helpful in untangling our sometimes dense prose, while secretarial and administrative support was given unstintingly by our wonderful Columbia team of Roy, Dorothy, Dante, and Blanche, and by Hayley Tedder at Cranfield.

We also want to thank our many colleagues, expert in their individual fields, who have lent their time in reviewing our interface chapters. These include Martin Christopher, Mike Fenlon, Atul Nerkar, Niall C. Piercy, Norman Toy, and Paul Zipkin. Some of our friends and colleagues were even kind enough to read the entire manuscript prior to publication, and for this we owe our thanks to Tim Ambler, Dean Butler, Sir C. K. Chow, Jeff Freeman, Jerry Jewell, Alan Kane, Simon Knox, Malcolm McDonald, Lynette Ryals, Nigel Stapleton, Ray White, and Russ Winer.

We have also been fortunate enough to have been mentored by some of the all time greats of Marketing, and notable among these are the late Abraham Shuchman and John Howard. Their seminal thinking on marketing has greatly influenced the development of our ideas. We also want to acknowledge those of our contemporaries as marketing academics whose work has helped us clarify our thinking. The ideas of colleagues such as Pierre Berthon, David W. Cravens, Peter Doyle, Peter Fitzroy, and Dan Jones have at various stages provided valuable insights into our task.

Finally, we wish to express our gratitude to our wives and families, without whom none of us would be able to continue our work. To Madge, Deanna, Nikala, and our loving children, we thank you for all you have given us.

# CHAPTER 1

# WHY TOTAL INTEGRATED MARKETING?

Marketing has lost its way! In country after country, senior executives have become obsessed with making their companies more customer-focused, market-focused, outward-oriented, or some permutation of those qualities—often to no avail. Companies cannot win in today's competitive markets by delegating marketing problems to a department. Success in the new marketplace demands integration of the firm's entire set of capabilities into a seamless system with the goal of exemplary customer satisfaction. In an era of total competition, commitment to customers must also be total—hence, the title of our book. We want you to rethink your company's entire approach to the marketplace. Nothing less will ensure your success in the markets of tomorrow.

Why do some companies drive home solid shareholder value over the long haul, while others struggle and fade away, even though their short-term performance was like a shooting star? Why are those same winning companies renowned throughout their markets for delivering superior customer value, while their competitors are just average? Is it merely coincidence, or is there more to it? How can some organizations get their act together around the things that matter most to their shareholders and their customers, while others fight internal battles, obsess over trivia, and let opportunities pass them by?

In this book, we search out some of the answers to these questions. One conclusion we have reached is that winning companies everywhere share an incredibly simple characteristic. They are the ones that really do get their act together around the things that matter most to their customers—they make a totally integrated offer of value. Their less successful competitors

1

cling to the models of the past with top-heavy bureaucracies, and their managers still believe that their functional specialization matters more than customer value.

This book about creating Total Integrated Marketing is a response to the problems of marketing in an era of revolution. The prospect is for more fundamental, dramatic changes than we have yet experienced or can even imagine. The information revolution has already transformed global competition: What happens in one part of the world reverberates in many others. The search for competitive advantage through innovative products, services, and methods; lower costs of production and distribution; and new organizational forms and relationships is unremitting. Under such conditions, the need for better marketing is overwhelming. But what is "better" marketing? Is it more advertising, brand proliferation, bigger marketing bureaucracies, slicker Web sites, or something much more basic and infinitely more powerful?

## WHY MARKETING?

This is a simple but critical question because many firms still consider marketing to be overhead. We have heard this question more than once! After plugging the marketing message for half a century, is there really any steam left in marketing? Is there anything left to say? Perhaps surprisingly, there is. Perhaps even more surprisingly, the reason is that many of us have missed the whole point of marketing.

The profound structural changes that characterize the world economy mandate the search for sustained marketing superiority. The economic success of many countries in the latter part of the twentieth century has driven many economies from scarcity of supply to scarcity of demand. Whereas low-level economies limit the scope of competition for the consumer dollar, rising affluence expands discretionary purchases dramatically, and it becomes correspondingly more challenging to induce consumers to buy any specific product. Choosing between a new computer and a European vacation may seem an absurd notion, but in high-level economies such choices between sectors are a reality for many consumers. As competition among sellers becomes intense, a focus on the customer moves from desirable to absolutely essential. It is as simple as that. The customer is inexorably taking center stage in the organization of business activities—witness the numerous articles in the business press about customer-based reorganizations.[1] Marketing is, above all else, preoccupied with customers. The need for better marketing is clear. This may be a self-evident message, but many companies appear not to have heard it or understood it.

## Marketing and the Profit Motive

When we work with executives, we sometimes ask them: "What are you in business for?" After the initial silence—and occasional wry comments and groans that greet such a basic question (surely we had figured that out, and couldn't we get onto more complex matters!)—the responses typically center around profit and profitability. Leaving aside the problems of profit measurement and time horizon that often bedevil the translation of this goal into reality, the almost universal focus on profit raises two critical issues. First, why is securing profits important, and second, what is the basic prerequisite for earning profits?

People's reasons for securing profits vary depending on who is answering the question: owner/managers, independent shareholders, or nonowner managers. For managers who own little or no stock in the company, the ultimate organizational goals are typically growth and survival as an independent entity.[2] Organizational survival enhances the manager's own likelihood of economic well-being, while growth may increase chances of the firm's survival and provide opportunities for career advancement. Independent shareholders are most likely to be concerned with the production of economic value—after all, economic value enhances shareholder wealth. In the near term, however, for both independent shareholders and owner/managers, organizational survival may be the critical objective. Certainly, for the more than 100,000 business entities (mostly owner/managed) that fail each year in the United States, and the many more that fail around the world, survival must be assured before shareholder value creation becomes a meaningful objective.

Economic value and organizational survival versus growth can create a serious conflict for owner/managers who believe that they can secure greater value if the firm ceases to operate as an independent entity. Allowing the firm to be acquired may produce greater immediate value than continued independent operations over the long run.[3] This conflict between corporate managers and shareholders is often starkly played out when contemplating hostile bids. Managers are inclined to value independence, whereas shareholders favor immediate value production.[4] Since in capitalist systems, owners' rights are generally regarded as secondary only to debtholders among the various stakeholders, the owners usually prevail.

## What about Shareholder Value?

Creating value for shareholders has become a corporate mantra in the past few years. It is a key requirement for firms capitalized in competitive financial markets, such as New York or London. These markets are remorselessly competitive—for capital is the ultimate fungible resource, flowing at the touch of a button from one instrument and even one country to another. Managers facing competitive pressures in product markets sometimes forget that unless the firm's financial performance remains competitive, its survival will be in jeopardy.

Good profit levels on an ongoing basis increase the chances of the firm surviving over the long term. This, however, ignores a more basic question: What is the prerequisite for making profits? What must be done to produce the profits that will enhance prospects of survival and growth? What key assets must an organization possess to generate profits on an ongoing basis? To answer these questions, we must switch our attention from capital markets to product markets.

The most obvious place to search for these critical assets is on the firm's balance sheet: cash; accounts receivable; inventory; land, plant, and equipment; and so forth. Although each of these assets may help to produce profits, frequently the asset itself is not essential. Accounts receivable are of little value if the customer cannot pay; nor inventory (finished goods, raw materials, work in process) if there is no market for the products; nor plant and equipment for making these unwanted products. In fact, the situation may be more serious. If a firm with a significant investment in plant and equipment to make products for a particular market experiences a sudden shift in demand, balance sheet assets may turn into strategic liabilities. Management may be best advised to write off its "investment" immediately and address some new opportunity. Too often, however, the prior investment binds the firm to its historic strategy and slows its market response. By contrast, a new entrant, with no such asset baggage may be able to move faster and secure significant advantage over its better established but slower moving rival.

## THE COST OF CARRYING EXCESS HISTORICAL BAGGAGE

In the 1980s, IBM consistently underfunded its commitment to personal computers, preferring to place its major efforts on mainframes—its traditional stronghold. This strategic decision not only resulted in Microsoft securing a stranglehold on operating system software, but also allowed the extensive growth of such PC start-ups as Dell, Compaq, Gateway, and Packard Bell. By contrast, shortly after Netscape's entry into Internet browser software, Bill Gates executed a strategic U-turn, and Microsoft wrote off a $100 million investment in software development as it sought to catch up and surpass Netscape. According to Microsoft executives, the change was instantaneous and worldwide. Stop what you're working on and start on this! No one bats 100 percent, not even Bill Gates, but some firms are flexible enough to change quickly and some are not.

## Customers as Assets

If you are even partway serious about Total Integrated Marketing, you have to take the view that the only asset the firm really needs over the long run is paying customers. Customers are the sole source of sales revenues—all firm activities are costs. Whatever traditional accountants may think, it is the ability of accounting "assets" to contribute to revenue generation that makes them assets, not their historical acquisition cost (less cumulative depreciation, etc.). If the firm has customers, it has revenues, and if revenues exceed costs, it makes a profit. The presence of customers uniquely allows the firm to secure whatever operating assets it requires to produce goods and services. If the firm has customers—or even good prospects of getting them in the future—it can obtain the capital, real estate, data processing equipment, and people to produce (or secure by outsourcing), finance, and deliver the goods and services. From this perspective, customers are a necessary condition for the production of profit, and are therefore the most important asset we can identify.

Securing and retaining customers is not only a necessary condition for making profits, but also a critical element for organizational survival and growth and, indeed, for creating economic value. The firm's value-creating potential, as measured by its market value, represents the firm's perceived ability to secure and retain customers over the long run, and this is the central job that management must accomplish. If it performs this job well, profits will result.[5] Hence, profits become not only a means of enhancing survival prospects, but also a measure of how well management is performing its most basic task. Profits provide the crucial link between performance in product markets and in capital markets. Using this logic, the difference between the firm's market value and the book value of its assets is a measure of marketing's value added.

Nevertheless, managers shouldn't make the common mistake of indiscriminately accepting everyone who wants to become a customer. Some customers may be too costly to maintain; others may fall outside the scope of the firm's mission; and others may not be able to pay. Better to select customers who can and will pay, than to spend money on sophisticated bad debt management! Careful selection of customers (targeting) is a key element in strategic marketing and a hallmark of firms that practice marketing well.

The individual firm is rarely alone in attempting to secure customers. Competitors seek the same customer assets, and each firm must continually struggle to target and retain the right customers while trying to ensure that competitors end up only with those it finds less desirable. Nor does our rationale mean that profits will necessarily result from attracting and retaining customers. If the costs of this activity are excessive (and intense competition is a factor that may make them so), there will be no economic profit. Although creating and re-creating customers is the key job the organization must accomplish, it is best viewed as a necessary, but not sufficient condition, to achieve profits and survive.

## IF CUSTOMER ACQUISITION COSTS EXCEED CUSTOMER LIFETIME VALUE . . .

A lesson we learned in the catastrophic dot-com crashes of the early 2000s is that even for an Internet-based enterprise, some of the basic rules still apply. One such rule is that if the costs of acquiring and retaining a customer are greater than the lifetime value of the customer in question, it is by definition impossible to make a profit. In Europe, for the sensational launch of the state-of-the-art fashion e-tailer Boo.com, crippling marketing and advertising costs in excess of $50 million attracted customers who simply did not spend enough. The spectacular crash of the $100 million company occurred within two years of start-up.

Our case for "Why Marketing?" is twofold. First, most of us operate in a world where customers are not forced to purchase, but choose to purchase. This fundamental change from a seller's market to a buyer's market

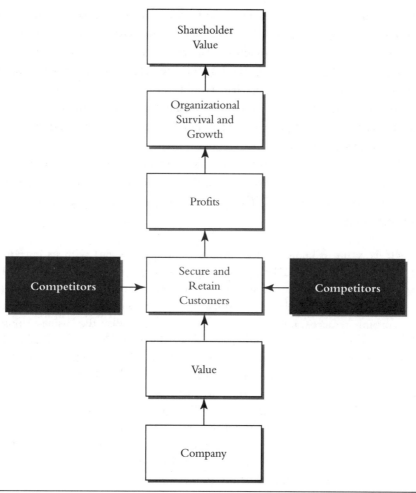

Figure 1.1   VALUE CREATION FOR CUSTOMERS AND SHAREHOLDERS

puts the customer in command and makes a customer focus essential. Second, securing and retaining customers is the activity or process that constitutes the central job description for the firm, both for managers and its employees. The key relationships are summarized in Figure 1.1.

## HOW DID MARKETING LOSE ITS WAY?

When you look around, you have to conclude that marketing has got itself into a bit of a mess. Many companies are thoroughly confused about marketing and think it is synonymous with advertising or promotional tactics such as offering frequent flyer miles along with purchases. For others, marketing is simply providing support materials for the sales force (or people believe that marketing is sales and vice versa). In recent years, some companies even seem to have had trouble distinguishing marketing and customer service. We take a hard line on the definition of marketing. Advertising, sales, and customer service may be a part of marketing but they can never be the whole.

To understand how marketing lost its way requires going back to its origins, as envisaged by the progenitor of the modern concept of marketing—Peter Drucker. In his book *The Practice of Management*, nearly 50 years ago, he opined:

[I]f we want to know what a business is we have to start with its purpose. There is only one valid definition of business purpose: to create a customer. It is the customer who determines what a business is. For it is the customer, and he alone, who through being willing to pay for a good or service, converts economic resources into wealth, things into goods. What the business thinks it produces is not of first importance—especially not to the future of the business and its success. What the customer thinks he is buying, what he considers "value" is decisive. . . . Because it is its purpose to create a customer, any business enterprise has two—and only these two—basic functions: marketing and innovation. . . . Marketing is the distinguishing, the unique function of the business. . . . Marketing is not only much broader than selling, it is not a specialized activity at all. It is the whole business seen from the point of view of the final result, that is from the customer's point of view. *Concern and responsibility for marketing must therefore permeate all areas of the enterprise.*[6] [Emphasis added.]

The only true role of marketing is as a guiding corporate philosophy for the business as a whole. This original conception of marketing has been neglected for many years.[7] In the late 1950s and early 1960s, however, marketing was the "hot idea" that engaged the imagination of senior executives, and consulting firms "marketed" the new approach enthusiastically. In 1961, Columbia Business School launched what was to become the most successful executive program in marketing management in the world. Only nineteen people came to the inaugural offering, but they were virtually all division or company presidents. The response of these and other senior executives to the exciting new marketing concept was to conclude that their companies needed it, and they did what senior executives typically do in this situation, they delegated . . . found somebody to "do" marketing for them.[8] This attitude changed the marketing concept—conceived as a philosophy for the business as a whole—into functional departments, often led by a person from sales or a recruit from an advertising agency.

The competitive conditions prevailing at that time meant that in many markets there was still a relative shortage of capacity, and the customer was far from being king. Shortly before he retired, a senior executive at Exxon remarked to one of the authors, "In those days, we made what we wanted to make and they lined up to buy it." This is a far cry from the competitive conditions that prevail in most major markets today. Through the 1960s and 1970s, functionalized marketing was an adequate organizational response to the conditions faced by many firms. This is no longer the case. The function that evolved because of marketplace change has instead become its victim.[9]

Whether your firm treats marketing as a philosophy or (as is more common) a departmental activity, there will undoubtedly be a set of activities that people with a marketing or product management title customarily perform (though people with general management or even sales titles sometimes handle these responsibilities). In the company's view, these tasks are what marketing is all about. It is essential, however, to view the marketing function in the broader context of a marketing philosophy. The way that marketing activities must be conducted today is radically different from the way they have historically been performed and demands a much higher degree of skill. These skills are not limited to mere technical excellence in classical modern marketing, but encompass reaching out across the boundaries that have traditionally existed within and around the organization. How else will you be able to draw on all the resources and capabilities required to win marketplace rewards in a hypercompetitive world? Without these skills, the effort will be neither integrated nor will it embody the total commitment necessary to win. As Ron Dennis, chief executive of the McLaren-Mercedes Formula One team once put it, "To come in second means being the first of the losers."[10]

At its simplest, the biggest reason we advocate Total Integrated Marketing as a management approach for winners is that it is a road map for dragging marketing processes out of marketing departments and putting them back where they belong—in the center of the company. You cannot really be a specialist in a company-wide management philosophy. It is foolish even to try. Instead, Total Integrated Marketing reverse-engineers by starting with customer value and working back to see what must be improved to deliver better value than competitors can provide. Most times, the answer is not that a bigger, more powerful marketing department is needed—usually it will be about combining marketing processes with others to create a seamless offer of value to the customer. To be even more direct—if I am your customer, be assured I have no interest whatever in your departmental structures, your specialist functions, your planning systems, your coordination problems—I positively do not care about any of those things. I just want a better deal than the next guy offers, or I'll buy from the next guy.

Total Integrated Marketing encompasses marketing as a philosophy as well as a set of activities that have traditionally been performed in marketing departments. In an early incarnation, lodged firmly in the marketing department, the function essentially referred to managing the "marketing mix"—the implementation programs that the firm would develop for a particular market or market segment. Later, in the era of "strategic marketing," the choice of markets and market segments, and the manner in which the firm positioned its offering(s) in those markets and segments, became logical extensions. The coming era of Total Integrated Marketing must embrace both, but it also requires that we go much further—orienting the firm as a whole to the changing customer, competitor, and general environment, and capitalizing on all its capabilities regardless of function. Illustrative of this transition, two McKinsey consultants, in discussing the changes taking place at Kraft, described the issues that the company had to face:

> The sources of customer value were no longer just marketing-based. The entire organization, from R&D to marketing, to packaging, to manufacturing and distribution, to field the sales representatives working the customers, was essential to identifying and delivering value to consumers.[11]

But to successfully orient the firm as a whole, and to achieve a high degree of interfunctional cooperation, senior corporate management must play a major leadership role. As a Kraft executive put it: ". . . no-one below the CEO possesses an integrative consumer perspective. No-one provides cross-functional leadership and no-one is fully accountable for anticipating consumer needs and responding quickly and effectively."[12]

If the entire organization is to develop an external focus, senior management leadership is vital. Senior managers must take responsibility for the organizational changes necessary to facilitate Total Integrated Marketing. Functional marketers, unlike quality advocates, have proven to be ineffective advocates of change; they lack the organizational engineering skills necessary to accomplish the task. To survive and win the competitive battle in the twenty-first century, Total Integrated Marketing must be the watchword.

## WHAT IS TOTAL INTEGRATED MARKETING?

Taking Total Integrated Marketing seriously is no small undertaking. In this book, we look at the task in three ways. First, in Chapters 2 through 5, we build a case that the marketing process provides the most powerful mechanism for real integration. We also lay down a framework for understanding and explaining the critical core elements of the strategic marketing process as well as the essential top management role of stewardship.

Second, in Chapters 6 through 11, we develop a framework for assessing the most critical interfaces for marketing processes: finance/accounting; operations; sales; research and development; customer service; and human resources. In each case, we examine the strategic and operational aspects of these relationships and provide a perspective for identifying conflicts to manage and collaborative opportunities to exploit. The overarching objectives are to build productive connectivity among specialists and to lay down the foundation for a corporate community focused on customer value.

Finally, we bring things together in Chapter 12 with an agenda for making Total Integrated Marketing a way of life in your company, emphasizing the implementation tools that you can use to achieve effective execution.

Our goal is to provide you with a framework for designing and managing change that will deliver superior shareholder value by outperforming your rivals in building customer value. That framework is Total Integrated Marketing.

# WOW! WHAT WAS THAT?

## Marketing in Today's Environment Is at the Speed of Light

To make Total Integrated Marketing work, you must abandon some of your strongest assumptions about marketing. The information revolution, still no more than a few years old, has brought unprecedented change, with a quantum leap in customer sophistication around the world. In the fierce competitive environments of the twenty-first century, globalization has affected how people and organizations buy, what they buy, how they experience their purchases, and how they live.

As corporations have attempted to cope with these changes, management pundits and stock-market analysts have been generous with their advice: Make some acquisitions, negotiate a merger, divest some businesses, pull out of some markets, put greater investment into other markets, outsource some operations. And, when workers are laid off—huge applause. In many cases, the value of such advice to companies is pretty much what they paid for it![1] We prefer the wisdom of Peter Drucker:

A company beset by malaise and steady deterioration suffers from something far more serious than inefficiencies. Its "business theory" has become obsolete.[2]

Maybe your company has so far avoided "malaise and steady deterioration" but many others have not. Instead, your bugbear may be the "fatal arrogance of success"—the danger that your company's worst moment of vulnerability occurs when short-term profits, market share, and stock values all look great, because that is when you get smug and complacent. One thing is certain for all corporations. The once-popular watchwords,"That's the way we do things around here" and "It's not broke, so why should we fix it?" have largely dropped off the agenda. The changes we face are so dramatic that companies must adopt new approaches if they are to stand any chance of coping with these enormous upheavals.

## THE LETHAL LEGACY OF THE TWENTIETH CENTURY

For much of the present generation's working lives, product standardization and the improved economics of volume production offered large market opportunities for producers. After World War II, reconstruction needs and relative supply scarcity brought enormous economic rewards. In that golden era, producers called the shots and it was almost difficult not to make money. In recent years, however, markets have matured, and emerging overcapacity has shifted market power decisively from suppliers to buyers. As economies have developed and competition has increased, buyers have enjoyed more choices. To address the shift from sellers' markets to buyers' markets, many companies took what they believed to be the ideals of the marketing concept to heart and became sophisticated practitioners of functional marketing.[3]

Now in the twenty-first century, customers are becoming demanding and divergent in their preferences to a degree that is almost bewildering to those steeped in traditional functional marketing principles.[4] As producers attempt to respond, they often proliferate product lines excessively and become locked in price and promotion battles with rivals. Consolidation of intermediaries has given distributors and retailers greater power, and sometimes manufacturers feel obliged to increase their own channel power through acquisition.[5] In addition to these pressures, companies are exhorted not only to be customer-responsive, but to address the broader needs of a variety of stakeholders.

All too often, the strategic moves of even leading firms do not represent acceptable long-term solutions. Instead, they just dissipate shareholder value through excessive downsizing, ill-considered acquisitions, deep cuts in brand portfolios, and overreliance on core competence, or "sticking to the knitting" (when rapid change is making those competencies obsolete d the knitting is fast unraveling).

However, the critical environmental forces of the late twentieth century that led to these actions are not going to disappear—far from it. Firms will continue to be beset by the traditional "five forces": rivalry from close competitors, the threat of new direct entrants, indirect competitors, pressures from suppliers, and pressures from buyers.[6] In addition, they will be subject to other external stresses related to economic changes, government action, sociocultural changes, technological upheavals, and terrorist threats. Yet probably the biggest difference will be in the impact of the information economy, which overarches many of the traditional forces.

Managing in the face of these critical environmental forces is not going to get easier. At any point in time, every company will need to address one or another critical imperative—perhaps the arrival of a new direct entrant, perhaps pressure from a powerful supplier, perhaps a change in sociocultural mores, or perhaps a downturn in the economy. But in the years ahead, the source of economic power will change from relative scale and supply shortages to something new and pervasive—information. The information paradigm describes an era where information quantity, quality, and accessibility explode. The information era is new and different from anything in the past. And we are only just starting to understand what it means for marketing. Do not be taken in by the disillusionment surrounding the crash of so many dot-coms; we are still in the earliest stages of the information revolution.

## MARKETING IN THE INFORMATION ERA: HOW THE RULES HAVE CHANGED

In the information era, many basic rules of competition have changed. Whereas the traditional five forces may have sufficed for the predominantly industrial era, the following five forces that will shape competition in the information economy are startlingly different in both their formulation and implications. [7]

### Moore's Law

In 1965, Gordon Moore, an engineer at Fairchild Semiconductor, noted that the number of transistors on a computer chip doubled every 18 to 24 months. This insight has become known as "Moore's Law," and the corollary is that the speed of microprocessors, at a constant cost, also doubles every 18 to 24 months. Moore's Law has held up for more than 30 years. It worked in 1969 when Moore's start-up, Intel, put its first processor chip—the 4-bit, 104-KHz 4004—into a Japanese calculator. It still works today for Intel's 32-bit, 450-MHz Pentium II processor—7.5 million transistors, 233,000 times faster. Intel predicts that a 1 billion-transistor powerhouse performing at 100,000 mips will be on the market in 2011.[8] For users, it's been a fast, fun ride. But can it last? Observers have been saying for decades that exponential gains in chip performance would slow in a few years, but experts generally agree that Moore's Law will govern the industry for at least another 10 years.

The most critical implication of Moore's Law is that as computing power becomes ever faster and cheaper, just about everyone in advanced western societies and many more people around the world will have affordable access to powerful computing. Furthermore, computer power will be built into devices other than computers themselves. Already, products as diverse as motor vehicles, surgical equipment, and elevators use computer chips to operate more efficiently, predictably, and safely. As costs decline, computer chips may be used in such disposable products as packaging, and even in "smart" interactive clothing that incorporates all the wearer's needs for music and video, Internet access, cell-phone operation, and automatic adjustment to external climate change.

## Metcalfe's Law

How useful is a piece of technology? The answer generally depends on the number of users of the technology, and how easily they can be interconnected. The first organization with a facsimile machine had no one to fax to, and no one to receive faxes from! One telephone is useless, a few telephones have limited value, but one million telephones create a vast network.[9]

Robert Metcalfe, founder of 3COM Corporation and designer of the robust Ethernet protocol for computer networks, observed that new technologies are valuable only if many people use them. The function known as Metcalfe's Law states that the usefulness (utility) of the network equals the square of the number of users. The more people that use software, a network, a particular standard, a game, or a book, the more valuable it becomes. As the technology's value goes up, it attracts more new users, in turn increasing its utility and the speed of adoption by still more users.[10] The underlying power of Microsoft, which has consequently attracted unwelcome antitrust attention, is that its Windows operating system is ubiquitous across continents, industries, and user types. The cost to a computer user of not using Windows is substantial.[11]

The Internet is the best illustration of Metcalfe's Law. Although its origins lie in the 1960s, it has gained momentum only in recent years. As more users join the medium, it becomes more valuable to all the users, thus accelerating its growth. Now, its potential to spread new ideas, products, and services is awesome. The online auction house eBay was profitable from the beginning, but as the potential buyers grow in numbers, they bid up prices to the sellers' advantage. For buyers, value also increases since the greater the number of sellers, the more choices there are available. No wonder eBay has been so successful!

It may be difficult to believe, but some companies that should be capitalizing on the network idea seem to miss the point. When AT&T reintroduced the videophone in the mid-1990s, it didn't "get it"—the phone was marketed individually, rather than in pairs such as, for example, to parents with children in college, or professional spouses (partners) working in distant locations. On the other hand, Microsoft clearly gets it big time—it prices and promotes new software releases to get the fastest possible diffusion among users, while quickly recovering development costs. The famed release of Windows 95 was almost a global party, with customers lining up outside stores to obtain the product at the earliest possible moment.

## Coasian Economics

In 1937, Ronald Coase, later a Nobel Prize winner in economics, made a critical observation about market behavior when he introduced the notion of "transaction costs" including searching, contracting, and enforcing. Transaction costs are a result of market inefficiencies. These costs should be added to the price of a good or service when comparing market performance relative to the nonmarket behavior within firms.[12] Transaction cost economics is a way to explain those activities a firm chooses to perform for itself, and those it will purchase in the market. In particular, transaction cost economics offers a useful explanation for the outsourcing decisions that many firms now face. Always widespread in the chemical industry (toll manufacturing), outsourced production is now the norm in the computer, electronics, athletic footwear, and garment industries, and is fast penetrating the pharmaceutical and biotechnology industries.[13]

In the past, improvements in communications technology led to increases in firm size. This enabled vertical integration, and firms could operate as larger entities even across continents. Such multinational organizations as General Motors, Siemens, and Unilever were essentially managed from a head office. What is sometimes overlooked is that new technologies, accelerated by Moore's Law and Metcalfe's Law, also reduce transaction costs and improve market efficiency.

The point is that more efficient markets may reduce optimal firm size. We may already be witnessing the first signs of this change as large firms, under the mantra of shareholder value, are breaking up into smaller units. In 1999, both Ford and General Motors sundered relationships with their in-house parts suppliers, setting them free as Delphi and Visteon, respectively. The Hanson Trust in Britain and ITT in the United States have broken up; and AT&T, which spun off the Regional Bell Operating Companies (RBOCs) in the 1980s as well as NCR and what became Lucent in the 1990s, is once more breaking itself apart.

In a turn-of-the-century interview, Coase observed that it was unclear which organizational entity was better equipped to control electronic commerce. Lower transaction costs favor a market solution, but lower intra-firm coordination costs and the potential for economies of scale and scope seem to favor a hierarchical solution.[14]

## The Flock of Birds Phenomenon

A further distinguishing feature of new communication technologies in the twenty-first century is that, in many cases, they neither belong to any one institution, nor are they controlled by any particular authority. This observation has been referred to as the "flock of birds phenomenon."[15]

When we observe a flock of birds flying in formation (or a school of fish swimming in a distinct pattern), we may be tempted to ask whether there is a "bird in charge" (or "head fish") and indeed whether its compensation package is adequate for its CEO responsibilities! Yet, naturalists explain that flocking is a natural phenomenon and that there are in fact no birds in charge (or head fish). Leadership of the flock changes as the lead bird tires and another member, having benefited from the favorable aerodynamics created by the flock, takes over in the lead. Similarly, all antelopes have white patches on their backsides; any individual can lead the flight from danger because antelopes gauge distance from the white patch in front.[16] In terms of communication, the network has become the processor.

Most humans have been conditioned to accept a controlling body or authority for the phenomena that they experience. For any one of us, this authority may be a large firm, a government, or a ruling institution. However, for the Internet and the World Wide Web, no one is in charge. These new information technologies are great mechanisms for democracy, but they are also anarchic. Society may have to develop new ways to deal with these liberating effects though to date most attempts to sanction the Internet have largely failed. The archetypal illustration of the flock of birds is the advent of P2P (peer-to-peer) computing. Napster and its close cousins Gnutella and Livewire are the best known examples, but experts are already hailing the possibility of whole new ways of using the network. Oxford University scientists have announced the identification of a molecule that could prevent anthrax infection. Over a million and a half computer users elected to use the anthrax screensaver, and by using the spare capacity of these cooperating PC owners, screening time was cut by many orders of magnitude.[17]

In the computer software industry, open source software (OSS) (i.e., basically free) is challenging the position of companies like Microsoft that cling to the idea they actually own intellectual copyright in software and people should pay for it. In 2001, the open source Linux operating system had already taken nearly 10 percent of the world market. But the real P2P revolution is that, aside from being free, online users amend, refine, and develop the programs on their own initiative—internal Microsoft documents admit to company concern that "the ability of the OSS process to collect and harness the IQ of thousands of individuals is simply amazing."[18]

The flock of birds phenomenon equalizes access to the Internet, unlike traditional media where only those with huge resources can have a significant voice. In a real sense, no one person or company has priority to the right of access, and no one, not even the largest corporation, can shout louder than any other. The smallest player, the individual, has a right and opportunity to be seen and heard. The practical implications are huge. For example, on October 16, 1999, Steve Jobs announced that "after a good night's sleep and digesting e-mails from many upset customers," Apple

Computer would be rescinding a retroactive price increase that it had intended to impose on customers who were back-ordered.[19]

## The Fish-Tank Phenomenon

Moore's Law and Metcalfe's Law combine to give individuals inexpensive and easy access to new media such as the Internet. Any individual or organization can set up a Web site and, theoretically at least, can be seen by the world. Many have noticed the "fish-tank phenomenon"—junk sites on the Internet showing a video from a camera aimed at someone's tropical fish tank.[20] It is tempting to suggest expunging this "junk" and leaving the Internet to the capabilities and resources of large organizations—but there is no one in charge to do this.

When we contrast the capabilities and resources of large organizations with the creative ability of millions of individuals—the power of the fish-tank phenomenon becomes apparent. Certainly, large organizations may have the resources to produce rich, complex Web sites, but the creative potential of millions of individuals working all over the world may be much more significant. Napster was the innovation of eighteen-year-old Shawn Fanning. Opposed by all the recording industry except BMG, Fanning's brainchild was not only a stunning example of the potential of the fish-tank phenomenon, it is also a powerful indictment of a huge industry's inability to get to grips with the implications of the new information economy. The failed attempt to sanitize Napster and turn it into a subscription service has done nothing to prevent the rapid growth of other file-sharing sevices much like Napster that provide free music, to the impotent fury of traditional recording companies and some recording artists.

Although the Internet may contain an enormous amount of junk—millions of individuals displaying their fish tanks—there is also unlimited creative potential. Many existing firms (small and large) will find themselves threatened by embryonic start-ups that previously were unable to gain market access. No longer will it be sufficient merely to observe close and known competitors; tomorrow's competitive threats may be anyone, from anywhere. In practical terms, the competitor that will hurt you most is not going to be the familiar "me-too" company using similar technology and offering products similar to those of your firm. Instead, the deadliest competitors will be interlopers you never heard of and probably would not have taken seriously, even if you had heard of them. Who knows what student in a dorm room is taking aim at your markets right now! Recall that, in early 2000, a Filipino student at his home in Manila launched the love virus that crippled computers around the world. Similarly, the miscreant who hacked into Bill Gate's credit card account and ordered him a large consignment of Viagra was a student with a $1,000 computer in the depths of Wales.[21]

## MANAGING WITH THE FIVE NEW FORCES

The new five forces of the information economy are very different from those that have dominated management thinking since the early 1980s. The technological effects of Moore's and Metcalfe's laws will bring hyper-accelerating change, spreading like a fast-proliferating virus. Indeed, the term "viral marketing" has already entered marketers' vocabulary as they begin to appreciate the word-of-mouth opportunities created by the Internet. Increasingly, boundaries will blur within and between firms, as well as across industries and markets. Decision makers will have to consider a world where computer chips are found not only in computers but also in many devices and articles that, in turn, are part of an exponentially growing network.

Because of transaction-cost economics, and the technological effects on firm and market efficiency, managers must now constantly evaluate the optimal shape, scope, and size of their firms. They must continually evaluate what activities should be performed in the market, and what functions the firm should conduct itself. Marketers will have to cope with the constant tussle between disintermediation (the demise of intermediaries whose functions are no longer needed) and reintermediation (the emergence of new intermediaries with new functions and competitive advantages). Even as travel agents come under increasing pressure, new intermediaries such as Expedia, Travelocity, and Priceline are appearing.[22]

The societal effects of the flock of birds phenomenon will bring communications democracy with the threat of anarchy, and the fish-tank phenomenon brings access to all. These phenomena will require managers to work in a new environment where control and governance are less clear and less structured than they have been throughout history. Managing in a world where significant issues are neither under the control of a government nor part of a large organization will be a new and often scary experience for many managers.

Managers may take cold comfort from our identification of the five new forces. They are more ethereal than those of the 1980s, and the impact on firms and industries is far less predictable. These forces are not neat and structured, nor do they offer much comfort for deciding the firm's strategic direction. Much recent writing on strategy emphasizes the effects of these forces and suggests that conventional management processes for strategy development will be insufficient, if not ineffective, in the years ahead. The inability to predict the source of potential competition will require constant revision of the firm's strategy. When competition is well or even partially defined, managers can examine and perhaps address it. When it emanates from the bedroom of a 17-year-old in another country, life gets much more difficult.

Our discussion of these five new forces has several implications:

- Change is too rapid for anyone to feel comfortable. More than ever, managers must beware of the anesthetizing effect of success—the fatal arrogance of success mentioned earlier. A firm's most dangerous moment of vulnerability is when short-term success is greatest.

- It may be worthwhile for you continually to seek ways to destroy your firm's value chain and "put it out of business." If you don't, someone else will.[23]

- Critical corporate capabilities are more often about knowledge, human resources, and the ability to innovate than about tangible assets.

- Increasingly, the "firm → customer" model of information flow will be supplemented by "customer → firm" and "customer → customer" models. Customers will become a greater source of information for the firm and will be involved in its product development efforts. And customers will form communities around firms, products, and experiences.

- As the half-life of ideas diminishes, the role of strategy will change. The traditional five-year plan will no longer be viable, and the value of the annual strategic planning process will be questionable. Perhaps strategy will become a one-page set of guidelines for action.[24] Resource allocation decisions may be less planned than incremental, and revisited far more frequently. Events, rather than the passage of time, will trigger strategy change. One thing is certain—the traditional periodicity of the company's own planning process is unlikely to correspond to that of its competitors.

■ Saving the toughest message for last, managers are going to have to learn to live with paradox. They will still have to cope with the old five forces, while grappling with the new five forces. The paradox is that, simultaneously, everything is different and everything is the same. Some fundamentals remain the same: Industry structure will affect the profitability of competitors, and only sustainable competitive advantage allows a company to outperform the average.[25] Those industry structures and company boundaries are now fluid, however; competitors are unknown and change daily; partnering and information exchanges replace traditional confrontational competition; competitive advantage may last for a shorter time than ever before; and the sources of customer value that underpin competitive advantage migrate almost hourly. One view is that strategy has become the art of surviving rapid transitions, success is surviving into the next round of the game, and successful strategies are those that generate options.[26] Life is never going to be the same again.

## MARKETING IN THE NEW ERA: HERE'S HOW IT IS DIFFERENT

The implications of the information economy for marketers and marketing in general are unimaginably far-reaching and ill-formed. Unavoidably, our ideas are speculative, but they will provide a springboard for readers to develop and continually rethink the implications for their own businesses.

### The Death of Distance

Frances Cairncross contends that "distance will no longer determine the cost of communicating electronically."[27] For any product that can be digitized—pictures, video, sound, and words—physical distance will have no effect on distribution costs. The same is true for many services. Many physical products will be identified, explored, and purchased remotely.[28]

Because American motor homes are very expensive in Europe, prospective buyers now routinely explore American dealers' Web sites to compare prices with their European options. For similar reasons, it is becoming difficult for international companies to maintain price differentials across markets in other countries, whether for autos, airline tickets, books, or computers. Very soon, traditional price discrimination strategies will be untenable. In the new era, consumers will routinely shop the global marketplace and arbitrage away unjustifiable price differences. Many industrial buyers already do; some are insisting on a single price and currency worldwide.[29] Resisting those demands is difficult now, and soon it will be impossible.

## Marketing at the Speed of Light

Think of a video running forward at high speed—this gives a sense of the pace at which managers have to work in the twenty-first century's competitive world. Marketers will need the precision and control of a Grand Prix or NASCAR driver as everything happens more quickly. And just as all parts of the race car must perform together, so must the organization behave seamlessly in a totally integrated manner. The quantity and quality of information about the market and customer behavior is growing exponentially, and because customers are unforgiving, managers will have to make course corrections in real time. As companies struggle to stay ahead of their rivals, the pace of new product introduction will increase. Even today, the effective sales life of a new notebook computer is only a few months. Within six months, the new product is outdated and being remaindered at the discount electronics store or on eBay. A better, faster, lighter machine is already on the market.

## Mass Customization and Segments of One

During much of the twentieth century, the desire to reduce production costs drove companies to seek market supremacy through economies of scale. Later, with the shift to a buyers' market, market segmentation became the watchword for firms practicing effective marketing. Today, the synthesis of customer supremacy and information technology is rapidly shifting the focus of businesses from market segments to market fragments to individuals. In Japan, the combination of features Toyota customers desire in their new cars is fed directly into the assembly process. About a week after placing the order, customers receive their "bespoke" vehicles.

Nor is Toyota unique. In Europe, the DaimlerChrysler Smart car (a two-seat city car) became the first car that customers configured and ordered exclusively online. Ford and General Motors are already involved in programs for Web-based vehicle ordering, and Levi's has supplied made-to-order jeans for several years. Services such as Amazon.com try to tailor their information products to customer requirements. For example, if you purchased this book from Amazon (or through its affiliates), Amazon will tell you about other books by the authors, as well as those on related topics.

## From Products → Services → Experiences

Many years ago, General Motors and other durable-goods manufacturers recognized that trade-in facilities and financing helped sell their products. More recently, many products have been turned into services. Consumers can lease or rent their cars instead of buying them; hospitals purchase images instead of the X-ray machines or CAT scanners that generate them; and some airlines want to pay per hour of operating life, instead of buying or leasing their aircraft engines. The transmutation of products into services has become a part of everyday life. However, because the ability of added services to differentiate among parity products is deteriorating, the experience economy has emerged as the newest stage of economic evolution.[30]

Many companies are creating customer experiences to build competitive advantage. United Airlines hosts a wine-tasting for its best customers in one of New York's top hotels—a private champagne and hors d'oeuvres reception that includes *Wine Spectator* editors. Saab rents the Lime Rock Raceway for a day and invites Saab owners to bring their cars (and drive the new models). If you want a hamburger and french fries, you can go to Planet Hollywood; the local restaurant; or the Harley Davidson, Rainforest, or Motown cafés. The food is pretty much the same, but the dining experiences are distinctive.

## The New Information Products

Many firms view the Internet as a means to augment their current businesses—a new way to promote or to take orders. Others, like Barnes and

Noble, keep their Internet businesses totally separate from their traditional business. In fact, the integrated "bricks and clicks" business model has proved to be a strong one. The British supermarket firm Tesco operates Tesco Direct, the most successful Internet grocery business in the world, as an integral part of its supermarket business and is licensing its technology to the U.S. Safeway chain. Tesco's strategy is based on the realization that the customer relationship is with the local store—the Web shop does not replace the physical shop, it supplements it. The Web page is designed around the local store; the products are picked and delivered from there. The proposition is "shop online from my local store."[31]

But there are other beasts in the jungle as well. These new players are different. They see the Internet as a revolutionary development for creating new products and businesses. The potential for radical innovation is unprecedented and seemingly without limit.

- Managers are sick of hearing about Amazon.com. They point out that the company has yet to make real money, and maybe should be called Amazon.org, because it is a not-for-profit organization. Many think that Amazon is an Internet book and video seller. It is not. It is a new business form, for which we do not yet have a name. Amazon displays the most advanced use of "collaborative filtering technology" to identify communities of customers with similar interests as targets. It has patented Amazon Associates as a business process and aims to become a broker, selling partner companies' products through the Amazon network. As well as expanding product lines and geography, Amazon includes an auction and zShops that allow small businesses to sell through Amazon. It also acts as an intermediary between buyers and sellers of used books. After forming an alliance with Toys "R" Us in a co-branded Web site, Amazon is looking for more bricks and clicks collaborations. The best description of what Amazon is comes from founder Jeff Bezos, who was asked by a shareholder what she owned: "You own a piece of the leading e-commerce platform."[32]

- January 2000 saw the announcement of the planned merger between America Online (AOL) and Time Warner (TW). Investors were initially confused as to the rationale. In fact, this represented the first large-scale partnering of old economy content (films, videos, news, music, information services) with the new economy context (Internet access). The goal was to create a business that dominated the home entertainment and information market, possibly to be bolstered by further merger with a telephone company for enhanced access to mobile media.[33] The record of AOL Time Warner so far indicates the difficulties involved.

■ Businesses such as eBay, monster.com, and contentville.com represent the new information-based players whose business models match so well the potential created by the Internet.

■ In all these cases, information-based business models have created a revolution in ways that were never predicted and that would never have happened in the old economy.

## Partners, Alliances, Networks

According to Andersen Consulting (now Accenture), the average large company that had no alliances 10 years ago has more than 30 today.[34] Two major factors are driving this change. First, as uncertainty increases, these networked relationships provide a hedge, albeit one that is sometimes short-lived.[35] Second, information technology permits firms to manage a network of far-flung relationships in ways that were previously impossible; outsourcing is part of this phenomenon. Because of transaction cost reductions, many service firms have been founded to perform functions that companies previously conducted internally. As brand owners continue to divorce themselves from manufacturing operations, contract manufacture is becoming one of the world's fastest growing businesses. Affiliations abound on the Internet. Amazon has in excess of 500,000 affiliate Web sites that send visitors to purchase books at Amazon, and throughout cyberspace individual Web sites maintain reciprocal hot links to their fellows.

## New Business Models

Business used to be straightforward. Companies made products and then sold (or resold) them. Profits were the difference between revenues and costs. Life is no longer so simple, and this traditional model is only one of many in the new economy. Examples of new business models include:

- Delivering eyes and ears. This media model will increase in popularity as the volume of electronic commerce increases and companies pay for online advertising, click-throughs, and so forth.
- Selling customer information. Web firms automatically collect data about their customers as an essential element of doing business. The data can be extremely valuable for other firms, whether they are in e-commerce, clicks and mortar, or even bricks and mortar.
- Making money on the accessories. Have you noticed the increasing charges for shipping and handling? You should, because that is where many dot-com retailers make their money. The margins on their core products are often razor thin or even negative. They don't make up the deficit on volume; they make it up on shipping and handling, if they make it up at all.

## Get Used to New Forms of Competition

We doubt that Barnes and Noble could have seen Amazon coming. Once Amazon started to become established, however, management should have taken the threat seriously. Early boasts about making the Internet revolutionary into "Amazon-dot-toast" were bold but unrealistic; so many managers seem to lack a sense of history. At Barnes and Noble, they should have remembered that in the mid-1970s, Emery Air Freight, then the leading freight-forwarder and the most profitable transportation company in the world, looked on from the sidelines waiting for Federal Express to go "belly up." In addition to the forces already discussed, three factors, taken together, suggest that markets will become much more competitive in the future making better competitive strategy mandatory.[36]

**Technology.** As noted, technology is transforming the way markets operate while proliferating solutions that serve customer needs. Figure 2.1 illustrates that not only are markets for new technology developing at a faster rate, but the latency period from inception to commercial launch is getting shorter as well. Put simply, the pace of technological change is accelerating. Not all technologies are electronic, but electronic media and the Internet are enabling information about new technologies to spread further and faster than in the past. And with competition accelerating, the drive for new technological solutions becomes more intense. As a result,

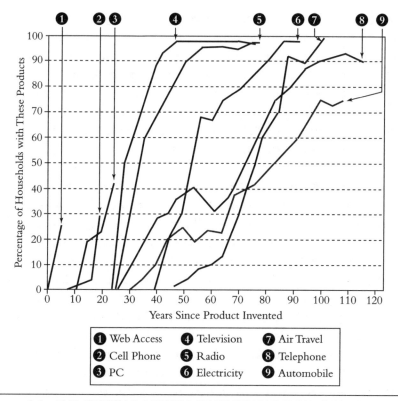

Figure 2.1 THE SHIFTING PATTERN OF TECHNOLOGICAL CHANGE. *Source data:* W. Michael Cox, Federal Reserve Bank of Dallas.

multiple technologies can address individual needs. Sutures are a good example. Used by the ancient Egyptians, they are the oldest technology for wound closure. Alternatives available today include staples, tape, glue, and zippers. Furthermore, laparoscopy and noninvasive therapies vastly reduce or eliminate the size and number of wounds to be closed.

Another example of technology-led innovation is the "smart" toilet. This product combines traditional plumbing with new electronics to provide a personal hygiene service. More telling, the product can analyze its contents and monitor the user's temperature and blood pressure! Suddenly, the product looks like a first-line medical diagnostic machine to monitor the primary health signs of the elderly, with huge implications for improved hospitalization practices in countries with graying populations and shortages of hospital beds.

**Deregulation and Privatization.** As Marxian thought retreats to the back-waters of history and liberal democracies gain ascendance, governments have retreated from control of, and direct participation in, business. As a result, competition has vastly increased in such diverse industries as transportation, telecommunications, and power generation and transmission. Indeed, deregulation has eliminated the barriers between certain of these industries as firms become full-range suppliers of utility services including gas, electricity, cable, and telecommunications.[37]

**Globalization.** As more countries join in free trade with the encouragement of the World Trade Organization and related bodies, competition is as likely to come from across the globe as from across the street. And as companies feel threatened in their home markets, many venture abroad in a cycle of growing global competition. Even as international boundaries to competition wither, however, other firms are forming global alliances or merging across borders, blurring their national origins and identity.

There are few better examples of the combined effects of these three factors than the turbulent telecommunications industry. Once the haven of protected domestic markets and stable technology platforms, 90 percent the $700 billion world telecom market is open to competition at the start of the twenty-first century. A shifting set of alliances dominates the industry. New competitors are entering with new technologies bringing high added-value data transmission services at the same time that basic voice transmission is becoming commoditized. Some commentators believe that Internet companies like Microsoft and AOL will surpass traditional suppliers like AT&T. With its latest plan to split itself up into four separate businesses, AT&T itself is likely to disappear.

## Only "Real" Perceived Value Will Count!

The availability of information heavily affects market efficiency. When markets are inefficient, suppliers' prices reflect not only the inherent value of their products and services but also customers' lack of information about alternatives. Whereas historically, information acquisition was difficult and expensive, the electronic revolution is rapidly transforming the process and making it cheap. This has already occurred in financial markets where real-time information is available on virtually a global basis. And in product markets, the Web provides a low-cost means of accessing information through such services as consumersearch.com, which offers product reviews in numerous categories. As inefficiency based on differential access to information is driven from all types of markets, the only sustainable price differences will be those reflecting differences in customer perceived value. Price differences due to lack of information will disappear.

Not only will information technology lower search costs, it will facilitate buyer/seller matching with intelligent search engines. The opportunity to profit from customer ignorance is rapidly fading. Put another way, we are embarking on what Bill Gates calls "frictionless capitalism." Companies can no longer make money from knowing that customers cannot, or will not, comparison shop. There are no exceptions: Even a senior executive of Wal-Mart, the world's biggest retailer, with formidable competitive strength, has predicted that the Internet will make retail margins razor thin.

## Forget Your Old Competencies: What Will Be the New Ones?

The core competencies necessary for success are changing rapidly as the customer-value frontier pushes ever outward. Overseas expansion and manufacturing strategies of Japanese auto companies have forced component suppliers around the world to master total quality management (TQM), just-in-time (JIT), and other new skills to remain competitive. Biotechnology has affected pharmaceutical companies and many have acquired ownership positions in emerging companies to ensure they possess competencies that are vital to their futures. Much of the spectacular growth in strategic alliances has reflected companies' needs to acquire new capabilities faster than they can develop them for themselves.

The revolution in information technology is a major driver of this phenomenon. Tesco has made information technology a core competence in the British supermarket industry. Less than a year after introducing its loyalty card (which pays a small rebate quarterly based on cumulative purchases), over 16 million households were enrolled. Average purchases per supermarket visit had risen significantly. Tesco subsequently developed a sophisticated, targeted direct-mail strategy and expanded into commercial banking with several innovative customer offerings.[38] Whereas most competing supermarket companies offer loyalty cards, only Tesco has leveraged the underlying information power to develop its strategy. Competitors who used the device simply as a sales promotion gimmick are now abandoning "loyalty" schemes.

## Don't Forget the Old Rules, Just Learn the New Ones!

As competition intensifies and the weak succumb, the survivors and new entrants are correspondingly smarter and more sophisticated. Consequently, the overall ability of these firms to practice classical marketing principles will increase. However, since all possess these capabilities, deriving competitive advantage from such practices will grow ever more difficult. Learning about customers by traditional methods such as focus groups and surveys will be insufficient, and firms will have to develop innovative ways of getting closer to customers. In the words of the Spice Girls, to identify "what (they) really, really want" will require new approaches to customer research. This imperative is a key factor ushering in ethnographic approaches in market research, for only truly deep customer insights are likely to lead to competitive advantage in the twenty-first century.[39]

For example, Elida-Faberge, Unilever's market-leading British personal care company, has formed a "youth board" and sponsors "immersion events" in fashionable nightclubs. To gain a better understanding of teenagers, executives take home study packs of teenage materials—one for girls included an All Saints CD, a pink inflatable picture frame, a teen bikini, and a packet of Tampax.[40] Even companies that managed to understand the Generation X consumer are being wrong-footed by the priorities of Generation Y.

## Get Used to Them Talking Back and Talking to Each Other!

The information economy, specifically the Internet, will transform marketing communication in more ways than one. Historically in consumer markets, one-way information has been the norm, with undifferentiated one-to-many mass communication. Not only does the Internet allow businesses to address individual consumers at relatively low cost, those potential customers can easily communicate with suppliers and with other consumers.

A British colleague of ours who runs her own Web site design company provides a provocative example of how tough it will be to deal with smart customers who answer back. Some years ago, she visited an early BMW Web site and found that it ran very slowly. Spotting an opportunity, she e-mailed BMW pointing out that such a slow site was running up customer phone bills—and would they like her company to improve it? The e-mail reply suggested that if she was worried about her phone bill, she was unlikely to be a potential BMW customer. Her response: "If your cars are as slow as your Web site, you know what you can do with them!" We have lost count of how many business audiences have heard this story.

"Talking to each other" may have more profound implications for companies. Word-of-mouth advertising has had a long history in the marketing literature, and over the years many companies have developed strategies to encourage consumers with positive experiences to pass them on to their families, friends, and colleagues. Companies also know that a bad experience is apt to be passed on more frequently (up to 10 times) than a good experience, hence the increased focus on service in the 1980s and 1990s. In the twenty-first century, these phenomena will increase in scope as the Internet makes it easier for customers to pass on both their positive and negative experiences. But direct e-mail communications will not be the only way to spread this information around. Communities of customers are already forming to share positive experiences, sometimes under company auspices, but also to exchange their own personal horror stories (e.g., chasemanhattansucks.com).

## SO WHAT?

Our message is that the information revolution is spawning the fastest, most complex changes the business world has ever experienced. The implications of these changes are so vast and far-reaching that neither our customers, competitors, suppliers, partners, nor our own organizations can be immune from them. The problem for managers in all these organizations is that at present we can only speculate about the outcomes of these changes.

The critical issue for all organizations, both today's and those that will be founded tomorrow, is how to deal with these as yet unknown implications. One thing, however, is becoming clear: The large, hierarchical, functionally organized companies that have been responsible for a large proportion of today's global economy are unable to deal with this challenge. Designed for an earlier era, they are too slow, too fragmented, too bureaucratic, and too inward looking to grasp the issues and respond effectively. (Unfortunately, most of us still work for these kinds of organizations!)

To succeed in such a fast-changing environment demands an outward orientation that the entire firm embraces; it must not be restricted solely to functions such as sales, marketing, and customer service. All must hear the voice of the market in an era of rapid change and intense competition.[41] When customers have the power, they will demand seamless perfection; to be successful in the twenty-first century, the corporation's watchword must be Total Integrated Marketing.

For companies to survive, they will have to be reinvented. Almost certainly, the organization of the future will be flatter, team-based, virtual, hollow, information-driven, and externally focused.[42] Yet, in the short term, many of us face the challenge of delivering solid customer value from organizations that are poorly designed for the markets they face. Although the tried and true basic principles of marketing remain, both the ways in which they will be used and the context within which they will be applied must change. Some corporations are already making dramatic changes, and in Chapter 3 we examine how companies can prosper in this new environment.

In the dramatically new environments that firms are facing, sticking with marketing practices of the past is not an option. As we struggle to drive customer value through traditional organizations, only Total Integrated Marketing provides the framework to make marketing real for customers. To prosper and enhance value for our shareholders, we must reinvent our organizations with new forms that harness the entire set of corporate resources in a seamless integrated fashion. Total Integrated Marketing is a philosophy essential to achieving these ends. Traditional thinking can only create business forms and alliance networks that are as myopic and inward looking as the organizations of the past. In the information economy, this prospect will surely consign our organizations to the scrap heap of history.

# THE STRATEGIC
# MARKETING PROCESS

## The Foundation for Total
## Integrated Marketing

Marketing departments as we have known them are a danger to corporate health. Yet, whatever the fate of those departments, marketing processes are fundamental to company survival and prosperity. For that reason, the foundation of all that follows in this book must be a sound, and shared, understanding of the strategic marketing process.

This chapter is not a cookbook of the latest portfolio models and analytic marketing techniques, nor does it deal with marketing implementation. Our purpose is to elucidate the strategic marketing process and to distinguish it from the kind of marketing that the majority of companies practice. We do not underestimate the importance of implementation and execution (much of our book deals with these issues), nor do we argue that this quarter's operating results and market share are unimportant (without achieving them, the firm might not survive). But these, per se, are not within the province of strategic marketing. Implementating, executing, and achieving short-term results may be part of operational marketing—they are certainly a responsibility of sales—but such actions and achievements do not constitute strategic marketing.

In this chapter, we first lay out our view of the strategic marketing process as a set of five tasks, or responsibilities. We then describe the essential principles for managing the process effectively. Our goal is to provide an overall framework that highlights critical issues for experienced managers.[1] These underlying tasks and principles provide the foundation for Total Integrated Marketing.

## THE FIVE TASKS OF STRATEGIC MARKETING

When we peel back marketing to its bare necessities, the strategic marketing process comprises the five essential tasks or responsibilities summarized in Figure 3.1.

When you have finished these tasks, you simply start again: Monitoring and controlling execution and performance feeds back into all the other procedures—securing support, offer design, segmentation and targeting, and opportunity identification. These processes are ongoing and interrelated, not a sequence of self-contained tasks to be completed and then discarded.

In this chapter, we stress the impact of Total Integrated Marketing in an effective strategic marketing process. We want you to be as convinced

Figure 3.1   THE FIVE TASKS OF STRATEGIC MARKETING

as we are that Total Integrated Marketing is not just another management fad. Instead, it is an essential and fundamental route to superior customer and shareholder value.

## Deciding Which Markets to Address (If You Don't Look, You'll Never Find!)

Strategy involves making critical choices about where and how a company should invest scarce resources. At the broadest and most general level, the firm must choose both industry and market. Choice of market ranks along with choice of technologies and products as one of the most fundamental company decisions. In fact, given the choice of owning a market or a factory, most senior executives would opt for owning a market.

Entry into completely new industries or markets involves high-level strategy decisions, but the marketing contribution is vital in the basic decision-making process.

Marketing insight plays two key roles in these decisions: opportunity identification and advice to corporate management on proposed strategic actions.

Identification of Opportunities.   Marketing is explicitly responsible for focusing attention outside the organization. Corporate and business strategies should focus and guide the search for market opportunity.[2] Marketing should scan the environment within these areas to identify new opportunities, then collect and analyze the appropriate data. Promising opportunities must be brought to the attention of top management for go/no-go decisions. Because redefining the scope of the business should take place periodically, opportunities that fall outside the previous scope should not be automatically discarded. Sometimes these new opportunities arise because of competencies that the firm must develop to operate effectively in its primary business.

### IDENTIFYING NEW MARKET OPPORTUNITIES

In operating its theme parks, Disney has developed considerable expertise in managing customer relationships. It now offers seminars to other organizations wishing to improve their own customer relationships.

> On the other hand, Boots the Chemists, the United Kingdom's largest drugstore group, failed badly in attempting to extend its brand into consumer products such as house maintenance and decorating. Those opportunities turned out to be an illusion.* This company is now painfully reinventing its core business as a health and personal care provider, instead of as a general retailer. This business scope is completely different: New services include in-store dental offices, massage and sports injury clinics, and travel and health care insurance. The common thread is consumer trust in a traditional health care specialist.
>
> *Marketing folks are fond of the saying, "There are no such things as problems, only opportunities to learn."

How well do most companies spot opportunities? Quite poorly, especially when they involve new customers. Why do companies obsess with present customers instead of seeking out new opportunities?[3] First, looking after current customers is less risky. A problematic effect of the customer relationship management (CRM) movement is that firms may be tempted to avoid the risks associated with new opportunities in favor of a focus on existing customers. Second, too many marketers equate marketing with serving customers better and achieving high levels of customer satisfaction. Superior customer service is fine, but this alone does not equate to strategic marketing. Third, firms rarely, if ever, consider opportunity losses. If current customer satisfaction is a more important measure than finding new customers, the behavior of managers and employees is highly predictable—and the company is at risk for eventual failure.

For these reasons, a serious audit of marketing activities should look for innovation. What growth rates characterize the firm's markets? How many new markets has the firm entered? What are their growth rates? What is the rate of new-product introduction? What innovations have been made in distribution, billing, order tracking, and improved delivery performance? The correct answers to these questions will confirm that the company is focusing less on current market shares or volumes and more on the activities that will create such positive results later. Too many executives spend their time looking backward rather than forward.

Proposed Strategic Actions.    Marketing plays a critical advisory role in many strategic decisions made at the corporate level. Such decisions as acquisitions, strategic alliances, new distribution systems, divestitures, and market withdrawal have important marketing implications. Managers frequently make these decisions strictly on financial grounds with at best superficial attention to marketing issues.

### AT&T AND NCR

An important element of AT&T's disastrous acquisition of NCR (NCR lost about 50 percent of its value under AT&T's parentage) concerned Teradata, a firm that made special database computers that were becoming popular with major retailers. Teradata threatened to cancel an arrangement that allowed NCR to use Teradata technology because it feared that its then biggest customer, AT&T, would switch to NCR. To maintain the technology, AT&T had to buy Teradata for over $500 million.* The realities of the marketplace can make nonsense of spreadsheets and financial models that ignore those facts of life.

* *The Economist* (March 25, 1996), 23–29.

The critical responsibility is to ensure that top management receives good advice based on sound marketing principles. Today, relatively few companies have a chief marketing officer—although all have a chief financial officer—which may account for many of the merger and acquisition disasters we read about almost daily.

## Choosing Market Segments (Going beyond the Obvious?)

Marketing's role in determining the scope of the corporate business portfolio is typically advisory. But within the markets the firm decides to address, marketing has a much more direct responsibility for identifying which customers the firm should serve—selecting market segments, customer types and roles, and in some cases individual customers. The trend toward direct marketing and key account management, or so-called customer management, illustrates how smart companies are evolving their strategic marketing capabilities.

Large companies typically achieve market and market segment focus only with difficulty. The options that surface tend to have different supporting constituencies (frequently related to organization structure), which can lead to protracted, if not destructive debates. Clear, explicit, and externally driven processes for assessing market and market segment options can serve shareholders' interests by preventing managers from making these vital decisions on political grounds.[4] Even within targeted segments, other customer choices are still necessary. These choices have both vertical and horizontal dimensions.

Vertical Choices.   Should we target the next level in the customer channel (e.g., an OEM or reseller) or bet the farm on the final consumer? In the auto industry, battery, tire, and even electric component manufacturers have sometimes carried their brands to the final consumer despite having been fitted as original equipment.

## INTEL'S CRITICAL CHOICES

As a computer chip producer, Intel historically focused promotional resources on its direct customers: personal computer manufacturers. In the early 1990s, however, it developed the highly successful Intel Inside program targeted at personal computer users. Its implicit message was, "All PCs are not alike—those with Intel chips are better." This change in strategy reflected the fact that the key decision makers in the PC market were no longer solely data processing professionals but included line executives and, increasingly, individual consumers. Once Intel had blazed the way in personal computers, rival AMD commenced television advertising, and other component manufacturers adopted similar strategies.

Perhaps the most serious vertical decisions concern channel redesign, for example, whether to target intermediary customers at all. This issue has become especially crucial with the advent of the Internet, which allows firms to bypass intermediaries and target end-customers directly. For firms with an existing channel structure, going direct raises difficult matters of channel conflict. Hewlett-Packard, IBM, and Compaq faced huge difficulties in competing with Dell's direct distribution when they had long-standing relationships with conventional resellers.

Horizontal Choices.   The horizontal issue revolves around which intermediaries and/or final consumers the firm wants to reach. The key considerations are the attractiveness of a particular target, and whether the firm has the capabilities to serve that target better than competitors. The particular customer segment that a firm chooses may be an excellent target, but without the necessary capabilities, success is unlikely.

## THE HONDA LEGEND

When Honda introduced the Legend in the United States, one of the firm's key markets, it chose not to sell this model through the same dealer system that was so successful with its Honda-brand vehicles. Arguing that the market segments for the two cars were very different, Honda boldly decided to establish a new brand name, Acura, and a new dealer system for the Legend and other Acura-branded automobiles.

**Organizational Roles in Buying.** Often, the varied organizational roles involved in the buying process complicate the customer-targeting issue. A company that targets manufacturing firms must decide how much and what type of effort (if any) it should allocate to such roles as the chief engineer, manufacturing manager, purchasing agent, and general manager, each of whose interests and motivations may differ from those of the others. Within a household, the choice of target may be mother, father, child, grandparents, or the entire family. Perhaps most difficult of all, the interests of parties to a purchase decision may not merely differ—they may even be diametrically opposed.[5] The Sony Walkman not only provides music, it also isolates the listener from other members of a (family) group. Parents who want to talk to their children may be frustrated. Yet under certain circumstances, such as long car trips, the Walkman can also function as a vector for improving family relationships! McDonald's choice of key customer target is evident from the happy meals for kids, the playgrounds, the choice of a clown as an icon, and even the firm-sponsored charity. Typically, when children are young and the parent pays, the child's role is as an influencer of the parental decision.

Choice of customer target is one of the most crucial market strategy decisions, but the most obvious marketing solutions may be ineffective. For example, the choice of heavy user is not necessarily appropriate. According to *Business Week*, McDonald's heavy user is a blue-collar male in his twenties who eats at McDonald's two or three times a week. Despite this reality, McDonald's key customer targets remain young children.

Furthermore, the obvious choice is often ineffectual precisely because it is obvious and all competitors tend to concentrate on this target. Among the reasons for Federal Express becoming the leader in overnight package delivery was its original decision to target the problem-owner, the harried and time-pressed professional, rather than the mailroom supervisor or logistics manager. Choosing the right target(s) for marketing effort is a major creative and innovative opportunity for strategic marketing.[6]

## Designing the Marketing Offer (The Mix Is Not Enough!)

Marketing offers have to be designed so that selected customer targets behave in the manner the firm desires. In many cases, the ultimate objective of offer design is to persuade customers to purchase the firm's products and services. For intermediaries, however, required behaviors may also include actively selling, holding inventory, providing services, or making strong purchase recommendations. Before undertaking marketing offer design, it is necessary to be clear about both customer targets and the customer behaviors the company is seeking.

The overall design of the marketing offer comprises a total benefit package. (This is where the absence of Total Integrated Marketing in companies can become obvious to customers, if not to the company itself.) Traditional functional marketing equates the tools available to perform this design task with the elements of the marketing mix.[7] However, the requirements of offer design and delivery go far beyond these traditional elements. The traditional marketing mix is often described as follows:

- *Product* benefits are delivered to satisfy customer needs. These benefits are designed into the product and the package.
- *Place* (location) benefits concern the convenience of purchase and use of the product or service.
- *Promotion* (communication) is the means by which the firm informs and persuades customers that it is providing sufficient product, service, and location benefits. For branded products, communications add value in and of themselves: Customers derive benefits from the reassurance (reduction of perceived risk), imagery, and status that are intrinsic to the brand.[8] Similarly, salespeople may provide positive relationship benefits, particularly in specialty retailing and many B2B markets.
- *Services* in this context are additional, more intangible benefits included in the offer, usually to further distinguish the firm's offer from competitors' offers. Services may be provided by the manufacturer or by an intermediary, or by some combination of the two.

- *Price* is the net monetary outlay required to secure the product or service. When compared with customers' perceptions of the benefits provided, price determines the net value that customers believe they receive before or after purchase.

Looking at a few of these traditional mix elements individually illustrates vividly why we need Totally Integrated Marketing. Consider first the *product* element. Suppose we decide that to attain advantage with our target customers, we need to offer quality that is superior to that of our competitors. Such a decision has major implications for design of the product, for the operations function, and for purchasing. In another market, we conclude that competitors are overpricing and underestimating the elasticity of demand. To set a lower price that can still generate shareholder value through volume gains, we will need to involve design, operations, and purchasing as well as finance and accounting. In today's competitive environments, the basis on which the firm chooses to compete must be driven right back throughout the business, or we shall fail. Total Integrated Marketing is not just desirable, it is essential.

There are also many possible interrelationships among offer design elements. Considering for a moment just the elements in the traditional marketing mix, the greater the perceived product and location benefits, the higher can be the price. A higher price might also be secured by differentiating a commodity product with additional services. New product features providing augmented benefits may give rise to different advertising and new location benefits. The requirement for interfunctional cooperation in strategic marketing derives directly from the intimate interrelationships that must exist within a successful marketplace offer.

The key issue here is design. Like the relationship between architects and builders, the design/execution interface may be a source of significant coordination problems. The focus of strategic marketing should be on benefit design: What would the customer like to receive? By contrast, engineering (product development), operations, and sales are generally more focused on features: What product or service characteristics are necessary to deliver the benefits customers are seeking?

For any given market, firms may need to design specific offers for multiple customer targets in several market segments. However, because firms have limited resources for these designs, they must weigh both strategic considerations—the degree of segment effort and likely customer response—to estimate the sales and profit returns for different offer designs. Since the potential marketing mix permutations for a given market segment run into the millions, no company's offer need be identical to that of a competitor unless it is pursuing an imitation strategy. Identical or nearly identical offers generally reflect lack of imagination and poor management. "Commodity" offers need not exist. Indeed, several companies have banned the word, arguing that its mere usage encourages unimaginative marketing approaches.

## Support from Other Functions (Strategic Marketing Cannot Stand Alone!)

In many organizations, marketing executives view this responsibility as ensuring that other organizational functions commit to supporting the offer after marketing designs it. The world is rarely that simple, however, and here we run into some fundamental paradoxes related to the traditional (functional) view of marketing. Total Integrated Marketing is not just about getting other functions to do what the marketing function wants.

Good strategic marketing requires two very different types of support: support for design and support for implementation. Support for design is shaped by considerations of technical, operational, and economic feasibility. A key marketing responsibility is to keep the organization focused on what targeted customers either desire, or are likely to desire, regardless of current feasibility. This constitutes a paradox that may generate considerable internal conflict. If marketing abdicates its missionary role, however, and concedes to strategies that are possible using the firm's current capabilities and competencies, it ceases to perform one of its most important tasks. It will not push the firm to evolve so that it can deliver competitive advantage in the future.

The second type of support is required for successful implementation, often described as "getting buy-in" or internal marketing.[9] In functional organizations, marketing typically has responsibility for offer design. However, it rarely has line authority over those organizational functions responsible for implementation. Like a chain, strategy is no stronger than its weakest link. If a key function does not play its part in the process, all other functions may expend effort in vain. Increasing competitive pressure requires firms to integrate and focus all capabilities on those opportunities they have decided to address.[10] Neither brilliant advertising nor a well-trained and highly motivated sales force can achieve success if the product is ill-designed or unavailable when the customer requires it.

Interdepartmental strife and rivalry hamper far too many corporations. Management must redirect precious time from dealing with external opportunities and threats to solving destructive internal conflict. Widespread use of the term "functional silo" indicates that the problem is pervasive. Most companies are far from achieving the "boundaryless" corporation that former General Electric CEO Jack Welch envisaged.[11]

### THE TRAP OF SILO THINKING

Examples of silo thinking abound. Faced with a new competitive threat, a major health care company decided that its three business units serving operating theaters should jointly develop an offer to satisfy the full set of customer needs. Despite agreement on this rationale, senior management in the three units could not agree on a coherent strategy and the attempt was dropped.

In contrast, we worked with a financial services company that needed to build collaboration between two warring divisions. It formed cross-divisional teams whose task was planning a regional rollout strategy. The effects were dramatic: improved collaboration, identification of new product opportunities, and shared interests in major corporate clients.

Securing support for offer design and implementation is frequently a vital but complex undertaking, particularly for new-product launches. For this reason, the notion of support lies at the heart of Total Integrated Marketing. It may be necessary to integrate such functions as the sales force, advertising department (and agency), customer service, credit control, market research, operations, product development, information systems, and human resources. The requirements for coordinating multiple functions have increased as the practice of outsourcing has grown. External entities may now have supplanted internal functions, with increased challenges in achieving coordination.

## Monitoring and Controlling Execution and Performance (Feedback and Learning Are Essential)

The next concern is evaluation—monitoring execution and performance, perhaps fine-tuning or modifying tactics, and where necessary, adjusting objectives and even strategies. Accomplishing this task requires sensitive market feedback systems. As the pace of change increases, antiquated management systems create implementation problems with ever-greater frequency. Inadequate design of such systems as compensation, planning, and objective setting can have dramatic—and negative—effects on results.

Management must ensure that performance objectives are appropriate to the firm's market situation. Performance versus objectives will usually drive behavior. Thus, objectives that are too high (or too low) will lead to weak effort allocation and poorly motivated employees. Sales-force compensation systems based on sales volume with a built-in ratchet provide a classic example of poor objectives. In these systems, success in one year leads automatically to higher targets in the succeeding year. Although these systems may work well in growth markets, they often generate great dissatisfaction and low motivation in mature and declining markets. Furthermore, since sales volume per unit of selling effort is typically easier to achieve with established products, newly launched products are often undersupported and, consequently, fail when aggregate reward systems are in place.

### WATCHING THE WRONG PERFORMANCE

The life insurance industry provides an example of poor performance dimensions. Agents' objectives and compensation are typically closely related to the number and value of new policies they have written. To keep new policy sales high, many agents roll over existing policyholders into new policies. Since new policies must be in force for several years to be profitable to the firm, such behavior creates immense profitability problems. The typical commission structure bias encourages many agents to seek new prospects rather than develop business with existing customers. As a result, many consumers purchase policies from several different companies but have a relationship with none of them.

Three broad types of performance objectives tend to dominate market considerations:

1. *Profit oriented.* Bottom-line profit, profit contribution, return on investment (ROI).
2. *Volume oriented.* Unit volume, sales revenue, market share.
3. *Intermediate.* Customer awareness, intention to purchase, customer satisfaction.

For most firms, profit-oriented objectives are the ultimate measures of success, and the rise of the shareholder value philosophy will increase pressure on marketers to analyze and document their strategies in financial terms.[12] For some profit measures, however, such as bottom-line profit, return on investment (ROI), and return on equity (ROE), the marketing group may have little control over many of the cost items in the performance measure. As a result, profit contribution or volume-oriented objectives frequently offer better direct measures of marketing performance. Furthermore, many marketing objectives are intermediate in nature. They do not provide profit or volume per se, but excellent intermediate performance should lead to future profit or volume.

For good strategic marketing control, three key questions must be answered:

1. *Performance.* Did the firm achieve its performance objectives?
2. *Execution.* Did the firm execute the agreed-on actions necessary to implement the strategy?
3. *Strategy.* Is the formulated strategy still relevant in the face of increasing environmental change and evolving firm competence?

Only if performance objectives were set appropriately, and the answer to all three questions is "Yes" should management should feel confident about the firm's trajectory. Any "No" answer implies that the firm should rethink its actions. If significant environmental change has occurred, good execution and performance may yet require a major change in strategy. As noted, "If it ain't broke, don't fix it!" is an inadequate maxim for continued high performance.

As markets evolve more rapidly, reviewing the appropriateness of performance objectives and realigning the support systems must occur more frequently than in the past. Rigid clinging to the annual planning cycle may result in slothful marketplace responses. Instead, companies should focus on these four principles in controlling marketing efforts:

1. *Proactivity*. Don't wait for disaster to strike before paying attention to poor performance or the quality of execution. Control plays a proactive role in the heading off of problems before they become serious.
2. *Continuity*. Exercise control continuously, not intermittently. Don't wait for the end-of-quarter results, because by then your assumptions may be invalidated.
3. *Objectivity*. Use objective measures rather than subjective feelings about how a particular group or person is performing.
4. *Flexibility*. Performance objectives involve assumptions about the future. If your assumptions are violated, it is likely that related performance objectives will not be achievable.

Control must focus on marketing efforts and effectiveness in the marketplace, not just on marketing department budgets. Too often, management focuses on financial results that significantly lag behind marketplace developments.[13] Nor is control a mechanism for marketing executives to beat up on the rest of the organization. The essence of Total Integrated Marketing is to control on the factors that most influence delivery of superior customer and shareholder value.

## PRINCIPLES OF STRATEGIC MARKETING

The preceding tasks are central to understanding marketing's proper role within the firm (though they probably don't describe what your functional marketing department does). Even if you accept our view of the key tasks, how managers go about executing these responsibilities is also critically important. Four underlying principles are fundamental to managing the strategic marketing process successfully, as shown in Figure 3.2.

### Selectivity and Concentration (Choose or Schmooze?)

Selecting and targeting markets and segments are prime marketing responsibilities. At its heart is the basic strategic principle of selectivity and

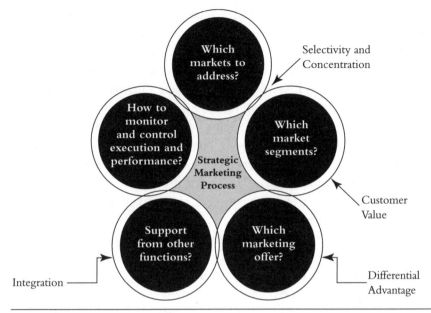

Figure 3.2   PRINCIPLES OF STRATEGIC MARKETING

concentration. This principle has two aspects: carefully choosing the market target (selectivity), then focusing resources on that target (concentration). Marketers preach selectivity widely but practice it much less often. The drive for volume and market share too often overwhelms sound strategic judgment.

The best-known marketing illustration of selectivity is market segmentation.[14] Segmentation has long occupied a venerable position in marketing. Much of the literature, however, focuses on methods for performing segmentation studies—how to analyze market information once gathered. Better descriptive understanding of a market only permits better strategy decisions: It does not guarantee them. The central strategic issue is not just developing a segmentation approach, but also acting on those results by selecting segments for effort and concentrating resources on them to the exclusion of alternatives.[15]

The principle of selectivity and concentration focuses attention on two key ideas: (1) Avoid spreading limited resources thinly over too many alternatives and (2) specialize in segments where the company can best leverage its distinctive capabilities to exploit an inherent advantage over competitors.

In business, the herd instinct prevails too often. Rather than leveraging distinctive competence or unique resources, imitation leads to the opposite situation: Followers compete on the bases early entrants established.

A concentration policy involves risks. Concentrating resources on some opportunities means relinquishing others. Some options that might have proved attractive will be rejected; others will be mistakenly chosen. However, the alternative approach of hedging bets—allocating small amounts of resources to all feasible options—is guaranteed to fail in competitive markets. For this reason, some experts have labeled this principle "Concentration and Concession," to emphasize that managers not only must concentrate resources in some segments, but also must deliberately concede other segments to competitors.

Our experience underlines an even more fundamental concern with making the principle of selectivity and concentration effective. Making the best possible selections requires the insight of the entire company, not just market research reports. Concentration involves coordinating the efforts of all organization members whose contributions affect the offer that the firm will make to selected customers. The alternative is to make poor market segment choices based on weak market understanding, with an ineffective focus on delivering superior value to selected customers.

## Customer Value (What Do They Really, Really Want?)

Very simply, success in targeted market segments relies on the firm's ability to provide perceived value to customers. The basis for this principle is also straightforward: Although firms develop, produce, and deliver products and services, customers perceive value only in the benefits that these products and services provide. For this reason, customer value increasingly drives product and investment decisions.[16] The delivery of value to customers undoubtedly should be a critical basis for evaluating firm performance. "Which customers?" however, will always be an issue, as will the underlying assumption that customers know their needs and wants. In recent years, there has been a welcome, if not always endorsed, questioning of these critical issues. Sometimes the questioning has been naïve and ill informed, but there is greater understanding that particularly in situations involving new technologies, existing customers' wants and needs may be misleading, conceivably fatal. Potential customers will typically respond to questions about their needs and wants, but because of their lack of product experience, their answers may well be seriously misleading.[17] Further, understanding customer value is always difficult, in part because wants and needs constitute a moving target.[18] As the environment changes and customers accumulate life (and/or organizational) experience, their needs change and the values they seek change also.

Because of these difficulties, world-class companies invest extensively in identifying customer needs and wants, and feed their results into product and service decisions. These offers should be continually modified and enhanced so that customers remain highly satisfied with the values they receive. The failure to observe this simple lesson has led some of the most successful retailers in the United States and Britain into crisis: Sears, Kmart, Sainsbury's, and Marks & Spencer have all fallen into this trap.

## Differential Advantage (Make It Unique!)

Differential advantage (sometimes called competitive advantage, "edge," unique selling proposition, or USP) lies at the heart of every successful market strategy. This principle indicates that the way to make high profits is to offer customers something they want but cannot get—or believe they cannot get or do not want to get—elsewhere. Differential advantage is the net benefit or cluster of benefits that achieves this goal. The intent is to design an offer that provides a sufficiently large and profitable segment with benefits that customers in that segment seek and that they believe competitors do not provide.

Today's markets are intensely competitive. Merely satisfying customer needs and wants is a necessary but insufficient condition for achieving the firm's goals: Competitive parity, even stalemate, is the most likely result. For long-term gain, the firm must develop an offer that is better and/or different in ways that are important to the customer. Some differentials are better than others, depending on how easily they can be imitated. Although many producers favor differentials based on product, other marketing-mix elements may be less vulnerable to competitive imitation. Marketers may secure a differential advantage from long-term personal relationships, better availability, communications, service, or elements that increasingly are not part of the traditional marketing mix, as described in later chapters. One approach suggests that sustained competitive advantage follows a roughly increasing linear pattern: product, manufacturing process, organizational processes (e.g., a parts delivery system), and people/people processes (e.g., customer relations, service from qualified technicians, and a willingness-to-serve culture).[19]

No matter how secure a differential advantage appears to be, historical evidence suggests that competitive activity will eventually erode it away. This is what the late Tom Bonoma, then a professor at Harvard Business School, described as "The Law of the West—There's Always a Kid with a Faster Gun." Consequently, maintaining a differential advantage is a constant challenge, and the search for rejuvenation must be ongoing. Ideally, the next advantage is "sitting on the shelf," ready to trump the competitor's ace. This is why the process for creating competitive advantage may be the ultimate sustaining advantage.

Creating and recreating differential advantage requires the firm to be always willing to outdate its own market offerings. Cannibalization is the price of sustained market leadership![20] Many large firms have a poor track record on cannibalization, no doubt because the political constituencies for current offerings are so strong. The advent of the Internet has highlighted this issue: "Old economy" firms with traditional distribution arrangements are struggling to integrate the Web's potential for dealing directly with end-customers. To the extent that firms are unable to swiftly make the tough cannibalization decisions (e.g., Barnes and Noble in book retailing) they allow the initiative to pass to the challenger by default.[21]

Finally, not all differences result in advantage. The business world is littered with examples of firms developing market offers that were truly different from those of competitors, but that failed nonetheless. Differences in the offer must create benefits that target customers truly value before a company can be confident that it has achieved differential advantage.

Sustaining differential advantage is not the sole domain of the all-seeing, all-powerful marketing department. It requires innovation, insight, and implementation throughout the organization. If the firm is unable to secure differential advantage, those competitors that more clearly understand the critical issues of Total Integrated Marketing will surely overtake it.

## Integration (Get It Together!)

Success requires that all elements in design and execution be carefully integrated and coordinated. The chain analogy is an apt and powerful metaphor. Just as a chain is only as strong as its weakest link, so a market strategy is only as strong as its weakest element. Poor advertising can ruin the chances of success for an otherwise excellent product; production problems destroy delivery promises; delayed promotional materials condemn a product launch to failure; a clumsy credit department drives customers away; and ineffective pricing raises havoc with sales forecasts.

Most executives readily agree in principle with the need for a carefully integrated plan and strategy. However, achieving such integration in practice is fraught with difficulty. Problems typically arise from different functions or departments squabbling over priorities. The result is mishmash or an offer so diluted by coalitions that it is impossible to develop a powerful, integrated benefit package. Organizations with a corporate-wide external perspective are most likely to achieve integration. Shared values incorporating a common belief that the firm must focus on serving customers better than competitors can promote the commonality of purpose required in a hypercompetitive world. Achieving integration requires agreements on priorities, as well as the development of close and cooperative working relationships among all the participants in designing and implementing the offer. These agreements are much more easily achieved with shared values. For functionally organized firms, significant organizational innovation may be required to promote interfunctional coordination. Such approaches as Quality Function Deployment (QFD), process teams, and multifunctional business groups can foster an integrated approach.

As discussed in Chapter 5, the design of a market strategy is a highly constrained problem. Once agreement is reached on the key elements of target market segments, customer value, and differential advantage, other offer elements must fall into line within very narrow limits. From the customer's perspective, this integration must occur to guarantee value creation and delivery. Once offer design is completed, the firm must ensure that management systems, organization structure, human resources, and action plans promote successful implementation of the integrated design. Marketplace success demands detailed planning to set the direction and timing of actions that, in the final analysis, are the only concrete manifestation of market strategies.

Yet again, the issue is Total Integrated Marketing. The alternative is to stand by and watch competitors get their act together better than we do, and to reap the rewards for doing so.

# CONCLUSION

In the strategic marketing process, five responsibilities, or tasks, describe the job: determining and recommending which market opportunities the firm should address; selecting target segments and customers in those addressed markets; designing the offer for customers in the selected segments; securing support from other functions; and monitoring and controlling execution and performance. The first three tasks are undoubtedly strategic, whereas the last two are focused on the operating aspect of the marketing job. Both are important, but in many firms marketing, perversely, becomes preoccupied with familiar operational issues, neglecting the tougher strategic decisions. As discussed in Chapter 4, this imbalance can create major problems for the firm and its shareholders.

To execute these tasks well is demanding. Four basic principles for managing the strategic marketing process make the job easier. These principles are closely linked to the five strategic marketing tasks (Figure 3.2). The principle of selectivity and concentration underlines the desirability of carefully and precisely selecting target market segments, then concentrating resources against those selected targets. The principles of customer value and differential advantage suggest that offers be carefully designed. These designs provide prospective customers with benefits they really value but cannot find in competitors' offers. Finally, the principle of integration highlights the crucial need to ensure that different elements making up the offer are designed and implemented in a coordinated manner. Unless managers achieve such integration, both within and without the domain of traditional marketing, their other efforts are doomed to failure.

This gets us back to our continuing theme—Total Integrated Marketing. Companies cannot achieve superior performance by placing marketing in a functional silo. World-class companies do not behave this way. Marketing must have a coordinated cross-functional, cross-boundary, cross-interest external focus that links together all parts of the organization and its external partners. This perspective is absolutely central for competitive success in the years ahead.

# MARKETING STEWARDSHIP

## THE VIEW FROM THE TOP

Who is the chief marketing officer in this organization? Why, I am . . . how could it possibly be anyone else?

Anonymous CEO

It may look a little curious at first sight. On the one hand, we are arguing that marketing has never been more essential to the survival and growth of organizations than it is now. But, at the same time, corporate marketing positions are relatively scarce at the top of many major corporations in the United States and overseas. Surely this is an important paradox—if marketing is more important than ever, why have corporate marketing structures disintegrated and what are the implications?

As to the "why," quite simply, the old-style functional marketing department has become an unhelpful anachronism in many companies. As for the implications, the declining influence and organizational status of the marketing department places ever more pressure on the CEO to view marketing issues as a key management responsibility.[1] There is little doubt that the chief executive is in effect also the chief marketing officer—and probably always has been, in successful organizations—and thus must create the conditions for Total Integrated Marketing to happen. In this chapter, we explore the role of CEO as steward of marketing practice throughout the organization.

Critics may say[2] that if the CEO is also the chief marketing officer, then he or she is also the chief financial officer, the chief IT officer, the chief operations officer, and so on. This criticism almost willfully misses the point. Such thinking belongs back in the Dark Ages of Management, when managers put everything in the company into neat little functional boxes and sat back to admire the pristine beauty of the organization chart. That

**55**

customers then had to sort out the confusion (getting one of the salespeople to sell them the product, someone else to get it to them, someone else to arrange the finance, someone else to come and maintain the products, and so forth) was largely ignored. Frankly, the world has moved on. The new rule is that suppliers exist to solve customer problems, not vice versa. Putting marketing in a functional box does not even get close to meeting this rule for most companies. That is where the CEO comes in.

In most companies, the reality is that no one but the CEO can ensure the implementation of the strategic marketing tasks and principles.[3] The strategically oriented tasks that focus on identifying market opportunity and selecting which market segments to target are critical. These decisions define the source of the firm's future revenues. But having identified the opportunity and selected potential customers, the firm must deliver value to them.

Much of Total Integrated Marketing reflects the crucial need to bring together all the activities in the organization that affect the value offered to the customer. For most, this includes a wide range of functional activities. But it also relies on the buy-in and leadership of the most senior people in the company, particularly the CEO.

## THE CUBE OF MARKETING

A method of explaining the requirements for Total Integrated Marketing to colleagues is to talk about the "cube of marketing": Squaring and cubing is a way to describe the impact of marketing on business performance. The argument is that the marketing impact grows and develops when we invest in marketing × marketing (marketing-squared), as well as in marketing × marketing × marketing (marketing-cubed). This is shown graphically in Figure 4.1.

- *Marketing* is the familiar strategic decisions and tactical actions to get our products and services into attractive markets.
- *Marketing* × *Marketing* (marketing-squared) is the less familiar task of integrating marketing issues into decision making throughout the firm's functions and business units. A large part of the challenge in building Total Integrated Marketing is that executives have to market marketing itself to managers in other functions up and down the company, and often in partner organizations.

■ *Marketing* × *Marketing* × *Marketing* (marketing-cubed) is the process of winning top management support for Total Integrated Marketing, particularly for the integration of marketing into decisions across the organization. Most managers need the legitimacy and organizational protection of top management sponsorship before they can invest time and other resources in cross-functional developments.

The underlying premise is that the full productive impact of marketing insights on business performance rests on cross-functional integration, with visible and substantial support from the organization's most senior executives. These are the internal marketing requirements for making Total Integrated Marketing a reality.

So, what are the marketing issues that should engage the CEO? *First*, the relationship between shareholder value and customer value takes top priority. The core operating responsibility of CEOs is to ensure that the firm delivers real value to its customers, which, in turn, will build shareholder value. The incidences of earnings manipulation brought to light in 2001 and 2002 leave little doubt that senior managers of some companies lost sight of this critical imperative. *Second*, the customer value imperative is

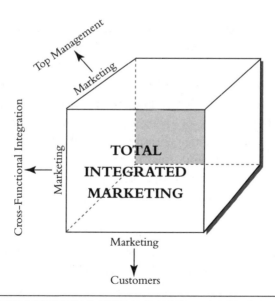

Figure 4.1   THE MARKETING CUBE AND TOTAL INTEGRATED MARKETING

linked to the crucial CEO role of managing brand and customer equity, and enhancing the lifetime value of the company's customers. *Third*, the CEO must manage the business system or value chain so as to balance creation of shareholder value against the delivery of customer value. This responsibility requires both adroitness and sensitivity to the trade-off between cost and value. The sum of these responsibilities makes an overwhelming case for the CEO's leadership role in establishing Total Integrated Marketing throughout the firm.

## SHAREHOLDER VALUE, CUSTOMER VALUE, AND TOTAL QUALITY MANAGEMENT

In many capitalist countries, particularly the United States, the shareholder value philosophy is deeply rooted: Management's job is to maximize returns to shareholders.[4] Most large public companies in countries like the United States, Great Britain, and Australia are financed in reasonably well-regulated, but extremely competitive, capital markets. Managerial underperformance is likely to provoke active opposition from shareholders, if not unfriendly takeover bids.[5] The shareholder value philosophy is also having a significant effect on the management of nongovernmental firms in France, Italy, The Netherlands, and Germany. Even in Japan, such conservatively run companies as Matsushita have instituted share repurchase plans, provided stock options for senior executives, and linked managers' salaries to share performance.[6]

Globalization and the consolidation that follows suggest the inevitable spread of the shareholder value philosophy. As share ownership spreads in a country, whether directly or indirectly (e.g., through actively managed pension funds), the emerging political power of the shareholder will ensure it continues.[7] Although, from time to time, management may talk about the firm's various stakeholders, the shareholder takes pride of place in the eyes of more and more senior managers.[8]

To add economic value and increase shareholder value, a firm must not only make a profit, but make sufficient profit to earn a return on its investment at least equal to its cost of capital.[9] Conversely, if the firm's ROI is less than the cost of capital, it is destroying both economic and shareholder value. The estimated value of the firm's discounted future cash flows should be greater than the disposable value of its tangible and intangible assets to justify its continued existence.

The calculation of shareholder value is based primarily on estimates of future cash inflows and outflows, and is grounded in economic rather than accounting concepts, hence the EVA (economic value added) acronym.[10] Accounting data has many shortcomings that have often led to incorrect managerial decisions[11]; the publicity this issue has received as the result of the Enron and Arthur Andersen debacles barely hints at the trouble that exists. But there is a major problem in traditional views of shareholder value. All cash inflows, with the exception of new investment or debt, come from customers who pay for something the firm sells. Unless these customers see value in the products and services made available for sale, they will be unwilling to part with their resources, typically money, to acquire them. The basis of all markets is this exchange, wherein both buyers and sellers receive value: Buyers prefer the seller's products and services to their own resources; sellers prefer the buyer's resources to their products and services.

As mentioned, the firm's ability to attract and retain customers creates its value. Within a competitive framework, we should ask why customers purchase from one supplier rather than another. The answer is simple: because they believe, rightly or wrongly, that they will receive better value from one supplier than the other. Customers assess this value by comparing the benefits they receive from one supplier for the price they pay versus the benefits they receive from a competitor at that supplier's price.

The creation of customer value is the crux in the creation of shareholder value. With striking parallelism, the Quality movement reached the same conclusion, albeit after a painful odyssey. Many companies went through a long evolution as they wrestled with the Total Quality concept,[12] and confronted the need to "align your entire organization (people and processes) with the evolving needs of your targeted market."[13] In retrospect, it is remarkable that the Quality movement saw the need for Total Integrated Marketing long before marketing executives came to the same conclusion.

*Business Week* (BW) provides some interesting evidence for the quality/value relationship. For several years, BW tracked the share price of winners of the U.S. Malcolm Baldridge Quality Award versus the S&P 500 share price index.[14] BW found that the share price of this relatively small sample of firms consistently outperformed the index by a factor of 3:1— stock pickers take note![15]

In fact, the apparently straightforward concept of shareholder value raises more questions than it answers. This is frequently the case with financial theory, whose focus on capital markets too often assumes away the complexities of product markets and, in this case, the real difficulty of forecasting future cash flows, let alone taking responsibility for creating them. To be fair to accountants, however, adoption of the balanced scorecard has broadened managers' horizons by including measures of quality, customers, and employees, in addition to traditional measures of business performance.[16]

As one of our colleagues has noted, "Top management needs to be deeply committed to marketing because marketing drives growth and shareholder value. The essential idea of marketing is offering customers superior value. By delivering superior value to customers, management in turn can deliver superior value to shareholders. Indeed this formula—customer value creates shareholder value—is the fundamental principle of capitalism."[17] Traditionally, however, the marketing discipline has not incorporated the shareholder value concept into the evaluation of marketing strategies. This is a major reason why, even as marketing processes have become more important, the influence of marketing professionals has declined.

The first challenge to the CEO is to work through the implications of the shareholder value-customer value link in evaluating the contribution of alternative marketing strategies to shareholder value. At the same time, the CEO must recognize that shareholder value relies on achieving superior customer value.

## MANAGING BRAND AND CUSTOMER EQUITY

As we have progressed into the twenty-first century, the valuation of firms has continued to evolve. During the nineteenth and for much of the twentieth century, value, notionally represented by the net book value of assets on the balance sheet, was heavily dependent on so-called hard assets such as plant and equipment. For the past several years, however, the gap between market capitalization and net book value has increased to enormous proportions—driven largely by the importance of intangible or "soft" assets. In the information economy, there is every reason to believe that this trend will continue. These intangibles pose a crisis for the accounting profession—placing a value on brands, customers, patents, or a skilled or productive workforce is much more difficult than recording the depreciated value of a piece of equipment.

The implications for the CEO are enormous. Consider, for example, the intellectual effort that professionals in both corporations and academe have devoted to determining appropriate capital investment decisions. These efforts have ensured that such acronyms as NPV (net present value), IRR (internal rate of return), CAPM (capital asset pricing model), EVA (economic value added), and WACC (weighted average cost of capital) have entered the permanent lexicon of modern management. By contrast, how much effort has been placed on the development of measures for such vital, but softer constructs as R&D productivity, brand equity, advertising effectiveness, or customer loyalty? This imbalance suggests the real dimensions of the issue. Managers always tend to focus more attention on things they can measure than on those they cannot. Although human resources are critical company assets, and their defection can have a devastating impact on the firm's stock price, for the moment, the focus of this discussion is the CEO's role in brand and customer equity.

The following definition of brand equity is currently accepted:

> A set of brand assets and liabilities linked to a brand, its name, and symbol that add to (or subtract from) the value provided by a product or service to a firm and/or that firm's customers.[18]

These assets and liabilities include brand awareness, brand loyalty, perceived quality, brand associations and image (or brand personality), use satisfaction, and other proprietary assets such as patents, trademarks, and channel relationships.[19] To this set of attributes, we may add brand resilience, related to brand loyalty.

### BRAND RESILIENCE

In the mid-1980s, although *Tylenol* market share plummeted to zero following a cyanide poisoning scare, it rebounded quickly when distribution and promotional activities recommenced. By contrast, *Perrier,* which suffered a similar problem related to benzene contamination several years later, has never recovered its preeminent position. Of the two brands, *Tylenol* demonstrated much greater resilience.

## Don't Confuse the Issue!

This traditional definition of brand equity poses a problem because it obscures who gets the value from the "set of assets and liabilities." It states that the value is provided "to a firm," "and/or that firm's customers"— indeed, the listed set of assets and liabilities seem to disproportionately represent values for the firm rather than values for individual customers. It is clearly valuable for the firm to have customers who are brand-loyal because typically a lower ratio of marketing expense then will be necessary to support a given volume of sales. However, the value of brand loyalty to an individual customer is far less clear. In one sense, value is created for the customer by the brand's ability to reduce search costs and to create expectations of securing additional functional, psychological, and/or economic benefits. However, brand loyalty may also have a negative aspect if it discourages the search for other more attractive options.

It is essential that the CEO understand the distinction between brand equity as value to the *organization* and brand equity as value to the *customer*.

## Organizational Brand Equity

Organizational brand equity is reflected in a series of cash flow streams the firm receives by attracting customers to its brand(s), now and in the future.[20] Current products or product lines do not constrain organizational brand equity, nor do current customers. One of the major contributions of this brand equity concept is that it both admits and endorses the notion that the brand may have customer-attracting properties in its own right, over and above any particular product or set of products to which it is currently attached. Alternatively, organizational brand equity reflects the difference between the price paid for the branded product and the price of an identical generic product.[21]

> **BRAND VALUES**
>
> In the mid-1990s, the brand name *Pan Am,* unattached to any airline, was sold for several million dollars. In 1997, Ralph Lauren's *Polo* brand raised roughly $767 million in an initial public offering (IPO) despite having negligible tangible assets.*
>
> * *The New York Times* (June 12, 1997).

The value of an asset does not describe the asset itself. To understand what the asset represents, we must consider the customer perspective, a subject to which we shall return.

## Measuring the Value of Organizational Brand Equity

The CEO, acting as steward, must be able to measure and track the value of organizational brand equity. For example, a firm that contemplates acquiring and/or divesting a business unit for which no market price exists must determine the value of the brands involved to set an appropriate price. Or, perhaps a firm wants to track the performance of its brands over time. Because it is relatively simple to improve profits in the short run by cutting brand support activities, current profits may be a poor indicator of future profits; hence, the need for a measure or measures of brand equity.

There are several approaches to valuing brand equity. Among the more popular are financial-market methods since they match the shareholder value perspective. The **Market Value** method views organizational brand equity as the difference between market value and balance sheet book value, plus nonbrand intangibles such as patents, know-how, and human resources.[22]

### FORD AND JAGUAR

In 1989, Ford paid $2.5 billion for the British car manufacturer *Jaguar*, whose book value was $0.4 billion. The difference, $2.1 billion, placed on Ford's balance sheet as "goodwill," mainly represents Jaguar's organizational brand equity.

The **Replacement Cost** method focuses on the anticipated cost to replace the brand, factored by the probability of success, whereas **Earnings** methods use earnings to develop measures of organizational brand equity.[23] For example, the Interbrand Group plc, employs two factors—annual after-tax profits less expected earnings for an equivalent unbranded product averaged over time, factored by a proprietary-developed multiple purporting to measure brand strength. Measures of brand strength are based on several factors including leadership (the ability to influence the market), stability (survival ability based on degree of customer loyalty), market (invulnerability to change of technology and fashion), geography (the ability to cross geographic and cultural borders), support (the consistency and effectiveness of brand support), and protection (legal title). Relatedly, **Product–Market** methods are based on the extra price commanded by a brand over a generic or unbranded equivalent.

Despite the precarious nature of some of the assumptions underlying brand valuation, the resulting values are of more than academic interest. Because of the problem of dealing with goodwill in acquisitions, in 2001 the United States joined Great Britain, France, Australia, and New Zealand in allowing companies to place the values of acquired brands on their balance sheets as "identifiable intangible assets."[24]

Apart from the difficulties associated with each of these methods, brand valuations may be wrong, just as with any item of value for which a liquid market does not exist.

## QUAKER OATS AND SNAPPLE

In 1994, Quaker Oats purchased the *Snapple* brand of fruit and tea soft drinks for $1.7 billion. Twenty-seven months later, it sold Snapple for $300 million, a loss of $1.4 billion, which, together with $160 million in operating losses in 1995 and 1996, amounted to roughly $2 million per day during Quaker's ownership. (Quaker's 1996 sales were $5.2 billion.)* Snapple's organizational brand equity obviously was not worth the $1.7 billion that Quaker paid.

* *The New York Times* (March 28, 1997).

Although these valuation methods provide interesting information, they are not terribly useful for day-to-day management of organizational brand equity. Valuation, especially about the revenue function, always rests on assumptions about the behavior of customers, and these assumptions must be subject to painstaking and frequent scrutiny. How many customers in the target market will buy? How often? How responsive will they be to the marketing programs we expect to use? What will be their reactions to the predicted blandishments of our competitors? How do we expect their tastes and preferences to evolve over time? How might government actions affect demand for our own and competitive products in the future? Assumptions about these and other issues are present, at least implicitly, in every valuation exercise. Thus, for most management purposes, more appropriate measures relate to the components of brand equity: brand awareness, brand loyalty, brand resilience, perceived quality, brand associations and image, use satisfaction, and other proprietary assets such as patents, trademarks, and channel relationships. For ongoing management purposes, changes in these measures are more important than their absolute value. This principle is reflected in the health checks that so many companies have put in place to monitor their brands.

## Brand Health Checks

These systems help remedy a major defect in measuring brand manager performance. Brand managers are too often evaluated on measures that focus solely on such results as profit, volume, or market share. This is rather like asking a corporation to show only an income statement. Organizational brand equity can be thought of as the balance sheet for the brand,[25] and provides assurance that good short-term results have not been achieved at the expense of the brand's future.[26]

Brand health indicators typically consist of trends in such criteria as customer purchase behavior, customer perceptions, marketing support, and profitability. In addition to historic trends, managers may also benchmark their brand's performance against competing brands. When the entire brand portfolio is assessed using the same criteria, management gets an accurate overview of the brand health for an entire business unit or company. A typical set of brand health measures is displayed in Table 4.1. Other measures might include perceived quality, brand associations, customer satisfaction, and brand loyalty.

Several methods are available for securing data to build these measures. Data for sales, advertising, and profitability are derived from the firm's accounting system. Competitive sales, advertising, and distribution data can be secured from industry-focused research suppliers. Survey research normally secures the perception measures. Brand health checks are not a one-time event. The health of a firm's brands should be measured on an ongoing periodic basis, say, bimonthly or quarterly, and the results used to make appropriate changes in the firm's market strategy and tactics.

Table 4.1   BRAND HEALTH CHECK MEASURES

| Type of Measure | Measure | |
| --- | --- | --- |
| Purchasing | Market share | Brand sales versus total market sales (units and dollars). |
| | Market breadth | Number of customers purchasing the brand. |
| | Market depth | Extent of repeat purchase. |
| Perception | Awareness | Degree of awareness of the brand. |
| | Uniqueness | Is the brand differentiated from competition? |
| | Quality | Perception of brand quality (actual quality in blind tests is also a useful measure). |
| | Value | Does the brand provide good value for money? |
| Market support | Advertising | Market share/advertising share. |
| | | Advertising/total marketing spending. |
| | Distribution | Extent of distribution coverage in target out less for retail goods, quality of display, especially in key accounts. |
| | Relative price | Price compared to competitive brands. |
| Profitability | Profit | Gross margin earned from the brand. |
| | | Economic value added (EVA) of the brand. |

## Customer Brand Equity[27]

Whereas the typical brand health check includes measures of organizational inputs, the ultimate value of brand equity to the organization depends critically on customer response to these inputs. Thus, the value of *customer* brand equity is the value that an individual customer receives from a branded product or service, over and above the value received from an identical unbranded (generic) product or service. This value may be greater than the price differential between the branded and generic product, as individual customers may be willing to pay more than the asking price for the branded product.

To manage brands well, senior management must understand and respect the source of this idiosyncratic value; it exists in the minds of customers. For this reason, we often advise clients that the reward for a successful brand strategy is loss of ownership! If they are successful, their customers own the brand. It is when we forget this simple lesson that things often go awry. To customers, a brand is a collection of perceptions that they hold about a product, service, or company. These perceptions embody values that together create meaning; this meaning represents a promise of the experience customers anticipate when they use the brand. If CEOs understand the perceptions and expectations associated with their brand, they are much more likely to make appropriate marketing decisions.

The extent to which customer brand equity is positive for substantial numbers of customers is basically a reflection of the nurturing of trust between the brand owner and its customers—both historical customers and newcomers. Anecdotal evidence suggests that, as with interpersonal trust, customer brand equity generally develops slowly over time, but fragile. Negative information from managerial mishaps can quickly dissipate it. Many companies in recent years have become acutely aware of the consequences of deterioration in customers' perceptions of these relationships. *Audi* cars were alleged to have slipped into gear causing several deaths, adverse side effects were reported from *Dow Corning* breast implants, *Intel's* first *Pentium* chip made incorrect calculations, and *Perrier* water contained product impurities.

## LOSING BRAND EQUITY

The Arthur Andersen debacle is a classic example of loss of equity. Clients hire accounting firms expecting them to conduct audits in a manner that complies with the law and accounting principles. Trust in the integrity of those audits is vital to the economy, for billions of investment dollars move around based on audited financial statements and the projections made therefrom. When that trust is violated, or even appears to have been violated, as with Andersen, the consequences can be so severe as to destroy the viability of the enterprise. The market value of professional services firms is more or less completely dependent on intangible assets, something that appears to have escaped the senior partners that ran this accounting firm.

Properly managed, the impact on organizational brand equity of well-nurtured customer brand equity can be extremely long lasting. In the liquor industry, the one hundred leading brands have an average age of over one hundred years! Although customer brand equity may build up slowly, it can endow long-term advantages to the brand owner. This characteristic raises serious basic questions for the CEO about the management practices of many companies.

Just as some decisions can lead to enhanced customer brand equity, so other decisions can undermine brand equity and cause it to decline. Activities that typically diminish customer brand equity are product proliferation; price-cutting, discounts, and excessive or inappropriate promotions; lower price component substitution; channel downsizing and proliferation; and channel/supplier squeezing. When brand management is delegated to junior brand managers and is embedded in an inadequate performance measurement system, the quest for increases in volume, market share, and even profit may actually harm customer brand equity (and ultimately organizational brand equity).[28]

## PROTECTING BRAND EQUITY

In discussing IBM CEO Lou Gerstner's tenure as head of the charge card business at American Express, where a high premium was placed on customer brand equity, Shelly Lazarus of Ogilvy and Mather said: "I learned a big lesson from Lou. Once you've set a strategy, you never *ever* violate it. Nobody ever got a free card, a discounted card, bundled pricing. Lou would say: 'This is a violation of the brand, and we're not doing it.' "*

* *Fortune* (April 14, 1997).

## Customer Brand Equity and the Lifetime Value of Customers

Just as organizational brand equity is reflected in the long-run value of the brand for the firm, so customer brand equity reflects the long-run value of the brand for the customer. To the extent that the brand delivers value to customers over the long run, they will continue to be customers and hence deliver value to the firm. The critical valuation from the customer perspective is customer lifetime value. In this view, the value of the firm is related less to the value of its brands than to the value of the customers that purchase those brands. This provides the direct link to the assertion in Chapter 1 that the only asset a firm requires is paying customers.

Technically, customer lifetime value (LTV) is the series of discounted cash flows that customers deliver to the firm over time. Empirical evidence shows that, in general, net margins get larger over time as customers increase their base product use, purchase additional products and services, and may pay somewhat higher prices.[29] (They may also engage in positive word-of-mouth that enhances margins from current and potential customers.) Retention rates also show some gains over time as loyalty increases with experience.

Although raising net margins over time is important, perhaps the most critical issue is customer retention. Customer retention is directly linked to customer brand equity. To the extent that the firm delivers value to customers, the brand equity that customers enjoy increases, and so does the likelihood that they will continue to be customers (higher retention rates). The metrics underlining the impact of retention on profitability are familiar.[30] It may be less well-known that retention rates vary dramatically in the marketplace. This really should not be news to anyone; as long ago as the early 1980s, some Japanese car companies were retaining over 70 percent of their U.S. customers, whereas some U.S. brands had retention rates below 30 percent.

In this way, customer lifetime values are directly related to the value of the firm. It is not quite this simple, of course, as managers have to be concerned about fixed costs and future potential customers. These customers also have value (and acquisition costs), for they are the ones the company expects to secure through its strategy. Their lifetime value is calculated in the same way as that of current customers, less acquisition cost.

Because of its relationship to company value, the customer LTV construct has important operating implications that should concern CEOs. For example, suppose you put your firm's promotional budget in two pots—one for promotional efforts focused on retaining customers, and one for securing new customers. In many companies a disproportionately large amount of the budget goes to customer acquisition, and too little goes to customer retention. What is the bottom line here? In the final analysis, customers are the only assets that the firm really needs.

Also, the value of the firm's customer assets, which can be measured using the procedures mentioned earlier, determines the value of the firm. It follows that not only should CEOs be seriously concerned about the firm's customers, they also should put systems in place to monitor their value and take appropriate actions to enhance retention rates and the margins received per customer.

This concept of customers as assets may initially come as a bit of a shock to the traditional finance department, which may more often think of customers as obdurate and troublesome slow payers. The asset view of customers, however, holds the potential to revolutionize the relationship between the marketing and finance functions, as well as between the firm and its customers. The concept of customer equity embodies the fundamental determinant of the firm's asset value, the prime reason it might be worth more than the disposal value of its tangible assets. This "stock" measure is an estimate of the stored value of the enterprise to its shareholders. Decisions that reduce this stored equity deplete the value of the business to shareholders—they are equity-destroying.

Yet, as noted earlier, customers do not appear on the firm's balance sheet. Furthermore, as company market values diverge ever more from the book value of their assets, the traditional balance sheet has decreasing relevance for the value of the corporation. The crucial link from the value of customers to the balance sheet is organizational brand equity. To the extent that the regulatory authorities allow the firm to account for its intangible assets, including brand equity, the balance sheet will more accurately affect company value. In any case, organizational brand equity must be measured and managed. This is a critical challenge for CEOs.

## LOSING CUSTOMER BRAND EQUITY AT BRITISH AIRWAYS

In the summer of 1997, the then chief executive of British Airways, Robert Ayling, permitted a labor dispute to escalate to a point that forced the cancellation of thousands of flights. In the months of the dispute, British Airways passenger route miles in its premier classes dropped 9 percent, and its stock price almost halved. Four months later, BA's traffic was still 1 percent down on the previous year, whereas its major competitors had seen increases. Ayling's failure to manage his labor relations better was enormously costly to BA's customer brand equity, especially among business travelers, for whom schedule reliability is essential. BA has since struggled to retrieve the situation under a new CEO.

Whether we approach valuation from the perspective of the brand (organizational brand equity), or from the perspective of the customer (customer brand equity leading to customer equity), the critical imperative is to place the customer at the center of investment and management priorities. This is the challenge for the CEO.

# IMPROVING SHAREHOLDER VALUE BY RAISING MARGINS

The firm's business system (also termed value chain) provides CEOs with a useful framework for guiding the implementation of Total Integrated Marketing and offers another link between the generation of customer value and the creation of shareholder value.

## The Business System (Value Chain)

In the most simple view, the business firm is no more than an organizational device for converting inputs (e.g., raw materials) into outputs (e.g., products and services for sale). The firm's business system consists of the activities involved in this process. Individual firms may identify a smaller or greater number of activities, each of which should add value in the conversion process. Figure 4.2 shows an example of a business system developed for a distribution business with several support activities. Typically, in addition to the value-adding activities noted in the figure, legal work, public relations, accounting, personnel, regulatory affairs, basic research, quality assurance, and finance must also be conducted, whether by the firm or an outsourced partner. Firms comprising multiple business units have several value chains. Any individual business unit may or may not share individual value chain elements and/or provide inputs and/or receive outputs from sister business units.

In considering the structure of a firm's business system, managers have four generic options for increasing shareholder value: They can increase the capture of value from customers, reduce costs, reengineer activities, or change the balance between outsourcing and insourcing.

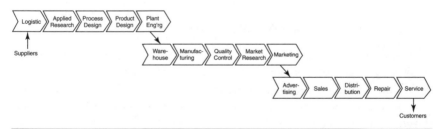

Figure 4.2 THE FIRM'S BUSINESS SYSTEM. Adapted from J. B. Quinn, *Intelligent Enterprise* (New York: Free Press, 1992).

## Increasing Value Capture from Customers

Capturing value requires the company to price its offer so that it is paid appropriately for the value delivered to customers. If products are underpriced, management can improve margins simply by raising prices. To implement such a change successfully requires a deep understanding of customers' perceptions of the value delivered. Alternatively, a price increase may be possible by finding ways to add value to the offer. The business system provides a framework for identifying areas where increased investment and other resources may produce value for customers in excess of cost increases.

## Reducing Costs

Cost reduction implies that the firm must examine its value–adding and support activities in an attempt to cut costs without affecting (and, perhaps even enhancing) the delivery of customer value. Table 4.2 illustrates the kinds of questions to ask.

In addition to the options in Table 4.2, perhaps the firm can reorganize the business system so that customers undertake some of its cost-incurring steps. Examples include banking with ATM machines instead of tellers, shopping at discount clubs with minimal floor help, and purchasing groceries at self-service checkout registers. There are many activities with widespread applicability such as order entry and tracking, purchase order management, product configuration, and even product development. When the new functions are properly designed, customers may perceive greater benefit in conducting activities themselves, enabling the firm both to reduce its costs and add value to its customers.

---

**REDUCING COSTS AND ADDING VALUE AT FEDEX**

Starting in the 1980s, Federal Express (FedEx) offered its customers package tracking at an 800 number. Today, FedEx's Internet-based system enables customers to track packages, schedule pickups, and generate and print airbills, complete with barcodes. As a result, customer value has increased, and FedEx has reduced its costs.*

*L. Downes and C. Mui, *Unleashing the Killer App: Digital Strategies for Market Dominance* (Boston: Harvard Business School Press, 1998).

Table 4.2   POTENTIAL SOURCES OF COST REDUCTION

*Necessity:* Is this particular activity necessary? Can we do with less of it, or without altogether? Particular areas for investigation are marketing and administrative transaction costs that firms incur in dealing with current and potential customers.

*Human resources:* Can we conduct the activity with fewer people (downsize, rightsize)? Can people whose wage levels are lower conduct the activity?

*Raw materials and supplies:* Can the activity be conducted with fewer inputs? Can we use lower cost inputs?

Frequently, companies overbuild products; detailed analysis of customer needs may allow them to use fewer and/or lower quality raw materials.

*Capital:* Do we need all of our assets? Can we sell/lease assets without reducing our competitiveness? Can we conduct the activity with less expensive capital equipment? Can we increase utilization of existing assets, for example, by multi-shift versus single shift working? Can we develop methods for reducing working capital, for example, by reducing inventory, shortening accounts receivable, or lengthening accounts payable?[31]

*Capital/labor ratios:* Would it be less expensive to substitute capital for labor (by using machines rather than people) or to substitute labor for capital?

*Geographic location:* Could we conduct our operations in a different country/ region where operating costs, for example, human resource, utilities, transportation, and taxes are lower? Where might this be?

## Reengineering Activities

Cost reduction assumes that, after making changes, the company conducts an activity in essentially the same way, just less expensively. Reengineering examines fundamental assumptions underlying the conduct of the activity and seeks alternative approaches. The reengineering perspective is that many company processes were put in place years ago, and frequently, the rationale for conducting an activity in a certain way has been lost in the mists of time. Furthermore, changes in knowledge, customer needs, firm requirements, and available technologies may allow for developing quite different, more effective processes.

The Internet is one vehicle for reengineering business systems. In many supplier/customer relationships, Internet technology has superseded purchase orders, invoices and shipping notices, telephone conversations, and faxes. In addition to direct cost reductions, companies often gain by inventory reductions.

### REENGINEERING TO CUT COSTS

Sun MicroSystems' traditional cost for issuing a reimbursement check was $35 per check. By moving to an Internet-based system for entering employee expenses and conducting the audit function in India (a low-wage economy), Sun was able to reduce the check issuing cost to $2.95, an annual cost saving approaching $1 billion.*

*Personal communication with one of the authors.

## Outsourcing

For each activity in the business system, management must decide whether to "make or buy." Should the firm conduct this activity in-house or have it performed by an outside supplier? Outsourcing has several advantages:

- Because the supplier specializes in the activity, has a broad variety of customers, secures economies of scale, and develops a large experience base, outsourcing may be less expensive; this is especially true if demand for the service is highly variable.
- If the outsourcing supplier provides the necessary capital equipment, it relieves pressure on the outsourcing firm's capital. This, in turn, enables the firm to vary costs that would otherwise be fixed, thus lowering its operating leverage. For capital-intensive firms, this can be a major benefit in cyclical downturns.
- Because the supplier may be able to provide its employees with a more extensive career path, they are likely to deliver superior performance.
- The supplier is more likely to push the technology envelope and so provide the firm with access to world-class capabilities.[32]

A potential disadvantage of outsourcing is that the supplier may be less committed to providing superior service than an internal department. Furthermore, unless the company has a carefully written outsourcing contract, management could find itself contractually bound to a supplier that is providing inadequate service.[33] These concerns may be fewer if the supplier operates in a competitive market and must strive for excellence to keep the business. Furthermore, the outsourcing firm may provide equipment to its supplier to secure some control over its operations. By contrast, the inside department may operate like the monopoly supplier it is.

Activities that are not central to producing customer value and securing long-run competitive advantage are candidates for outsourcing. These activities have to be conducted well, but even though outsourcing may reduce costs and increase value, competitive advantage typically does not accrue because outsourcing suppliers often also sell to the firm's competitors.

Among areas that have seen significant outsourcing are support activities such as security services, payroll administration, mailroom, invoicing and bill paying, pension administration, inventory management, software development, data system management, and oversight of corporate assets (e.g., vehicle fleets and industrial equipment).[34] Many marketing activities may also be outsourced including development of advertising campaigns (to advertising agencies), selling activities (to agents and brokers), and customer service. Increasingly, major companies are outsourcing production activities.

### OUTSOURCING MANUFACTURING AT SARA LEE

Sara Lee Corporation, a major producer of cakes (*Sara Lee*), handbags (*Coach*), sweatshirts (*Champion*), frankfurters (*Ball Park*), bras (*Wonderbra*), and panty hose (*L'Eggs*) decided to outsource virtually all its manufacturing activities and become basically a manager of brand assets. One underlying assumption in Sara Lee's business model is that the strength of its brands will inhibit finished product suppliers from attempting to sell products directly to end users. If this assumption does not hold, then sometime in the future, the branded product seller may find it has to deal with a significant competitor.

Another far-reaching example of production outsourcing is Volkswagen's new Brazilian plant. Suppliers manufacture complete subassemblies on-site placing Volkswagen, whose workers are in a distinct minority, merely in the role of an assembler. Notwithstanding these examples, the firm should not outsource activities that represent core organizational competencies.

### RISKS IN OUTSOURCING

A previous Sara Lee attempt to outsource production ended in disaster. From 1969 to the early 1990s, the glove division grew from $6 million to $220 million (operating profit, $35 million) and *Aris-Isotoner* gloves had 75 percent of the department store market. In an outsourcing move, the firm closed its Manila plant. However, the replacement "low-cost" producers cost 10 percent to 20 percent more, delivery time increased, and product quality dropped. By 1997, operating losses totaled $120 million, and Sara Lee had invested over $100 million to keep the firm afloat. In June 1997, Aris-Isotoner was "virtually given away" to Bain Capital; Sara Lee simply did not understand that the Manila plant was Aris-Isotoner's critical core competence, its crown jewel.*

* *Forbes* (October 20, 1997).

The CEO's stewardship of these decisions is vital. Properly executed outsourcing should enable the firm to devote greater intellectual and financial resources to those business system activities that really deliver customer value and hence secure competitive advantage in the intermediate and long run. Improperly performed, the result can be disastrous.

## Insourcing

Insourcing is the opposite of outsourcing. Just as outsourcing implies that the firm takes an internally conducted activity and places it with an outside supplier, so insourcing takes a purchased activity and conducts it in-house. All the value-added and support activities noted in Figure 4.2 may be conducted either in-house or out-of-house; and at any point in time, an individual firm has a mix of such activities. A particularly interesting example of insourcing is the move of some major corporations to develop their own in-house financing operations, eliminating the need for investment banks to conduct debt and equity underwriting.

Prime candidates for insourcing are activities that are central to producing customer value and securing long-run competitive advantage. These derive from the firm's core competencies, and as long as they match up with customer requirements (needs and wants), they remain the activities that the firm should most likely perform internally.

Far too many attempts to define core competencies have been seriously misdirected. Managements often approach the issue by defining what they are (or even, were) good at, without assessing the relationship to customer needs and wants. That way, the exercise ends up looking inward and backward, instead of outward and forward, as should be the case. A firm's core competencies should not be regarded as fixed; they should evolve over time as the environment changes and strategies are developed to satisfy customer needs more effectively than the products of competitors.

To make appropriate outsourcing/insourcing decisions, management must benchmark the company's performance of business system activities against external "best in class" benchmarks. Highly specialized activities will be within the firm's own sphere of activity, but for commonly performed activities such as billing, shipping, and routine legal work, best-in-class benchmarking principles should be applied. Further, management should benchmark not only the cost of performing an activity, but also the value added to the customer by the activity. Figure 4.3 brings together the concepts of *relative customer value added* and *relative cost* in a matrix that provides guidance for the outsourcing/insourcing decision.[35]

Each of the four cells suggests a different course of action:

- Activities in *Cell A* represent the core of the firm's value chain. The firm is delivering high customer value yet incurring low relative costs. Management should attempt to continue to add value while maintaining the excellent cost relationships.

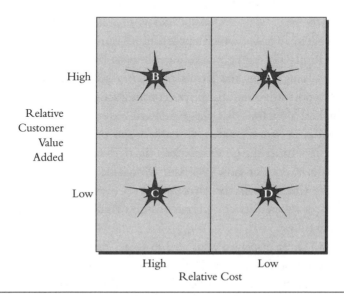

Figure 4.3   VALUE/COST ANALYSIS MATRIX

- In *Cell B,* the firm delivers high customer value but its costs are also high. The major goal for this cell is to reduce costs.

   Activities in Cells C and D offer low customer value. If this value is unnecessary, the firm should contemplate ceasing the activity. If the value, though low, is necessary, different options should be considered.
- *Cell C* activities are strong candidates for outsourcing since the costs are high.
- *Cell D* activities could continue at their current low costs unless there are ways to enhance the value customers receive. These activities need not be outsourced unless even lower cost options are available.

## THE LEADERSHIP ROLE

In Chapter 2, we laid out one view of the new set of environmental forces that corporations face as the information economy takes hold. Of all the responsibilities the CEO assumes, none is more important than trying to understand the implications of these changes for the organization and making the necessary decisions that enhance shareholder value. Perhaps the most critical decision is where the firm should seek its revenue opportunities. One of marketing's core responsibilities is to make recommendations to senior management about which opportunities to pursue. But the CEO has the responsibility for telling marketing where to look in the first place.

We are talking about the firm's mission, a statement that guides the search for opportunity and that places constraints, for the midterm at least, on the market domains that the firm will explore. In many cases, the firm's mission is closely related to markets and products that it currently offers, but sometimes the CEO may lead the firm far away from its historic revenue base. Consider how William Woodside transformed American Can into the financial services firm Primerica (now part of Citigroup), or how Nokia developed its cell-phone business from a Finnish mining and lumber operation.

The CEO must display the leadership to set direction and to have the entire organization fall in step. The CEO is vital to the change process that places the customer at the center of all firm activities and creates the environment in which Total Integrated Marketing becomes a reality. We are convinced skeptics in attempting to divine what CEOs really mean when they periodically make public pronouncements. Although many executives say the right words, these words often prove to be empty platitudes. It is **behavior** that matters. When Tom Peters admonished executives to "walk the talk," he called attention to a pervasive management problem. Saying one thing and doing another is the most common reason executives lose credibility.

When it comes to exhorting the organization to practice Total Integrated Marketing, CEOs must "walk the talk." They must demonstrate to the entire organization, its partners, and allies that the customer really is at the center of all its activities. Managing this change is a great challenge to any organization—many try but few succeed! Embedded in the firm's policies and procedures, its structure and human resources are immense pockets of organizational inertia, forces of resistance to change so great that they are almost inevitably underestimated. Consider the cases of tire maker, Firestone, and securities firm, Bache. In the 1970s, both made severe errors that raised concerns over senior management's ethical behavior and judgment. Directly or indirectly, these errors led to takeovers by Bridgestone and Prudential, respectively. Yet, years after these acquisitions, both Firestone and Prudential-Bache witnessed a recurrence of the very problems that led to their failures in the first place.

Perhaps the most critical message for the CEO is the close interconnection between customer value and shareholder value. As the firm improves the value it delivers to customers, it increases customer brand equity, and improves the retention rate for current customers and the acquisition rate for new customers. Furthermore, by understanding the value that customers receive and by making sensible decisions in such areas as cost reduction, reengineering, outsourcing, and insourcing, its margins should also improve. Improved customer retention and increasing margins constitute a winning combination. This combination enhances the lifetime value of customers, and is reflected in superior organizational brand equity and shareholder value.

This model is powerful and simple, but execution is difficult. Environmental turbulence will bring shifting customer needs and enhanced competition. The firm will only succeed if it can harness the entire set of organizational capabilities to secure and retain customers. This effort demands driving the total integration of the marketing effort from the top. For CEOs, the time is now; you do not have the luxury of waiting!

# MARKET STRATEGY

## THE FORCE FOR INTEGRATION[1]

The output of the marketing process described in Chapter 3 should be a market strategy, and we have repeatedly used the word "strategy" in building the case for Total Integrated Marketing. We want you to understand what strategy is really about for several reasons. First, it is one of the most abused and misunderstood words in the management vocabulary, and it is important. Second, sorting out strategy around the marketplace provides you with a structure that explains why Total Integrated Marketing is an essential management approach—and in practical terms that will allow you to articulate and demonstrate this need to colleagues and CEOs. And let's be honest—if we cannot convince colleagues across all areas and at all levels that strategy matters and is powerful, then they are unlikely to want to be part of Total Integrated Marketing.

Part of the problem in pinning down what people mean by strategy is that it exists at several different levels in the firm (e.g., corporate strategy and business-unit strategy). It is not surprising that strategy seems to mean different things to different people at different times. Our interest is in market strategy.

We focus on the basic building block: strategy for a market segment (or, increasingly, for a single customer). The important point is that different customer requirements demand different marketing approaches, even if the basic products/services offered to the various market segments are similar.

### DIFFERENT SEGMENTS FOR THE SAME PRODUCT

Imagine that two similar consumers visit an electrical appliance superstore early in the evening, and both are looking at kitchen ranges. A reasonable assumption might be that both have similar needs and requirements—a new range. In fact, one is building a new house and is looking at possible appliances for a high-technology kitchen assembly to be installed over the next few months. The other potential buyer has just received a call from home informing him that a broken water pipe has flooded the kitchen and destroyed the range, and what will they give the children for dinner that night? These two buyers have different needs and priorities, creating a problem for the salesperson. They both need a range, but there is a big difference between designing a state-of-the-art kitchen for a dream home and finding an emergency replacement before the entire family budget disappears into McDonald's and Domino's coffers, and the potential buyer hears from a divorce attorney.

Many executives fail to appreciate the importance of adapting marketing approaches to the needs of buyers in different parts of the market. The first step is to look at what constitutes a good strategy and what it should do for the company.

## THE FUNCTIONS OF A STRATEGY

Our work with many corporations has convinced us that a poorly developed vocabulary poses a formidable barrier to successful strategy development and implementation. In today's global marketplace, strategies must frequently be coordinated across geographies and cultures; this magnifies the vocabulary problem. When your European counterparts act as though they do not understand what you mean by strategy, the reason may be that, to them, the term means something else.

To keep it simple, we define just three central concepts: objectives, strategies, and programs; if you get these right, you will be well on your way to building strategic clarity. The following definitions are drawn directly from their original usage in military vocabulary:

- *Objectives* are the results we want to get from the operation of our business.

- *Strategies* describe in a general way how we expect to develop and allocate our resources (deploy our capabilities) to achieve these objectives.
- *Programs* describe the specific actions we will undertake to implement the chosen strategy.

## Why Have a Strategy?

The cynics who suggest that strategy is just how you explain what you have done after the event are sometimes right—strategies do not always exist before the fact. A firm may achieve success, and an after-the-fact examination of its actions reveals a pattern that someone designates as a strategy. The phrase, "Success has many authors," illustrates this approach.[2] Although we agree that managers should learn from experience, we assume the superiority of a properly thought-out strategy. Such forethought typically demands accurate insight into how a market is likely to change and how customers and others will react to the firm's actions as well as those of competitors. As the business environment changes rapidly and becomes more complex, strategy development becomes more essential and difficult. If you need convincing, consider the spectacular crashes of so many of the dot-com pioneers at the start of the twenty-first century. Then ask yourself how much of the problem simply reflected lack of an effective strategy.

### STRATEGY AND THE DOT-COMS—BAD IDEAS DON'T GET BETTER ONLINE[a]

In the late 1990s and the early 2000s, headlines across the world proclaimed the crashes of the dot-coms that had promised so much and delivered so little. Underpinned by investor frenzy and commercial models of short-term greed, many dot-coms failed to distinguish between doing what was technologically feasible and providing customer value. For many, first-mover advantage and the strengths of being "virtual" turned out to be myths. Customer acquisition costs were astronomical and customer retention poor—the latter accelerated by poor levels of customer service and inadequate fulfillment systems. Michael Porter concludes that many dot-com pioneers perished because they tried to compete in ways that "violate nearly every precept of good strategy."[b] The fundamentals of business strategy remain true: Industry structure affects the profitability of competitors, and only sustainable competitive advantage allows a company to outperform the average competitor. He suggests cogently, "In our quest to see how the Internet is different, we failed to see how the Internet is the same."[c]

[a] Based on Nigel F. Piercy, *Market-Led Strategic Change: A Guide to Transforming the Process of Going to Market,* Oxford: Butterworth-Heinemann (2001), pp. 190–196.

[b] Michael Porter, "Strategy and the Internet," *Harvard Business Review Review,* March 2001, pp. 63–78.

[c] Ibid.

## What Does Having a Strategy Do for Us?

At its simplest, firms benefit from strategic clarity for four reasons: It provides direction for integrated effort; it guides the development and allocation of scarce resources; it helps to identify and secure competitive advantage; and it provides the basis for achieving coordination.

**Provide Direction.**  Good strategy provides managers with direction on where to take businesses during some future time period. Typically, the longer the time horizon, the more broad-based the strategy. The content varies with level, but the purpose is the same—to guide the firm in directions that generate shareholder value.

**Guiding the Development and Allocation of Scarce Resources.**  Because resources are limited, strategy must define how to develop and allocate them to take the business in the desired direction. Usually, there is a particular resource that imposes more limits than others—capital, manufacturing capacity, sales-force time, shelf space, or technology. These limitations are most evident when different organization units share resources, which is quite usual at lower levels of strategy development. Clear and effective strategy is essential at the market level, where management must allocate resources across market segments, as well as decide which customers to target and how to compete with rivals. Resources must also be allocated across product development, advertising spending, and sales-force effort.

**Identifying and Securing Competitive Advantage.**  A well-developed market or market segment strategy clearly defines why customers should buy from that firm rather than from competitors. Many company strategies do not meet this test. Too often, management fails to explicitly assess potential competitor response to strategies being formulated.

In business, firms do not typically seek the capitulation or annihilation of competitors; they attempt, instead, to reduce competitors' options, particularly if they pose major threats. Any strategy that cannot withstand reasonably predictable competitor responses should be rejected. Management may need to develop contingent, or "what if . . . ," responses to alternative competitive scenarios and lay out further potential moves. This process leads to both high-quality strategies and the ability to act preemptively.

To achieve operational competitive advantage, every strategy should meet one of the following criteria, in descending order of preference:[3]

- *Competitor cannot do.* If possible, the strategy should commit the firm to actions that competitors cannot duplicate, typically because they lack a key resource or ability.
- *Competitor won't do.* Somewhat less desirable is a strategy that competitors could match, but are unlikely to pursue. To be confident of such a judgment requires considerable insight into competitor resources and management. Perhaps previous experience has convinced the firm that competitors will not choose this option, or market analysis suggests they are placing resources behind other products and markets or will not replicate this strategy because of cash-flow considerations.
- *Competitor is relatively disadvantaged.* Competitors will likely duplicate the firm's strategic moves, but this action will create disproportionate benefit for the firm. For example, price reductions may be a possible strategic action for the low-market-share competitor in an inelastic market. However, should the high-market-share leader follow the across-the-board price cut, its high volume will lead to significant opportunity loss, at least in the short term. Conversely, when a large competitor increases fixed-cost expenditures, such as R&D, market coverage, advertising, technical service, or product-line breadth—small competitors attempting to match these actions generally suffer because the larger competitor can spread its fixed costs over greater volume.[4]

**Achieving Coordination.**   The final benefit of a clear strategy—critical but all too often elusive—is coordinating the actions of organizational units so that they are all pulling in the same direction to implement chosen strategies. A good strategy must integrate the functions that provide resources for strategy implementation, but because the requirements of each market segment are unique, integration must be achieved at this level.

In most organizations, the potential for conflict and discord among key functional managers is significant. Very often, the actions of these managers are appropriate for their organizational positions, consistent with existing reward structures, and based on their individual backgrounds and training. To develop a solid strategic direction, however, the firm must resolve these conflicts. Many companies achieve harmony through compromise, whereby each functional area gives up a little to secure an agreement with which no one is happy but with which all will live. Alternative conflict-resolution methods are for top management to make a decision, or for functional managers to exercise political power to secure an agreement most to their liking.

The problem with all these decision-making methods is that they tend to be internally rather than externally focused. Although one functional area may seem to gain advantage, the firm as a whole does not win, the competitors do. In many firms, sales managers are driven to reach sales quotas, manufacturing directors to run efficient plants, research directors to design better products, human-resource directors to upgrade personnel quality, and finance directors to improve profitability (particularly by limiting investment). Performance standards and criteria (especially traditional measures that have changed little over the years) may be out of kilter with what is necessary to win customers and beat competitors in the twenty-first century.

Total Integrated Marketing requires genuine team support around the direction embodied in the strategy, and the reward system and evaluation criteria must match that direction. The strategy-development process plays an important role in encouraging functional managers to take a holistic view of the business; this requires significant skill in building relationships, managing group processes, and coordinating activities. Creativity must be valued, while conflict and contention should be seen as natural and healthy. Once managers achieve consensus, however, the action shifts to program planning and execution. At this point, strategy resembles a yoke or harness:

Just as the yoke keeps the oxen (or horses) pulling as a team, so the strategy ensures that all important functions necessary to executing the market strategy are moving in the same direction.

An important purpose in formulating market strategy is to encourage managers to look outward to the environment and focus on external issues instead of succumbing to insidious yet ubiquitous internal perspectives. But even if management is convinced of the need for a clear strategy, this leaves the question of what it is.

## ELEMENTS OF A MARKET STRATEGY

This section covers the elements of strategy for a market segment. At a minimum, the framework can serve as a template against which managers can test their own strategies for completeness. It may also be viewed as a model to guide strategy development. At its simplest, a market-segment strategy contains four major elements and several subelements:

1. Performance objectives:
   —Strategic objectives.
   —Operational objectives.
2. Choosing a strategic focus.
3. Positioning:
   —Choice of customer targets.
   —Choice of competitor targets.
   —Selection of core strategy/key buying incentive/value proposition.
4. Implementation:
   —Description of supporting marketing-mix programs.
   —Description of supporting functional programs.

The first two major elements, performance objectives (strategic and operational) and selection of a strategic focus, establish the broad direction of the strategy. The third main element—comprising customer targets, competitor targets, and core strategy (sometimes known as the three Cs of market strategy)—determines the product's positioning in the target market segment.[5] The final element, the marketing-mix and functional-support requirements, deals with the planning and integration of the programs (or tactics) necessary to implement the strategy successfully.

Objectives, strategic focus, and positioning are conceptual devices. Responsibility for their development lies with those who plan strategy, typically possessing such titles as business or marketing director, or product or brand manager. More and more, however, cross-functional business teams are developing these strategies. In any case, strategy implementation requires the actions of many people throughout the organization; that is the ethos of Total Integrated Marketing. Only if strategy development is agreed on and well articulated can it provide the total integration that will coordinate individuals' actions to achieve appropriate implementation. One of the best ways to ensure this integration is to encourage wide participation in strategy development. Coincidentally, the quality of the strategy that emerges from such a process is almost invariably higher than when development is constricted to a few individuals.

## Setting Performance Objectives: What Do You Want to Achieve?

**Choosing Strategic Objectives.** The choice of strategic objectives is a fundamental decision because it establishes, in a qualitative and directional sense, the results the firm wants to attain during the planning period. Typically, strategic objectives are grouped into three broad categories: profitability, cash flow, and growth. Although improvement in each of these areas may be desirable, trade-offs exist. Since significant growth typically requires increased spending, both expenses and capital (fixed and working) are likely to rise, with consequential short-term declines in cash flow and, sometimes, net profit. Although the impact of these relationships depends on growth rate and investment intensity, achieving maximum possible profits, cash flow, and market share all at the same time is impossible in the real world. Before the strategy-development process can proceed, management must prioritize objectives. Is growth in sales volume or market share of greater concern than cash flow or profit, or vice versa? Management must address these strategic trade-offs for each targeted market segment.[6]

Strategic objectives are usually stated qualitatively but should nonetheless set an unambiguous direction for the business in the segment. A typical statement for a segment of the breakfast-cereals market might take the following form:

- In the "young family with children" segment, our primary objective is to increase profits from sales of our "Cold Chunks" brand of ready-to-eat cereal. Our secondary objective is to maintain market share.

**Guidance in Choosing Strategic Objectives: You Must Set Priorities!** Setting priorities among objectives is a difficult task. However, it is easier to attain the firm's objectives by concentrating efforts in attractive markets where competitive advantage is considerable versus in markets without these conditions.

Empirical evidence guides consideration of priorities. Results from the PIMS study[7] show that sales growth and market share are high in early life-cycle stages and lower in late life-cycle stages; by contrast, return on investment (ROI) and cash flow are negative in the start-up stage and become positive later. Priorities among strategic objectives will change across a typical product life cycle. In the early stages (introduction and early growth), firms often set objectives of growing at, or faster than, the market growth rate. As market growth slows (late growth stage and/or when market share is considered sufficient), firms may choose to improve profit margins and/or return on assets (ROA). During the maturity stage, and especially when decline appears imminent, cash-flow concerns are likely to predominate. These guidelines are not cast-iron prescriptions for choosing primary strategic objectives (setting such objectives contrary to the received wisdom can be an effective destabilizing competitive move). Rather, they reflect the behavior of many companies if we assume that, on average, business results reflect objectives.

Whichever trade-off is selected, that objective is central to all subsequent decisions. Because it is such a critical choice, top management and business-unit (or division) managers typically exert significant influence on market-level objectives. These often are based on capital market expectations although this happens somewhat less frequently at the individual segment level. Managers primarily concerned with the product/market area should also be active participants in setting objectives, and decisions must be based on a thorough analysis of conditions in their markets.

Inevitably, setting objectives causes conflicts based on tension between characteristics of the product/market opportunity and capital market pressures for profits. Trained to focus on the marketplace when setting strategic objectives, marketing and product managers typically concentrate on such dimensions as market growth, market size, competitive strength, and current market position. They must temper this focus with consideration of shareholder value and the competitiveness of the firm in capital markets.[8] Far too often, however, this takes second place to arbitrary and unthinking actions by managers driven to conform to a budget that may have, but typically has not, considered the true interests of shareholders.

**Choosing Operational Objectives: Give Us the Numbers.** Strategic and operational objectives differ in specificity. Whereas strategic objectives establish, qualitatively, the general direction the firm wishes to take, operational objectives are quantitative, providing the numbers that tell how much is required and in what period of time. Therefore, the operational objective should specify the amount of sales volume (or market share), profit (or profit margin), or cash flow to be produced over each year of the planning period. To continue with our breakfast-cereal example, a complete objective statement may appear as follows:

## Segment: Young Family with Children

|  | Strategic Objectives | Operational Objectives |
| --- | --- | --- |
| Primary | Increase profits from sales of our "Cold Chunks" brand of ready-to-eat cereal | • From: $15 million in 2003 to: $20 million in 2004 $25 million in 2005 $25 million in 2006 |
|  | while maintaining revenue market share | at 25% from 2003 through 2006. |

*Whereas operational objectives are typically set per annum in the strategic marketing plan, in the annual marketing plan they are typically calendarized by quarter or by month.

Operational objectives provide a specific goal (or end result) to be achieved and offer a means of evaluating performance. Objectives should be challenging to the managerial team but should also be realistic.[9] Over the years, we have learned that objectives beyond the reach of managers are likely to act as disincentives (or demotivators) instead of as a positive force. At early stages in strategy development, operational objectives must be viewed as tentative. The feasibility (or otherwise) of operational objectives can only be fully assessed after the company has developed the strategy and programs, and has projected revenues and costs.

A Final Note.    Objective setting is critical because such decisions frame the entire strategy. Top management frequently states objectives in terms of profits required over the planning period: "Over the next three years, $45 million must be delivered to the firm's bottom line!" The problem with such an objective is that no one may have asked—let alone answered—the most basic question: "How might the achievement of this objective affect performance on other important dimensions?" If achieving these profits destroys the ongoing value of the business by running down assets (tangible or intangible), it is likely that it will not have served shareholders' interests. Likewise, if profits are achieved, but market share goes down significantly, the consequences will probably be similar.[10] There is nothing wrong with an aggressive $45 million profit target per se. But achieving this objective by cutting new-product development, advertising, or sales promotions may jeopardize the long-term viability of the business. It is best to address such trade-offs explicitly.

## Choosing a Strategic Focus: You Must Make Choices!

Choosing a focus provides broad direction for achieving the strategic objectives. The "tree" of strategy alternatives has almost an infinite variety of branches, but defining objectives prunes that tree to a manageable size and sharpens focus. Although fully developing the strategy still requires an enormous amount of work, the problem is significantly simpler.

There are many options in selecting a focus. It is useful to array the strategic options logically, in a way that is related to the likely marketing challenge. To do this, we have constructed a means–ends chain that depicts alternative ways of realizing the goal of long-term profit (see Figure 5.1).[11] For a start, this distinguishes between growing profits through increased sales volume and increasing productivity to enhance profitability.

Increasing Unit Sales Volume.    Four broad strategic alternatives are available to increase unit sales volume; two focus on existing customers, two on new customers. The most profitable way to grow almost all businesses is to focus on the existing customer base. First, stop losing so many customers

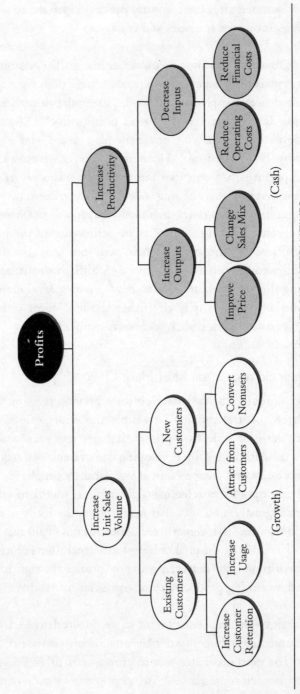

Figure 5.1 DEVELOPING STRATEGIC ALTERNATIVES

to competitors! Second, how about doing a better job of increasing usage by, or cross-selling to, existing customers? In these two options—as well as a third, attracting competitors' customers—the customer is assumed to have already purchased the product form and is therefore familiar with the basic product-form benefits. By contrast, if the firm targets nonusers, it cannot assume any familiarity with the benefits, and customer decision making is notably different.

*Increasing retention (reducing defection) of existing customers.*   The customer list of any business is a little like a leaky bucket. If the firm can plug some of the holes by reducing the defection rate, the business will grow faster. Such thinking is central to customer relationship management.[12] Indeed, some organizations employ retention managers. At NASDAQ, these managers attempt to halt successful companies' defection to the New York Stock Exchange. Loyalty programs designed to reward repeat business such as airline frequent-flyer programs are now common, but even small organizations can benefit from such initiatives. In Hong Kong, many retail stores have formed loyalty clubs typically based on a loyalty card that clerks "chop" (nick) with each purchase.[13] Improved customer service is one of the most effective ways of reducing defection. At some companies, customer retention is a major goal of the customer-service function.

*Increasing use/cross-selling existing customers.*   For this alternative, too, the firm already has a relationship with its customers. Several tactics might encourage usage: Enlarge the unit of purchase,[14] increase the rate of product obsolescence,[15] find new uses for the product,[16] and provide price incentives to purchase larger quantities.[17] For firms in business-to-business marketing, an effective approach is to help customers grow at the expense of their competitors. Such strategies include distributor training programs, joint promotion strategies (often seen in retail outlets), provision of advertising and promotion allowances, and "spiff" monies (cash incentives) earned by retailers' and distributors' salespeople. Some of the best-known examples, however, involve customers incorporating the seller's brand on their products in return for the seller's advertising direct to final consumers; synthetic-fiber manufacturers are especially adept at this approach.

### CO-BRANDING FOR GROWTH

In the late 1980s, Australia's BHP, then the world's most profitable steel company, launched television advertising in its "Strengthening Australia" campaign to support manufacturers that co-branded its steel. This highly successful campaign was reintroduced in 1999.

Firms are now using advanced technology to explore their databases for opportunities (often extending across product categories) to secure increased usage by current customers. Financial-services companies have been in the vanguard of this trend. Such efforts range from targeted selling and marketing efforts to such simple examples as that provided by Fidelity, the mutual-fund giant, which has made it extremely easy for customers to transfer funds from one Fidelity fund to another.[18] However, the traditional brand and product-management structures of many companies are not conducive to the cross-selling model that is an important component in the economic logic underpinning the customer–relationship management concept.[19]

*Attracting competitors' customers.* This alternative is the predominant option (implicit or explicit) in many market strategies. It assumes that the firm and its direct competitors are fighting for the same customer and that the customer is now using a competitor's product. These users may include the firm's own past customers who can only be lured back with difficulty. Further, actions necessary to regain a previously lost customer may be different from those required to attract a first-time customer.

Of all the alternatives, attracting competitors' customers is the one most likely to lead to competitor retaliation. Yet when few nonusers are available for targeting (as with credit cards), it may be the only way to increase unit sales. Rarely does any one firm or its competitor earn all the customer's business. Customers often split their business among several suppliers. The task then becomes one of increasing the share of the customer's business (so-called share-of-wallet in credit cards) rather than seeking a total switch from the competitor to the firm. Targeting competitors' customers often overuses the price weapon; instead, management should be asking, Why does this customer prefer to buy from the competitor?

*Attracting nonusers in the market segment.* Converting nonusers in existing segments requires a different approach from those just discussed.

Both the firm and its direct competitors may have been trying to sell to these potential customers, but for one reason or another, they have not purchased the product form at all. Selling to these customers is a twofold task: First, they have to be convinced to purchase the product form rather than some other technology with which they may be comfortable and, second, to purchase the firm's offering rather than those of competitors. In new markets, most customers are by definition nonusers—hence the heavy costs of new-market development.

*Selecting the route for unit growth.*   Choice of strategic alternative is closely related to the stage in the product-form (category) life cycle and the firm's competitive position. Early in the life cycle, few customers have ever tried the new product form; as a result, most sales must originate with nonusers. As the product form moves from introduction into maturity, the proportion of nonusers decreases accordingly. The focus then shifts to current and/or competitors' customers, depending on the firm's competitive position. A leader with high market share typically focuses on current customers simply because they represent the bulk of the market. For similar reasons, firms with smaller market shares focus on competitors' customers.

*New market segments.*   Whereas the four previously discussed strategic alternatives focus on increasing unit volume within an existing market segment, a further growth alternative is to broaden the firm's horizons to focus on new markets or market segments. Because our focus is primarily on developing strategy within a market segment, we did not include this alternative in Figure 5.1.

Increasing Productivity.   In Figure 5.1, we define productivity (in terms an engineer might use) as the ratio of outputs to inputs. Increased productivity (or efficiency) can result from either increased outputs for a given input or reduced inputs for a given output. For our purposes, output is defined as sales revenue; inputs are costs and assets. (In this formulation, we assume that unit sales volume is held constant.)

*Increasing outputs (inputs constant).*   Two strategic alternatives are available to increase sales revenues while holding unit sales volume constant. Most straightforward is to improve prices by such means as increasing list price, reducing discounts, and/or reducing trade allowances. A second avenue is to improve the sales mix by selling higher volumes of more profitable product variants and reduced volumes of less profitable ones; the customer mix may also be modified to deemphasize less profitable customers. Many means are available to execute each alternative.

*Decreasing inputs (outputs constant).* The reduction of inputs to increase efficiency is the more obvious approach. Cost reduction possibilities may be widespread, including both fixed and variable costs. This particular route to improving profits has received a lot of attention through such methods as downsizing (rightsizing), reengineering, and outsourcing.[20]

The second alternative is to improve asset utilization by cutting the financial costs of doing business. Current assets such as inventories and accounts receivable can often be linked not just to a segment but also to specific customers. The outsourcing movement is leading to suppliers' having ownership of fixed assets at customer sites, so that asset management can be segregated even further by customer. Some organizations have managed working capital (accounts receivable plus cash less inventories and accounts payable) so carefully that the number has turned negative. Insisting on faster payment from customers can reduce accounts receivable, while inventory reduction forms part of the growing field of supply chain management. A feature of these systems is that the supplying firm is linked directly to data on product sales further down the distribution system, tying its production operations to ultimate demand. It can then reduce raw material, work in process, and finished-goods inventories. Improved distribution may also reduce inventory in the pipeline from supplier to final customer.

**Strategic Alternatives.** Within a market segment, the firm has four basic ways to improve sales volume and four basic ways to improve productivity. These eight ways are the only methods to improve long-run profits, though many different tactics (programs) may be used to implement any of them. In addition, some alternatives are mutually contradictory. The firm is unlikely to increase volume by targeting competitor's customers at the same time that it reduces marketing costs by cutting advertising and decreasing sales commissions!

The focus selected should be closely related to the primary strategic objective. If the primary objective in the segment is to increase growth or market share, likely alternatives are shown on the left-hand side of

Figure 5.1. Conversely, if the objective is increased cash flow, productivity (right-hand side of figure) is favored. A strategic objective of increasing profits would likely require a balance between the two. Whereas within a company, it is possible to pursue several alternatives simultaneously, focus is essential within a segment. Attempting too much within a segment prefigures subsequent failure.

## Positioning: A Make or Break Issue

Positioning is the heart of the market strategy. It has the power to transform your chances of success. Yet, many marketers use the term loosely, sometimes treating segmentation and positioning almost interchangeably. In contrast, developing strategy for a market segment means that the firm has already targeted the segment. Developing positioning involves key decisions within the segment about customers, competitive framing, and the benefits that the firm will offer.

The purpose of positioning is to create a unique and favorable image in the minds of target customers. To create this image, the firm must make decisions about the following three issues:

1. Choice of customer target(s).
2. The framing of competitor target(s).
3. The core strategy, key buying incentive, or value proposition for the customer.

These decisions are highly interrelated, but we necessarily discuss them sequentially.

Choice of Customer Targets.    This decision has several dimensions:

- Choice of system by which the firm's product reaches the ultimate customer.
- Choice of level at which the firm targets the bulk of its marketing effort (e.g., original equipment manufacturer, distributor, retailer, or consumer).
- Choice of specific decision influences at each level targeted (e.g., purchasing agent, engineer, or production manager for a manufacturer).

*Choice of system.* Whether the firm makes a completed product/ service or a component/raw material for some other product, several entities may be involved before the final product reaches the end customer.[21] Whereas a component manufacturer may sell products to finished-goods manufacturers (or to subassembly manufacturers that in turn sell to finished-goods manufacturers), finished products may pass through distributors, wholesalers, and retailers before reaching end users, or they may be sold directly—the system traditionally used by Avon and Amway.[22] Although well-established channel systems exist in many industries, innovative channel decisions frequently secure competitive advantage.

## DELL'S DIRECT MODEL

In the mid-1980s, Michael Dell realized that as the personal computer market matured, experienced computer buyers no longer needed the reassurance and information provided by traditional distributors. Dell bypassed that traditional system and marketed directly to sophisticated final consumers. By 2001, Dell Computers enjoyed the number one market-share position in PCs, with annual revenues in excess of $30 billion.

Even if a firm employs a conventional distribution system, the firm must choose particular channel members.

*Choice of level for effort.* In addition to specifying the channel system, the firm must make choices about the appropriate target(s). Should a firm selling finished consumer products place the most effort on working with retailers (a push strategy) or on persuading consumers to purchase (a pull strategy)? Should a component/raw material manufacturer place major efforts on the manufacturer that converts its offerings into completed products or on consumers that may purchase those completed products? In Tasmania a few years ago, a copy-paper manufacturer distributing to Australian firms through a conventional paper distributor system switched focus, developed a brand name, and successfully targeted Australian secretaries.

A firm rarely can afford to apply equally high effort at all levels, nor is this always wise. It should designate the level receiving the largest effort as the primary customer target and others receiving less effort as secondary targets.

*Choice of specific decision influences.* Having targeted channel and level, managers must identify the buying influence(s) to address. For example, if a consumer household is the target, should the focus be on the husband, wife, children, grandparents, or some other member of the extended family? College Savings Bank, offering certificates of deposit indexed to college-cost inflation as a means of saving for college education, targets both parents and grandparents.[23] Conversely, many children's products such as ready-to-eat cereal directly target children.

Analogous decisions are necessary when an organization is the target of effort. A well-known floor-covering manufacturer decided to target efforts at retailers instead of distributors or consumers; however, rather than offer greater retail margins to the store, it provided spiffs to the salespeople. Similarly, in selling to a manufacturer, firms must allocate effort among such organizational positions as operations manager, design engineers, marketing and sales, purchasing agent, and general manager.

**Be Creative in Targeting.** Choice of customer target is a crucial market strategy decision; however, the obvious choice may be an ineffective option. Those unskilled in marketing practice often believe that the appropriate target is the one "who has the money." Paradoxically (as discussed later in this book), a better choice may be the one who doesn't! Furthermore, the obvious choice may be ineffectual precisely because it is obvious and is also the target for competitors. In the development of market strategy, taking a contrary position can often pay great dividends.[24]

Several considerations guide choice of target. First, the prospective target should be seeking the values built into the firm's offer. Theoretically, designing an offer with a target customer in mind—as advocated in this book—should ensure a good match, but in the real world this does not always occur. Sometimes target customers are difficult to reach, and significant creativity must come into play. In many institutional buying situations, designers, engineers, senior managers, sales and marketing managers, and operations managers are likely to be responsive to added value.[25] On the other hand, the procurement system typically tends to confront sellers with purchasing professionals, whose major interest is short-term cost minimization. The marketing and sales challenge is to overcome these obstacles.

Second, although selected targets should be influential in the overall buying process, they need not necessarily be decision makers. Often in business-to-business marketing, overeager sellers neglect the decision maker's subordinates, with fatal results. Such targeting is shortsighted for the following reasons:

- These individuals frequently determine which suppliers enter the buyer's consideration. Set-membership is a necessary, though not sufficient, requirement for would-be sellers.
- Although junior set-members, from executive to shop-floor user, may not have "yea" power in a decision, they frequently have "nay" power—the firm should cast a broad net, at least for marketing communications.
- Eventually, senior executives move on, and their subordinates may replace them. The firm may build significant obstacles for itself by failing to treat these subordinates appropriately, especially if competitors have been streetwise.

## LOOKING TO THE LITTLE PEOPLE

Unable to gain access to critical decision makers at a major retailer, the national account manager for an office supply company assiduously called on lower-level personnel who were correspondingly neglected by the incumbent supplier. When, eventually, these junior executives were promoted to senior positions, the relationships built up over many years paid handsome dividends.

The final criterion for choosing an ideal customer target is to seek an influential individual who will personally benefit from, but does not personally carry the cost of, the purchasing decision. Examples include:

- Children as a means of influencing parental decisions.[26]
- Business travelers, whose companies pay for airline and hotel services.[27]
- Architects, interior designers, product designers.[28]
- Accountants, financial advisers, and lawyers for customers with investable funds.
- Politicians and regulators, who always want the best for their constituents, but who are spending taxpayers' money.

Such targeting may raise ethical issues. Some may view targeting intermediaries with family or political links to government buyers as ethically questionable; others may object to advertising to children. Regardless of your own ethical position, you should recognize that customer targeting is an area where a marriage of analysis and creativity can pay major dividends.

**Framing of Competitor Targets.** We use the term "competitor" broadly to include both current and potential competitors, as well as direct (similar products and technologies) and indirect (meeting the same customer needs with different products or technologies) competitors. Targeting a segment defines a firm's competitive set—those organizations that currently (and in the future will) seek to meet the needs of the same customers that management is pursuing. However, positioning can produce very different competitive frames.

Competitive positioning depends in part on the firm's strength in the market segment. Large, strong firms typically can be less delicate in positioning. Coca-Cola has more positioning leeway in the soft drink market than Cadbury-Schweppes. For small competitors, appropriate positioning is vital. One way to frame the competitor-targeting decision is to divide competitors into two categories: those that the firm would like to compete with and those that it wants to avoid. This partitioning may also help in devising the core strategy and in guiding the sales force.

### STRENGTH FROM EFFECTIVE POSITIONING

Honda repositioned the motorcycle from primary use (transportation) to secondary use (leisure) and transformed an industry. Its competitor targets changed dramatically.

Guinness took a drink with a limited, traditional market and vastly expanded its use by positioning it as a friendly beverage for younger consumers. It leveraged the brand's heritage through the experiential aspect of more than 2,000 Irish pubs around the world.

The perception of available opportunities also affects competitive positioning and can be fundamental in shaping a target customer's perception of the offer. A simple example from the soft drink category (Table 5.1) illustrates these distinctions. Positioning creativity can have a dramatic impact on sales.

Table 5.1   SOME POSITIONING ALTERNATIVES

| Claim | Type | Opportunity Implications | Customer Implications |
|-------|------|--------------------------|------------------------|
| "7-Up tastes better than Sprite"* | Comparison with individual direct competitor. | One lemon-lime soda must substitute for another. | Compare us. |
| "7-Up the best tasting lemon-lime soda" | Subcategory superiority. | The whole lemon-lime subcategory. | The best choice when drinking. lemon-lime soda. |
| "7-Up, the Uncola" | Out of category. | The cola category. | The alternative to drinking cola. |
| "7-Up, the real one—the only one," etc. | Implied or claimed uniqueness. | All beverages? | There's no other drink quite like it. |

*In the United States, such a claim (including naming a competitor directly) may be used as advertising if acceptable statistical data is provided to support the claim. The "Pepsi Challenge" was conducted on just such a basis. This type of advertising is prohibited in many countries.

**Core Strategy/Key Buying Incentive/Value Proposition.**   The final positioning element can be called core strategy, key buying incentive, or value proposition. It describes how the firm plans to compete for its targeted customers. It must provide a convincing answer to a deceptively simple question: Why should the targeted customer prefer the firm's offer to that of competitors? The firm must decide where it will place its efforts in terms of benefits it offers customers.

To develop a successful market segment strategy, the firm should ideally:

- Focus on satisfying important customer needs.
- Attempt to meet these needs better than competitors.
- Where possible, offer benefits that are difficult for competitors to imitate.

Other actions are likely to offer only temporary advantage. In designing the core strategy, the firm makes the principles of customer value and differential advantage (see Chapter 3) operational in a market segment.

## CORE STRATEGIES

The following examples are companies with clear and effective core strategies for their customers:

- FedEx delivers on time ("when it absolutely, positively has to get there overnight").
- Apple's Macintosh computers are easy to use.
- Calls made with Sprint are exceptionally clear ("you can hear a pin drop").

Terms such as "key buying incentive," "unique selling proposition," and "value proposition" come close to representing the critical concept, but none captures it as well as "core strategy."[29] Externally, core strategy is the firm's key competitive weapon in capturing the customers it seeks; internally, it defines the task for implementation programs. From the customer's perspective, it defines why the firm's benefits are superior to those offered by the competition. For the firm, it provides the organizing framework for the marketing mix and other functional activities.

If the firm targets more than one customer type, more than one positioning execution will be required. Many consumer-goods firms target both retail distributors and consumers. The core strategy for consumers revolves around a specific set of end-user benefits. Detergent manufacturers may offer consumer targets such functional benefits as clean clothes, stain removal, or "whiter whites" and/or such psychological benefits as reinforcing their caring for the family and being a good parent. By contrast, the positioning for retail distributors is likely to focus on such benefits as potential profits, promotional support, ease of doing business, inventory turns, and product delivery.

For branded consumer products, the key customer target has always been the consumer. Designing a core strategy for consumers necessarily imposes constraints on the possibilities for alternative targets. Because establishing the brand with consumers typically involves heavy spending on advertising and promotion, the firm may be unable to offer retailers the margins they desire. By contrast, manufacturers of private brands have selected retailers as their key target. They price low to create retailer margin opportunity and limit their advertising and promotion to the intermediary level. Although firms may design positioning statements for more than one customer in a market segment, they typically select a key target for the core-strategy design and limit their options with other targets.

Developing Positioning Statements. This is probably the most laborious and difficult element in developing strategy. We described positioning in the linear, sequential format that written communication imposes; whereas in reality, it is a complex, creative, and highly interactive process. It usually requires many cut-and-try attempts and simulated testing to achieve a satisfactory combination. In segments where the firm has a strong advantage, the core strategy may dictate the choice of customer and/or competitor targets. More often, the complex process begins with a preliminary choice of customer target, followed by a series of consistency checks to arrive at well-integrated positioning (Figure 5.2). Ries and Trout capture the complexity of developing positioning when they state, "Positioning is not what you do to a product—positioning is what you do to the mind of the prospect."[30]

In developing positioning strategy, we also recommend developing a common framework for use across the firm. One such framework requires statements that implicitly or explicitly distinguish the firm's offer from that of competitors and that fit the following format:[31]

| | |
|---|---|
| Convince | [Customer Target] |
| that they will receive | [These Benefits (Core Strategy)] |
| because we have | [These Capabilities/Features] |

Clear positioning statements have major value. One of the most common complaints advertising agencies make about their clients is that they have not clarified their strategies. Although positioning statements are not advertising, they provide excellent guidance for the firm's agency. Without such guidelines, the agency's creative personnel have enormous difficulty and may well misdirect their talent.

Whereas positioning statements help to guide and coordinate the firm's efforts in the marketplace, they are absolutely crucial in achieving Total Integrated Marketing.

## Strategy Implementation: You've Got to Make It Happen

In traditional functionally organized firms, marketing managers commonly fail to secure adequate support from other parts of the company. Unless the firm has embraced the marketing concept as a philosophy, or

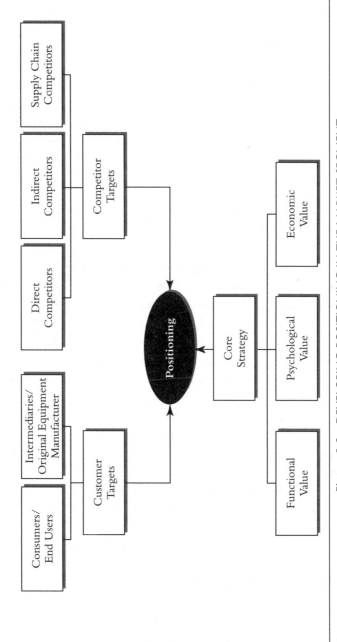

Figure 5.2  DEVELOPING POSITIONING IN THE MARKET SEGMENT

the marketing department has been an unusually effective advocate, other senior functional executives, and even general managers, may understand little of the external orientation and its implications. Far too often, the internal task remains undone.

The marketing group may do a superb job of analyzing the external environment, setting performance targets, selecting strategic alternatives, and developing positioning statements. However, unless others in the company coordinate their actions to support and actually deliver the benefits specified in the core strategy, the firm will fail in the segment. Success requires not only that we align the traditional marketing mix, but that we also integrate other key functions with the core strategy. The following subsections illustrate these relationships.

Supporting Marketing-Mix Programs.    Almost every basic marketing book advocates the need to integrate the marketing mix—the implementation elements of product, promotion, distribution, service, and price (see Chapter 3). Most books then neglect the concept, however, in favor of "disintegration," by structuring their content around a separate discussion of each element. Integration cannot be conducted in a vacuum; rather, the marketing mix should be integrated around the core strategy. We use as an example a firm that bases its core strategy on the benefits that flow from superb product quality. Other elements of the marketing mix should focus on supporting this theme.[32] We examine the implications of the core strategy for each element.

Since the product in question must be of high quality, performance and durability, appearance, and brand name should reinforce the quality concept. Likewise, advertising copy should focus on quality with supportive choice of media and format. Sales promotional materials (e.g., brochures and display racks) should likewise be of high quality, and to the extent possible, the firm should try to obtain only "appropriate" publicity. Selling strategies must reflect the core quality benefits and if intermediaries are involved, the firm should carefully scrutinize the number and quality of distributors. (If quality is so high that the firm seeks exclusive positioning, then it should use just a few distributors of the highest possible caliber.) If the firm offers truly high-quality products, the need for service should be minimal, but when needed, it should be superb. Finally, high quality allows considerable pricing discretion. Depending on the firm's customer and competitor targets (and its strategic objectives), price may range from very high (specialty positioning) to competitive levels (more aggressive). The company should avoid low prices, since too low a price renders quality claims unbelievable to many customers.[33] Further, although the production of good-quality products does not necessarily imply high costs, very high quality almost always does, such that setting low prices may be committing financial suicide.

Had the firm selected some other core strategy such as low price and widespread availability, a completely different set of marketing-mix implications would prevail. The core strategy provides the parameters for developing the individual marketing-mix elements. Since many different individuals and departments may be involved—advertising agencies, sales department, sales-promotion experts, public relations department, and market-research suppliers—coordinating the process is a complex task.

Supporting Functional Programs.    In an era of total competition, attending to the marketing mix alone is simply insufficient. Whereas generations of marketing students were taught that if they got their four P's right they would be okay, today's reality is quite different. To win in the twenty-first century, the whole firm must constitute a competitive weapon, targeted and honed to the requirements of the particular segment that managers hope to capture. It is therefore essential to establish support from other functional areas to implement the proposed strategy. If one or more functional areas cannot (or will not) meet these requirements, management must revisit the core strategy. To go ahead without this support will be to commit a cardinal sin of marketing: making promises to customers (for that's what the promise of benefits does) that the firm will not fulfill.

Offering customers superb product quality has important implications for other functions of the firm: For engineering—product and process design; for manufacturing—process control and scheduling; for purchasing—procurement policies for high-quality inputs; for finance—provision of necessary funds and agreement on appropriate pricing; for technical service—provision of superb backup; for customer service—billing, shipping, and follow-through; for transportation—scheduling and loss/breakage control.

Managers must build a genuine consensus that commits functional areas to meeting these requirements or the strategy will fail. Customers do not care which department or individual is at fault. If they fail to receive the benefits they anticipate, they rightly believe that it is the supplier's job to deal with such issues. The failure to integrate successfully across organizational elements to delight the customer is epitomized in phrases familiar to millions of consumers: "That's not my job." "You'll have to speak to my supervisor." "I can't do anything about that." "I'm sorry, but you'll just have to wait." "We've tried to get it changed, but they won't listen." These responses and their ilk have passed into the lexicon of marketing failure, testimony to the wide gaps that so often separate the high ideals of a strategy from its successful implementation.

One result of the decline of the formal marketing function or department is that as critical customer-related responsibilities move away from the control of marketing executives, the coordination and integration issue multiplies in importance and difficulty:

- Market research was for a long time the last refuge of the beleaguered marketing executive—at least we "own" the information! Increasingly, technology means that information is a by-product of operations. Customer relationship management technology spans departments and systems to integrate customer information; point-of-sale scanning systems combine with loyalty programs to replace many traditional market-research needs; Web sites operated by IT (Information Technology) capture customer data instantly; key account-management teams have the real customer "understanding."
- As the company Web site has moved from mere "brochureware" toward interactive marketing and e-commerce, so the control of the Web site has too often moved from marketing to IT or e-commerce specialists.
- In many situations, the driving force behind product quality, price, and availability is supply chain management, not marketing.
- Particularly in high-risk and high-technology markets, the key to adding customer value is through alliances and networks; these are not usually controlled by marketing.
- The move in many major organizations from product branding to corporate branding means that brand-management decisions have moved upward and beyond the traditional marketing department's area of influence.

- There is some suggestion that only a minority of marketing departments even retain oversight of the customer–service function.[34]

If ever there were a time when the coordination and integration of all company processes and functions around customers and markets was a top-management priority, that time is now. If ever there were a time when top management needed carefully planned and implemented Total Integrated Marketing, that time is now!

## CONCLUSION

In this chapter, we have reviewed the functions (or purposes) of a market strategy in detail. The content of strategy is often poorly understood; many managers equate it to the marketing mix. In fact, marketing-mix programs are a consequence of the market segment strategy. Strategy at the segment level is the guts of the firm's marketing effort and the key to its success. Yet without tremendous effort in implementation, we are unlikely to achieve the internal consistency required for that success.

Consistency of performance objectives and strategic focus, consistency of positioning elements (customer targets, competitor targets, core strategy), consistency between the strategy and implementation programs, and consistency across functions and departments are all vital to success in today's marketplace. The intellectual capability to develop a sound strategy plan may be a necessary condition for success in a competitive environment, but it is not sufficient. Success cannot be achieved unless organizational units work together to deliver the benefits of the core strategy to customers. Without Total Integrated Marketing, the entire effort will come to naught; in the competitive markets of the twenty-first century everyone must market.

# MARKETING AND FINANCE/ACCOUNTING

## BUILDING ALLIANCES AROUND THE REAL VALUE DRIVERS

This chapter, as well as the ones that follow, confronts the relationships between marketing and the main functions in the firm: finance/ accounting, operations, sales, research and development, customer service, and human resource management. If Total Integrated Marketing is going to become a reality for your company, then you need to examine each of these relationships and ask:

- What are the current and potential conflicts here, and how can we overcome them?
- What is the potential for the joint delivery of enhanced value to our customers and our shareholders through better partnering?

Sadly, this approach is sorely needed. Traditional marketing departments have not worked very effectively with other functions: Now there is a price to be paid.

And, let's be honest about this—marketing people often are not very popular with their colleagues. A British study found that the majority of executives in nonmarketing disciplines considered their marketing teams' performance adequate at best, and often poor. Survey participants commented: "Marketers should be more communicative . . . more pragmatic

**111**

and less egotistical." In particular, finance directors commented that their marketing peers were "brash . . . wide-boys[1] . . . flash . . . uncontrollable . . . into freebies . . . never in the office . . . overenthusiastic."[2] In a similar vein, research at Cranfield School of Management concerning non-marketers' perceptions of marketing people, suggests that they want to deliver the following messages to their marketing colleagues:

- You're not accountable—you act like the "chosen ones," deserving of fast promotion, but showing little company loyalty and incurring high costs.
- You're (a touch) arrogant in your dealings with the rest of the company.
- You're always "at lunch" or "in meetings."
- You're slippery, expensive, and untouchable.[3]

However, even if being perceived as "untouchable" by peers doesn't worry the marketing person (what do peers know, after all?), there is a far more serious consequence if others in the company have this image of marketers. There is growing evidence that when marketers try to share their insights and information with other departments, they are frequently ignored or misunderstood. In many cases, they struggle just to get their voices heard.[4] It seems that not only are marketers disliked, no one believes what they say either! Nonetheless, in this book we focus on exploring the impact of Total Integrated Marketing on customer value, not on getting everyone else to do what the marketing department wants it to do.

We start by looking at the relationship between marketing and finance. Of all the functional relationships involving marketing, this one is most often explosively unproductive and damaging, revealing more about interdepartmental politics than about company performance. A study from the KPMG/Institute of Practitioners in Advertising underlines this depressing reality.[5] The vast majority of finance directors complained that they could not measure the effectiveness of their companies' marketing efforts. Fully one third of the respondents admitted that if costs were under pressure the marketing budget would be the first one they would cut. To be fair, on the other side of the equation, marketing executives often dismiss finance specialists as "bean counters" and "balance sheet mechanics" who contribute little to company effectiveness.

In fact, when things go bad and stock values dive, finance VPs can be busted just as easily as marketing VPs. In 1999, when the failure of British Telecom's marketing strategy in the United States drove down stock price dramatically, the headcount culling focused on headquarters finance staff.[6] In June 2000, when the failure of global convenience retailer W. H. Smith to hold market share led to disappointing profits and a stagnant stock price, the retail arm's marketing director and the finance director departed from the company simultaneously.[7] Those who study strategic alliances tell us that effective alliances display mutuality of interests—something has to be there for both partners. Few can doubt the mutuality of interest between marketing and finance, but much needs to be done to mend this often-fractured relationship.

Our approach is based on understanding that the pivotal issue for enhancing a company's performance is value—customer value and shareholder value. A deep and profound understanding of the drivers of value for a company is a powerful basis for alliance between marketing and finance. It supersedes interfunctional rivalry and political divisions—or at least it should if managers want the company to gain the strength of Total Integrated Marketing.

The critical requirement is to focus on the marketing tasks that the **firm** must accomplish, not on the marketing department. First, we examine the essential strategic relationships stressing the role of customer value in the creation of shareholder value. The fact that many managers fail to understand that the firm's ability to create and re-create customers is crucial to enhancing shareholder value is very alarming. Researchers have found that "on average, boards devote nine times more attention to spending and counting cash flow than to wondering where it comes from and how it might be increased."[8] Nonetheless, financial expertise can play a decisive role in developing effective market strategy, and we illustrate its role as a key capability.

Then, we turn attention to the operational challenges that an uneasy relationship between finance and marketing can create. We look at how misuse of the shareholder value concept can jeopardize the future of the company, and we explore how issues like credit management and price adjustments can affect the relationship between the firm and its customers. We end the chapter with recommendations for better management of the finance-marketing relationship.

## STRATEGIC RELATIONSHIPS

### Customer Value, Shareholder Value, and Short-Term Profits

In Chapter 4, we described the relationship between shareholder value and customer value and presented powerful evidence that delivery of real value to customers is a critical driver of profit performance. So why do so many firms make stupid and shortsighted decisions that hamper delivery of customer value? The answer is straightforward: Quite simply, management failure to distinguish between shareholder value creation and accounting profit is at the root of most of these blunders. Even the much-vaunted measure of economic profit falls short of the goal. Just adding a charge (computed at the company's cost of capital) to the accounting profit reported by an element of the business does not ensure shareholder value creation.

Let's go back to basics. The fundamental determinants of value for shareholders are not reports of last period's profits, but expectations about future profit streams. Although last period's profits may influence future expectations, in many cases there is little relationship between profits in the past and expectations of profits in the future. The experience of many dot-coms until early 2001 amply confirms this point. More recently, even though Amazon has claimed to make operating profit, it is a long way from making positive net profits; yet its market capitalization is still several billion dollars. For better or worse, the company's stock price largely reflects investor expectations about the future, admittedly heavily influenced by management pronouncements and the judgments of investment analysts. The stock price is a barometer for judging managerial decisions.

But investor expectations are not just about next year's profits. Because of the time value of money, the anticipation of a given level of profits next year is weighted more heavily than the same anticipated profit level in later years. Yet, in most cases, the discounted sum of expected profits next year is almost always going to be much smaller than the discounted sum of expected profits in subsequent years. Far too often, managers make decisions that are based on their measurable and predictable (they hope) impact on next year's profit, rather than thinking ahead about long-run profit and considering the impact of decisions on the market value of the firm. The harsh truth is that decisions based solely on the criterion of maximizing the next period's accounting profit will almost certainly not be value maximizing for shareholders, even if they make traditional accountants feel comfortable.

Firms that repeatedly make important strategic decisions using these criteria inevitably are vulnerable to competitors, not least because their decision criteria are transparent and their actions so predictable. And after the Enron debacle, who believes the accounting profits anyway? We wholeheartedly admire much of what Jack Welch achieved during his tenure as CEO of General Electric (GE). Yet Mr. Welch presided over most of General Electric's more than 100 straight quarters of earnings growth—give us a break, Jack! Were there no ups and downs at all?[9]

**Customers as Assets.**   The concept of customers as assets[10] initially may come as somewhat of a shock to conventional finance executives who were brought up to see customers as obdurate, troublesome, slow payers. However, this simple idea holds the potential to revolutionize not just the relationship between the marketing and finance functions, but also between the firm and its customers. The customer equity concept embodies the fundamental determinant of the firm's asset value—the prime reason it may be worth more than the disposal value of its tangible assets. Thinking of customers as assets also has enormous implications for the firm's information systems. Whereas many firms are still struggling to get reliable estimates of direct product profitability, truly integrated marketers are online with systems enabling them to estimate the past and future profitability of their relationships with individual customers or, at least, groups of customers.

**The Underlying Investment Problem.**   The topic, "Investment Opportunities," sounds like a subject made for finance experts to wax lyrical, whether the investment decision concerns an acquisition target or a proposed new plant. However, we must first discard the potentially highly damaging and archaic concept that equates investment with traditional notions of capital expenditures. Economic theory mandates a cash flow view of all economic decisions, and cash flow analysis provides the essential underpinning to the whole concept of shareholder value. The definition of what constitutes an investment is basically arbitrary and has been unduly influenced by government regulations and accounting traditions.

Many forward-looking accountants, influenced by financial theory and the advance of the shareholder value philosophy, have become passionate advocates of the need for change, if not radical reform, in the use of data based on traditional accounting assumptions.[11]

Many decisions on marketing expenditures such as setting the advertising budget are, in principle, just as amenable to shareholder value analysis as an acquisition decision. Yet, in practice, the problems are not with financial theory, but with putting the theory into effect. All cash flow estimates involve forecasting future cash inflows and outflows. The latter create some problems, but the most troublesome issues revolve around revenue forecasting, especially for really new products or for the estimated impact of a particular proposed advertising or promotional campaign.

This is where financial and accounting managers can benefit from a better understanding of marketing. Frequently, assumptions underlying the forecasts incorporated into financial models are not subject to rigorous analysis, and executives tend to accept projections at face value. Sales forecasts always contain assumptions about both customers and competitors and are sure to be more robust if the data are exposed and discussed explicitly, instead of being glossed over. The failure of many product launches can often be traced back to the superficiality of the review stage, rather than to technical failures of the product or faulty advertising campaigns.

A further problem with investment decisions is the still-prevalent practice of using point estimates and certainty-equivalents, rather than explicit risk examination. Modern finance theory embraces such risk assessment, and approaches for considering risk and uncertainty are widely discussed. Yet, point estimates prevail in most companies, however, and the consequent surprises can play havoc with shareholder value. In the review stage, finance managers should always ask, even if their marketing colleagues do not, what might be the most likely competitive responses to the initiatives, and what would be the impact on the point estimates. Going further, they might introduce time-honored approaches to dealing with risk,[12] or educate their less aware colleagues in some of the contemporary thinking.[13]

A somewhat different approach involves throwing out forecasting in its entirety. For example, rather than base the decision for an advertising campaign or a new product launch on a point estimate of sales volume, an alternative is to ask first what sales level would be necessary to make the campaign or launch worthwhile. Then, the second question is: "What is the probability that this sales level will be met or exceeded?" The answer determines the go/no go decision, based on the decision makers' appetite for risk.

Planning and Budgeting.    The problem of missed forecasts leads to one of the most contentious yet important elements of the marketing-finance interface: the damaging confusion that exists over the distinction between planning and budgeting—and their very different philosophies.

Two of us spent a significant, yet ultimately depressing, part of our professional lives studying how large U.S. manufacturing companies plan and budget. A major conclusion, that subsequent years have given us little reason to change, is that most do so poorly, with little evidence of a beneficial effect on performance. We observed, however, that a few companies did achieve positive results by placing emphasis on understanding external conditions that affected their markets and developing appropriate strategies. They saw budgets as an output of this process, rather than the be-all and end-all. On the other hand, those companies that pursued a financially driven budgeting process performed less well in two vital respects. First, they achieved lower average returns; a result consistent with picking poorer investment opportunities. Second, they had higher fluctuations in their returns a predictable outcome from encountering more surprises because they failed to anticipate external events that could affect their markets. By contrast, the companies with the more strategic type of planning achieved higher returns at lower risk—exactly what should happen with good planning . . . better choices, fewer surprises.

We are not arguing against budgets for they are essential to directing and managing the enterprise.[14] Numbers, however, do not have a life of their own—they are the estimated consequences of the decisions we take or plan to take. Managers working in accounting and finance should take note of this simple but vital insight, and those who ignore it should be so reminded. Understanding markets, customers, and competitors will help you ask better questions, get better plans, and develop budgets that the company can meet. A succession of unmet budgets is a sure sign of organizational pathology. Pressuring for results is no substitute for sound thinking!

Forecasting.    In general, marketing could do a far better job of forecasting. In most organizations, the finance department takes the marketing plan and develops the financial plan. The CFO takes the marketing projections, then works backward to raise the short- and long-term capital needed to implement the plan. If sales projections are badly in error, then the financial plan will inevitably be out of kilter. If actual demand exceeds forecast, the CFO may have to pay excessively high interest rates for the extra capital required to satisfy demand. If actual demand is far lower than forecast, the company may end up with excessive inventory (perhaps to be disposed of at a loss) or, if quick adjustments can be made, even surplus cash on hand. The CFO may be forced to invest this cash at lower interest rates than the borrowing cost. Either way, the shareholder loses.

Market fluctuations occur all the time and are the major reason we advocate incorporating risk rather than just using point estimates. Here is a place where close working relationships between marketing and finance can help manage the inherent differences between forecasts and actuals.

Response to Budget Shortfalls.    Most companies set budgets at the beginning of the year, then manage against these budgets during the operating period, making adjustments as needed. Sometimes, however, market forces get things out of alignment and belt tightening is necessary. In many organizations, the finance function likes to be fair—"Everyone should cut their expense budgets by 15 percent." This may be "fair," but in most cases it makes no sense whatever. If the world has changed since the budgets were initially formulated, the strategic situations of the product and/or business units have also changed. In the present circumstances, perhaps the budgets of some areas should be cut 15 percent, but not necessarily every unit because their strategic situations are not identical. In fact, perhaps some budgets should be cut by 25 percent and others left alone, or even increased. What is certainly true is that the so-called fair decision is easy to work out. Doing the necessary analysis to develop a strategically appropriate approach to cutting budgets is far more difficult, but more rewarding.

## The Approach to Marketing Expenditures

In their desire to increase reported profits, financial experts seem to misunderstand some of marketing's fundamental truths. When things get tough, one of their most common approaches is to cut back on advertising and other promotional product support. The traditional finance and accounting mind-set often sees advertising, promotion, and other marketing expenditures only as expenses. Even worse, it is difficult to measure effectiveness of this expense, and hence to know whether the firm received value for money. So, the immediate effect of a cut in advertising support will often be an increase in reported profit for the next period, and a self-satisfied accountant. However, a wealth of empirical research shows the substantial impact of advertising both in the short and long term.[15] The result, then, of cutting back on advertising, may easily be a loss of market share and deteriorating shareholder value.

Accounting and financial managers must understand that for many products and services, advertising and promotional communications play a major role in securing and maintaining sales revenues. The imagery created through advertising and other promotional communications may be a critical factor, if not the only factor, differentiating the branded producer from its competitors. The offer that the consumer buys comprises not only the product and related services, but also the associated communications. In several product categories, consumers cannot distinguish one product from another in blind tests. Food and drink products are a classic case: No matter what your friends and colleagues may say, see how they perform blind in identifying brands of beer. Most drinkers cannot distinguish one brand from another. The communications component of such product offers is undeniably important in maintaining the price premium that branded manufacturers enjoy. In some personal product categories, especially perfume, image is everything. Flavor houses can, and often do, quickly enable follower companies to duplicate the exact composition of a new fragrance, but if the innovator has developed a good promotional strategy, competitors can never command its market position or price premium.

The supposedly rational model of thinking that often characterizes the financial (and, frequently, the technical) mind is nothing of the sort. It actually denies reality by failing to recognize that appropriate marketing communications are not just expenses; instead, they are value-adding for customers, and hence for shareholders. It may seem irrational; it may be hard to measure; but it is the reality of the marketplace. There can be no greater arrogance than to deny reality because you do not like it or cannot understand it. The penalty for such arrogance is often severe.

Nowhere is the denial of the value of advertising and promotion more dangerous than when launching a new product. It is not being the first to invent, the first to market, or even the first to distribute that creates the advantage for the innovator. An increasing body of evidence suggests that being first in the mind is what counts, and communication is the vital tool for getting there. Markets cannot work properly without information, and at no time is information more critical than when the firm is attempting to create a new market, whether for a new brand or whole new category.[16] The new product success rate of most companies is abysmal, yet few companies knowingly launch defective products.[17] The reasons for failure lie in the misunderstanding of market dynamics and typically revolve around unexpected responses from customers or competitors.

All too frequently, companies underfund their new product launches. Typically, the managers who lead these organizations accept the legitimacy of investing in technology or production capacity, but do not understand the necessity of investing in market development. The growth of shareholder value-based management has exacerbated this tendency in some companies. At launch, all new products consume resources, and if they are evaluated on the criterion of economic profit, a long-term perspective is essential or they will show up as value-destroying. In their incubatory and developmental stages, it is necessary to protect new products from the normal regime of value measurement.

To deal with these problems, the firm needs accounting, finance, and marketing specialists who understand the drivers of customer value. We join enthusiastically with our financial colleagues in their plea to bring more accountability and analysis to marketing decisions. The tools of finance are invaluable here, and once a company has shifted to any form of cash-flow analysis, the irrelevancy of an arbitrary distinction between investment and expense is unmasked for all to see. The heat is on for all marketers, and they must expect to provide sound financial justification for their recommendations.[18]

## Expenditures in Other Areas

Marketing expenses are not the only concern. How do you deal with plant expansions or R&D expenditures in economic downturns or even recessions? In the economic downturn, revenues are reduced and, all things being equal, profits will also go down. No problem: It is easy to fix this situation just by cutting R&D expenses; now sales revenues are reduced but so are expenses, and the profit picture doesn't seem so bad. Is anything wrong with this mode of thinking?—you'd better believe it! Suppose your competitors are thinking the same way—you've missed a marvelous opportunity to gain an advantage in new product development. But then suppose they know you are thinking this way, but they decide to hold (or even increase) their new product R&D expenditures. Suddenly, you are at a disadvantage and when the upturn comes, you are behind the eight ball.

### INTEL'S PERSPECTIVE ON SPENDING

In February 2001, Craig Barrett, Intel's CEO, said he had seen a sharp slowdown in American manufacturing but that Intel would not reduce its $12 billion spending budget (for research development and production). Said Barrett, "You never save your way out of a recession. The only way to get out of a recession stronger than when you went in is to have great new products."*

* *The New York Times,* February 28, 2001.

## Managing Products

Setting Objectives.    Despite the popularization of product portfolio management for the past twenty-odd years, a depressing number of companies still operate with an "every tub on its own bottom" philosophy. Essentially, this philosophy holds that each product must pay its own way, and that maximizing profits for each product is the best way to ensure that the firm as a whole optimizes its profit performance. The alternative portfolio management principle does not disagree with the overall objective—optimization of the firm's profits—but suggests a different tack based on setting different objectives for products, depending on the their strategic situation. Thus, some products' objectives should focus on maximizing profits but others should maximize growth or market share, and perhaps others should maximize cash flow.

Objectives such as growth in volume and market share that require investment in facilities, equipment, and marketing effort typically will not maximize profits and frequently lead to negative cash flow. For cash flow and profit objectives, however, lack of investment and marketing effort will inevitably have a negative impact on growth and market share. Finance and marketing must be on the same page for product portfolio management. For marketing and product managers seeking to position the firm in fast-growth markets, also trying to meet short-term profit goals from the finance department is often too heavy a burden. This area cries out for both finance and marketing to understand the strategic imperatives and to set objectives that mirror the firm's strategic realities.

Dropping Products.   Although many companies understand the wisdom of investing in products with high growth potential and may waive profit goals in the short run, they face an equally insidious problem at the other end of the product life cycle. Here they have to decide whether and when to kill products and remove them from the product line. Once again, product profitability is typically the critical criterion, but in this case the problem is one of measurement.

Usually the profit statement for a product shows sales revenues at the top, then a set of cost items, and a figure for profit at the bottom. In most companies, if there is a profit they retain the product, and managers work harder in the next period to try to increase that profit. But suppose the ink is red. Just like a bull that sees a red flag, in charge the accountants demanding the product be dropped. After all, if the product is losing money, then getting rid of it will increase the company's profits. Right? Not necessarily!

For the sake of argument, assume that a particular product has been in the product line for many years and is showing a $200,000 loss—for most of us that's big money. But, before dropping the product, management takes a closer look at the costs: Variable manufacturing costs, selling costs, fixed manufacturing costs, and so forth are all fine; but then—R&D, $500,000, and Marketing Research, $300,000. When was the last time the R&D department did any research on this product?—about five years ago! For years, marketing has been asking futilely for product improvements to stem market share erosion. To be fair, R&D wanted better customer input, but then, nobody ever did any marketing research. Yet a charge of $300,000! What's going on here?

What's going on in many companies is allocation. Many professions have an oath that captures the essence of what that profession is about. Just as doctors have the Hippocratic oath, many accountants adhere to their oath—"If you see a cost, allocate it!" The $500,000 R&D and $300,000 marketing research expenditures don't really exist. What exists is $20 million for company R&D and $5 million for marketing research. The $500,000 and $300,000 charges are merely allocations to the product based on some allocation formula that did not do anything for the product is question.

Now, what is going to happen if the firm drops the product? Well, the company will no longer have to contend with the $200,000 loss. But now, some other product will have to carry the burden of the R&D and marketing research allocations. Dropping the product is not going to affect the firm's aggregate R&D and marketing research budgets. When these allocations are factored in, the impact on the company is not an increased profit of $200,000, but rather a negative impact of $600,000 ($500,000 + $300,000 − $200,000).

This is not an argument for maintaining loss-making products in the firm's portfolio. It is rather an argument for sensible financial management of the product line. To be fair, some firms have adopted activity-based costing (ABC) methods to deal with the arbitrariness of cost allocation systems. They should be able to avoid this sort of problem, but many other companies cannot. They have dropped mature loss-making products from their product lines, only to find that the firm is worse off than before, because of the allocated costs that continue to be incurred after product deletion.

## Pricing Decisions

Most marketers understand that the most important consideration in the pricing decision is perceived customer value. This value sets the upper bound on the customer's willingness to pay. In general, however, marketers have been singularly ineffective in implanting this idea elsewhere in the firm, particularly in the offices of their finance colleagues. Recent polls of executives show that cost-plus methods are still the most common approach to setting prices.[19] It is certainly acceptable to check prices against estimated costs and to calculate expected profit margins, and it is fine to look at tracking studies. However, to use costs (usually historical) as the prime basis for setting prices is totally illogical.

What does cost-plus pricing really mean? First, you figure out your product costs. Then you add a predetermined margin percentage. Sounds simple? Well, it is if you can calculate the product costs. But this may require some heroic leaps of faith, in part because of allocation problems. In any well-recognized cost accounting textbook, there are scores of allocation procedures—percent of sales, percent of labor costs, percent of capital employed, and on and on. Which is correct? None of them! They all suffer from being arbitrary and having little to do with the resources actually consumed in making the product. The ABC methods have certainly helped, but they don't solve all the problems.

Nonetheless, suppose that you come up with a product cost that you find comfortable and you add your margin, and now you have a price. Economic theory tells us that you face a demand curve for your product. In general, the lower the price the higher the volume you will sell and vice versa. Based on the price that you select, you can anticipate selling a certain volume of product. Fine, but now think back to your product cost. This cost will vary depending on the volume you sell, because the fixed costs will be spread out among more or fewer units. So the price you set is an important contributing factor in determining your costs. But since your estimate of costs helped you determine price in the first place, this reasoning is totally circular. Cost-plus methods should be consigned to the trash can.

If the illogicality argument doesn't grab you, how about the argument of economic madness? First of all, customers don't give a hoot about a supplier's cost. This data is totally irrelevant, except possibly insofar as they can use it to strengthen their bargaining position. Second, from a practical point of view, cost-plus pricing hides two major errors. Suppose the value to the customer is greater than the cost-plus price. This leaves revenue and profit margin on the table for the customer and may reduce organizational brand equity. And if the value to the customer is less than the cost-plus price, the customer will not purchase. But the customer might have purchased at a lower price that would still have given the firm a worthwhile profit.

Make no mistake, the critical determinants of choice are perceptions of relative value for prices charged . . . period, end of discussion![20] Of course, customers are not the only players—the firm must build competitors' reactions into the pricing decision. Competitors are part of the market reality and a strong influence on the perceived value that customers place on any offer. Nonetheless, at the end of the day, customers will base their purchase decisions on perceived value delivered—certainly not on the supplier's costs.

## PRICING AN INNOVATION

Strategic pricing for demand creation may be a powerful way to get high volume quickly and to establish a market position that competitors will struggle to equal. The Swatch watch transformed the wristwatch from a purely functional item for telling time, into a mass-market fashion accessory. The product combined an accurate timepiece with colorful, creative design and emotional appeal. At the time of launch, cheap, high-precision quartz movement watches from Japan and Hong Kong (priced at around $75) dominated the mass market. The Swatch was launched at an aggressive price of $40. This price encouraged consumers to buy several watches as fashion accessories for different outfits and moods, but also left no profit margin available for competitors to imitate the Swatch and undercut its price. The Swatch project team had made a strategic price decision, and then worked back from the price to arrive at a target cost and designed a suitable manufacturing system.*

*W. Chan Kim and Renee Mauborgne, "Strategy, Value Innovation and the Knowledge Economy," *Sloan Management Review,* spring 1999, pp. 41–54.

If there is one area where shareholders and the firm can benefit most directly from getting marketing ideas out of the traditional function and into the business, surely it is the pricing decision. Astute marketers should ask themselves whether they have really done a good job in this area. The trend in many companies to move pricing decisions upward and away from marketing departments underlines this failure. While managers commonly profess an understanding of the concept of pricing to customer value, few put it into practice. The Internet-based reverse auction pricing systems will probably do more to make the point than generations of marketers by underscoring what customers really think a product is worth.

## Working Capital Management

Extending Credit.   Another cause of recurring conflict between marketing and finance/accounting in many organizations involves working capital, specifically, the extension of credit to customers. Many companies manage this process poorly; they totally disconnect it from other customer-facing functions. This is not how customers see the credit function. For many customers, how you manage credit is the most important test of the level of customer service you provide. Treating credit with a bureaucratic instead of a strategic mentality means taking a big risk. There are several signs of this tendency.

*Criteria for granting credit.* First, what should be the criteria for granting credit and should they tend toward tightness versus looseness? In many companies, the goal of the credit department is to minimize bad debts, and the managerial reward structure reinforces that goal. Of course, the best way to minimize bad debts is to avoid credit altogether. Insisting on cash with delivery or, better yet, cash with order totally avoids the bad-debt problem. However, unless the product offerings are unique and demand is high, these options are just not viable in today's world.

### YOU CAN'T WIN THEM ALL . . .

In a midsize industrial company that manufactured fire and smoke alarms, the sales force faced anger and frustration from several major customers. The problem was that an energetic credit department was pursuing payment so aggressively that on occasion it demanded payment before products had actually been delivered. The sales director—having read books on customer care and the like—decided that the solution was to take the credit manager out to meet some major customers and to discuss the problem. This he did—and his best account generously provided an excellent lunch. On returning to the factory, the sales director said, "Now, do you see the problem?" and the credit manager said, "Yes, I do. If they can afford lunches like that, they can afford to pay us quicker," and returned to her office with renewed vigor. This problem required a different solution!

The goal of credit is to enhance sales, but relaxing credit standards to encourage sales to additional customers also increases the probability of bad debts. The critical issue is where to draw the line between customers that are creditworthy and those that are not. In choosing criteria for this decision, most companies focus solely on minimizing bad debts. Frequently, they take this position because bad debts are so visible. The problem is that they fail to focus on the invisible losses that the firm suffers because of an overly tight credit policy. These are opportunity losses, the sales and profits that the firm did not earn from consumers and organizations that would have become its customers had the credit standards been somewhat looser. These losses are rarely measured or remarked on. A good start would be to discuss this issue with salespeople: They probably have a good idea which accounts they cannot get because of company credit policies. The conclusions may be frightening.

## CHANGING CREDIT PHILOSOPHY

During General Motors' (GM's) low point in the early 1980s, the success of General Motors Acceptance Corporation (GMAC) largely kept it alive. At a retirement dinner for GMAC CEO Tom Murphy, a Columbia Business School alumnus, we asked him how he had made GMAC such an important factor within GM. The core reason, he said, was a change in management philosophy (accompanied by changing several managers). He alleged his problem at GMAC had been too many people who thought their job was to minimize bad loans, and not enough who realized that they had to sell the loans in the first place. This is what he changed.

Too many companies fail to realize the strategic power of credit extension in capturing customers. As noted, finance may be an area of distinctive competence that can endow the firm with significant advantage. To fail to use this competence appropriately is a betrayal of shareholder interest. For a significant period, GMAC was the lowest cost borrower in the United States, excluding the federal government. Failing to capitalize on this advantage could have jeopardized the very existence of General Motors.

*Decisions on granting credit.* Not only are opportunities lost because of firms' unwillingness to extend credit, they are also lost because of the sheer amount of time they take to decide whether to extend credit. This problem is particularly common with new customers, a behavior that seems designed to demotivate the sales force. It is difficult enough to persuade customers to switch from competitors, but to lose customers because the credit department has no sense of urgency is galling in the extreme.

*Credit as a strategic weapon.* The firm's ability to craft different options for the payment of goods and services for different kinds of customers can become a major strategic weapon. Imaginative companies realize the advantage that this flexibility creates for them. Over and above working with credit terms per se, such companies include currency flexibility, barter arrangements, offsets, training, buybacks, and the like. By more closely meeting customer requirements, an entrepreneurial and outward-oriented finance department can be a great asset to doing business in the global marketplace.

## CREDIT IN DEVELOPING THE TELECOMS

The telecom industry provides an excellent illustration of the way things were, compared with the way things can be. When telecoms were poorly regulated monopolies, billing and credit were secondary, bureaucratic accounting functions. Firms paid little attention to customer care—consumers put up with bad treatment or did without a phone. As governments deregulated and privatized their telecom companies and new competitors entered, billing and credit have become a critical customer interface, concerned not just with collecting revenues faster, but with stimulating demand by using imaginative tariff structures. One reason MCI's "Friends and Family" tariff was so effective in the United States was that, for several years, competitors lacked the necessary accounting systems to imitate the strategy. New generation systems track customer use of diverse products and services to integrate fraud control, churn management, and customer care. These systems compile customers' usage of services and invoice them with an aggregate bill. New customer offers, such as discounts across fixed and mobile networks, are constantly evolving to improve value in critical market segments that are identified with data-mining techniques. In some countries, telecoms (e.g., British Telecom) have leveraged this capability to become suppliers of other products like electricity and gas utilities. Add to this the impact of an Internet-based relationship with the customer, and bureaucratic accounting functions arrive at the front edge of the firm-customer relationship.*

*G. Naim, "Humble Invoice Becomes Mission-Critical," *The Financial Times* (October 9, 1999).

*Dealing with slow payers.* It's one thing to grant credit, but it's quite another to ensure that the firm collects what it is owed. Obviously, companies want to get paid, but managers need to understand that the customer they are trying to collect from today will be the same customer that they want to do business with tomorrow. How many of the readers of this book would junk their local phone companies just as soon as possible if they were to have their telephone service cut off for late payment of a single bill, after years of on-time payment?

### TAKING THE CREDIT FOR LOSING ACCOUNTS

Buttonwood Company,* a leading manufacturer's multimillion dollar key account, was having some short-term cash flow problems. The supplier's key account manager was well aware of this and had advised the credit department of the situation. Nonetheless, the credit department, following bureaucratic procedures, sent dunning letters to the account and instructed manufacturing to stop all future deliveries until the debt was cleared. Aside from offensiveness, stopping supplies actually threatened the customer's ability to operate and was not very friendly. Buttonwood dealt with its cash-flow problems—they were short-term and temporary. It then switched all its supply contracts to one of its supplier's closest competitors.

* Disguised name.

The credit department is a critical direct interface with the firm's customers and important to the maintenance of a good customer relationship. However, many credit departments seem unaware that, among their other functions, they serve a critical customer service role. Rather than viewing their function as one of saying "no," they should substitute a thorough going customer service philosophy. Strategically managing credit with a customer service philosophy constitutes a major challenge but will surely pay dividends for companies that are successful. It is just a further example of the competitive strength that Total Integrated Marketing can unleash.

Supplier Payments.    Just as we suggest a different perspective for the granting of credit, so a parallel caution may be in order on the payments side. Since working capital has to be financed, lower working capital is generally better. This explains the traditional focus, noted earlier, on having customers pay sooner rather than later (except in industries such as credit cards where profits are heavily based on credit transactions). The traditional parallel prescription for suppliers is to pay creditors later rather than sooner.

This traditional prescription might make sense for less important supplies where the firm has multiple potential suppliers and is basically indifferent about the one it chooses, making its decision on such criteria as price and delivery. However, current procurement trends have led to a rationalizing of many firms' supplier bases—in part under the influence of total quality management and supply chain collaborations. In addition, increased competitive pressure has mandated further outsourcing, while information technology has facilitated management of the resulting web of collaborators, often tabbed the network economy.

Under such conditions, traditional supplier payment practices make little sense and may destroy the relationships on which networks and collaborative supply chains rely. As the firm's dependency on suppliers increases, it must ensure that its supplier base remains solvent and able to supply whatever is needed. Paying long to a supplier that goes under in the meantime does not put the firm ahead. Furthermore, as the countervailing power of suppliers increases, an alienated supplier may well jeopardize the firm's ability to serve its customers. The language of supplier-customer is being replaced by that of partner. When both firms seek similar long-run goals, stretching payments to improve a working capital position is non-partner-like behavior.

## TOTAL INTEGRATED MARKETING: MANAGING THE FINANCE/MARKETING INTERFACE

### Role Relationships and Teamwork

The hostility that often marks the finance/marketing interface flows directly from the role relationships created by traditional corporate organization structures. Historically, many of these role relationships arise from a control—if not punitive—culture that emphasizes external control instead of self-control. In many companies, product and market managers develop plans and budgets, but these go to finance for review or even approval. This process casts the finance department in the role of corporate police officer. Some finance executives relish this power, but this role almost guarantees conflict and antipathy. We might even draw a parallel with the traditional approach to quality in which manufacturing operatives did not check their own work. Rather, specialist quality control inspectors were hired for that purpose. In contrast, the more recent quality movement places this responsibility in the hands of those actually doing the work.

Instead of perpetuating the counterproductive "us versus them" attitude, firms need to foster team-based approaches to strategy and plan development. Some level of conflict can be healthy because it raises critical issues and improves decision making. But too much conflict tends to turn the discussion inward and away from a focus on external imperatives. Having a well-trained member of the finance function on the business team allows members to raise potentially contentious issues early and can dramatically improve the quality of economic decision making. As with other nonsequential innovations, it can also save time and effort. We discuss this issue further in other chapters of the book.

## Measurement Systems

A second key area for producing conflict and internally oriented diversion of effort lies in measurement systems, where finance usually (and appropriately) has a heavy input. First, recall that profit may not be the best objective for a product or product line. Portfolio approaches to managing the business require tailoring objectives to the strategic role that the firm expects a business segment to fulfill. Second, studies on measurement suggest that companies should consider using softer measures that encompass a much broader purview of the business than that provided by the traditional finance or accounting perspective. The balanced scorecard movement is the best example of this trend as it tries to capture measurements that may be important for long-run profits.[21] The brand health check measures discussed in Chapter 4 represent another illustration. It is vital to realize that a poorly chosen objective may result in the entire strategy being distorted.

The underlying issue derives from the observation that profit per se is a poor control measure. Profit is nothing more than a residual. It is a consequence of other things done well—volumes sold, prices maintained, costs controlled, and so on. Greater focus on the determinants of profit rather than the profits themselves provides better and more actionable insights. Too much focus on a lagged outcome measure, such as profit, tends to produce dysfunctional consequences for the business system that attempts to generate those profits.

## PROACTIVE FINANCIAL MANAGEMENT

How then, should the twenty-first century finance or accounting manager change to reflect the philosophy underlying Total Integrated Marketing? A critical fundamental is to look outward, rather than inward. After all, the stock market sets the ultimate benchmark of corporate success, reflecting an underlying principle that can be usefully extended. When marketers measure performance, they are concerned with sales volume and revenue measures, which are critical aspects of the sales force. But, importantly, they also focus on market share—both revenue share and volume share. These measures have the enormous benefit of benchmarking the firm's performance against competitors, while controlling for exogenous factors that affect the market as a whole.

Benchmarking performance, either against sectoral competitors, or the market as a whole, is a vital concept. Too many accounting and financial managers remain fixated on internal comparisons such as how well the firm is doing year-to-date versus last year. Frankly, who cares? Performance this year versus last year is essentially meaningless.

## HOW WELL HAVE WE REALLY DONE?

An actual statement from a CEO: "We have done a rigorous analysis versus our performance in the same period last year. So far we are 15 percent ahead of last year in both revenues and profits. I want to congratulate all those who have supported me in achieving this stellar performance." What the CEO apparently failed to notice is that the market grew at 30 percent over the year, that his firm's market share has dropped by five percentage points, and that its chief competitor had a profit increase of 60 percent. Is the firm's performance really that stellar?

What is important for managing the organization is not how well it is doing versus last year but how well it is doing versus a rigorously developed budget. And it must be a budget that is not just a projection of last year's numbers, but is the outgrowth of a strategically focused plan. The analysis used by the quoted CEO should have picked up the incipient growth in the market and surely should have included performance measures such as market share and other benchmarks.

The underlying issue goes back to the inward versus outward distinction raised in Chapter 2. In the twenty-first century, the action is fast paced. Next year will always be radically different from this year, and yet more different from the year before. Our measurements should reflect this reality and be outward and forward, not inward and backward.

A second lesson concerns a key role for finance and accounting managers. They constitute the primary corporate link for relationships with shareholders and the financial community and can use many concepts of strategic marketing advantageously. Investors often rely on the recommendations of analysts when they decide to trade shares. Thoughtful analysts in turn base recommendations on their understanding of a company's strategy and how it will affect future returns to shareholders. Positioning that strategy to them can have significant influence on their recommendations. This input is of special importance when the company is attempting to raise capital in the public markets for the first time with an IPO. It also comes into play in mergers and acquisitions when interested parties (e.g., Hewlett-Packard and Compaq) need to be able to assess the value of the prospective merger or acquisition candidate.

Consider market segmentation in this light. Homogeneous markets exist only as a theoretical ideal to permit simplistic economic analysis. As with product-markets, markets for shares are characterized by heterogeneity of size, return requirements, risk preferences, trading preferences, service requirements, and emotional involvement. Consider trading preferences: Some investors prefer to trade stocks heavily (day traders are the prime example) and hold them only for short periods of time. Other investors hold for the very long run. Put another way, companies can influence the composition of their shareholder base. Indeed, when there are very large institutional shareholders such as Calpers and CREF, the tools of key account management may be appropriate.[22]

## GETTING LONG-TERM INVESTORS

Given the choice, most companies prefer to have owners that hold shares for the long run. One approach to achieving this aim is to invest heavily in an investor relations department that provides high levels of service to shareholders. Warren Buffett has another approach. Have you tried to buy a share of Berkshire Hathaway lately? The last time we looked, it would have set you back about $75,000. Why doesn't Mr. Buffett split the stock? Because he believes, rightly or wrongly, that the high share price attracts long-term investors. (Of course, his educational annual general meeting also helps.)

A third lesson is that accountants must practice marketing within the organization. Quality guru W. Edwards Deming made the point that internal processes have "customers" too, and that accountants who provide information to line managers need to start thinking of them as customers. How is it in your organization? Do reports on expenditures such as telephone, travel, and entertainment arrive (on paper) months after the periods to which they apply? Are invoices for employee expense reimbursement and external suppliers paid months late? Many companies lack the systems support necessary for good economic decision making. The fact that firms such as SAP and Oracle have built very large businesses based on providing such information is prima facie evidence of the failings of many companies' internal systems.

It is wholly in the spirit of Total Integrated Marketing not to limit the accountant's role to internal constituencies. It should embrace a broad external perspective that includes assessing the relative cost positions of the firm's competitors. For example, although accounting skills are vital to developing an analysis of business systems (as discussed in Chapter 4), companies often pay consultants large fees to perform this task when their own executives could be performing some, if not all, of the work. Bringing a better understanding of competitors' costs and business systems is just one example of how accounting can contribute more value to the firm.

## CONCLUSION

For accounting and finance alike, the goal must be to look forward and outward much more than in the past. Crucial changes should come in applying marketing concepts to customers, in actively engaging their expertise to estimate the asset value of customers, in modifying measurement and reporting systems to meet the criterion of shareholder value creation, and in ensuring that the credit department does not become a major source of lost opportunity. Perhaps most important of all, they must discard the corporate police officer role. Becoming active participants in strategic decision making is the best way to ensure that the company's finance and accounting expertise is wedded to the creation of value for customers and shareholders alike.

# MARKETING AND OPERATIONS

## DELIVERING "THE GOODS"

The relationship between marketing and operations has always been crucial, largely for self-evident reasons[1]—most people accept that having products to sell is an advantage. Whereas the firm's marketing efforts lead customers to expect benefits that its products and services will provide, operations is usually the driving force in actually delivering them. Environmental changes are placing enormous pressure on the performance of traditional operations systems, leading to a radical rethinking of models for organizing and managing the operations function. Customer demands for increased value, rapid response, and tailored solutions require new approaches to managing the entire supply chain. Great rewards are possible for firms that adopt these approaches, and an early demise awaits those that do not.

In this chapter, we work through the key marketing/operations linkages that underpin the delivery of customer value, and then study the convergence of those trends that have created the supply chain revolution. In the traditional view of operations, the challenge is manufacturing and delivering products on time, but the new view focuses on creating a whole new way of doing business. The interface between marketing processes, operations, and supply chain systems is not simply a one-way street for keeping marketing promises through enhanced product and service quality. The challenge is just as much about working with new business models created by integrated supply chains based on interorganizational collaboration. The need for a market-based philosophy to penetrate supply chain design is critical; Total Integrated Marketing now spans the supply chain, not just the company.

Unilever Chairman Niall Fitzgerald has remarked that today's consumer wants the product, where she wants it, when she wants it—nothing else will do. The firm's ability to satisfy these customer requirements is a function of the quality of its operations and logistics systems. Fitzgerald's goal can only be achieved with a seamless integration of sales, marketing, operations, logistics, and customer service. Astoundingly, this aspiration still remains elusive for many companies, although it has been central to the success of such a diverse group of firms as Singapore Airlines, Amazon.com, Dell Computer, and FedEx.

Beyond this seemingly modest aspiration, changes in information technology and better understanding of cost economics are revolutionizing supply chain management, which is now more tightly integrated and managed than ever before. Traditional manufacturers benefit from modern-day transportation systems' improved cost and performance. In addition, the Internet and the World Wide Web are dramatically changing the distribution of information-based products and services, as well as the basic assumptions about marketing services. Furthermore, the "lean enterprise" and integrated supply chains are changing business practices in industries as diverse as computers, airlines, health care, and groceries. We are only beginning to grasp the impact of these developments on customer value, let alone what they mean for the marketing/operations interface.

## STRATEGIC RELATIONSHIPS

In Chapter 2, we noted the trend toward increased competitive intensity in many industries and such related changes as the speeding up of technological and product life cycles, and the shift toward greater customer power. These environmental imperatives have placed tremendous pressure on company profits and enormous stresses on companies' operations and logistics systems.

The different measurement systems, objectives, and reward structures for operations and marketing personnel have caused many difficulties in the marketing/operations interface, especially in the matching of supply and demand. In general, marketers focus on measures like market share, sales volume, and profit; and they want fast, on-time, and in-full deliveries to achieve their objectives. In contrast, cost reduction was the traditional focus for operations. The adoption of total quality management has improved this state of affairs. The new-model operations manager is extremely conscious of customer and shareholder value, and the total quality discipline has highlighted the importance of keeping delivery promises. Yet, while objectives are beginning to move into alignment, considerable difficulties still exist at the interface.

## Matching Supply and Demand

**The Problem.**   Since the Industrial Revolution ushered in the era of mass production, the generally accepted system for operations and logistics has been to manufacture products, place them in inventory, then ship them when orders arrive. To implement this process, huge quantities of inventory occupied the industrial landscape—from raw materials, through work-in-process, finished goods at the factory, and finished goods in transit and at both wholesale and retail distributors. The operations research discipline developed, in part, to deal with the problem of assessing appropriate inventory levels.

Manufacturers tried to develop inventory control models that optimized the trade-off between long production runs, low setup costs per unit (spread over large volumes), and high inventory costs on the one hand; and short production runs, high setup costs per unit (spread over small volumes), and low inventory costs on the other. They also had to consider the related trade-off between the real costs of holding inventory and the opportunity costs of being unable to meet demand if inventory is not available.

For this system to operate well, accurate forecasts of the level and composition of demand were essential. The firm produced goods against this forecast that moved through the distribution system in the anticipation of sales. However, there are major questions about how well this system ever worked.

### TRYING TO FORECAST WHO DOES THE FORECASTING

During a seminar we led at one of the world's largest computer companies, it emerged in discussion that a sales forecasting department was reporting to the production director. When we asked about this somewhat unusual organizational location—in particular, why the sales forecasting group was not in the sales or marketing department—the production director replied: "Oh yes, they've got one too. But we can't believe a word they say so we have to have our own for production scheduling!" (We have worked with other companies that are even worse—they also have accounting departments that operate sales forecasting systems because they don't believe marketing or production!) What is it like in your company?

What is certain is that however well this system may have operated in the past, it will operate worse in the future. Sales forecasting has never been easy, but at least when change is slow and evolutionary, the forecaster has a fighting chance of being in the right ballpark. However, as markets undergo rapid rates of innovation and structural change, past history is less and less relevant for making forecasts, so the traditional model tends to fall apart. The firm must either increase inventory to deal with demand uncertainty, or miss profits because the requested product is not in stock. Product design changes leading to excessive inventory of the now "old" product can present enormous disposal problems for the firm and its distributors. The new designs also generate significant conflict in the distribution system because the value of the old product is reduced overnight.

A second problem concerns greater competition, which increases pressure on profit margins. Decreased profit margins mean decreased returns and, hence, reductions in shareholder value—right? Well, not necessarily. It depends on whether we look at return on assets (ROA) as simply Profits/Assets, or as ROA = Profits/Sales × Sales/Assets. The point is that Profits/Sales is profit margin and Sales/Assets is asset turnover. It may be an inevitable long-term consequence of higher levels of competition that profit margins will fall. However, if asset turnover can be increased, it may protect or even enhance ROA. More effective management of working capital can make a big contribution to increasing asset turnover, and improved operations and logistic systems have proved to be a critical tool for achieving this.

It is one thing, however, to consider the problem from the manufacturer's perspective; the perspectives of customers—their ideas about value—may be quite different from the firm's.

## THE REAL COST OF BEING "OUT OF STOCK"

One of the authors was present when a senior executive of Asda (now Asda/Wal-Mart), a large British supermarket chain, briefed executives from a packaged goods manufacturer. He used the stockout example to underline the differing perspectives between a brand manager and store management. To the brand manager, a stockout represents the unfortunate loss of a single sale to a particular consumer. To the store manager, the same stockout means the consumer may go to a competitor supermarket, particularly if the missing brand is strongly preferred; and then the consumer's entire basket of supermarket purchases may be lost, possibly forever.

Essentially, there are two ways of solving the supply/demand matching problem: improving the current system and changing the system.

## Improving the Current System

The basic approaches to improving the current system are better forecasting and avoidance of artificial demand swings.

Better Forecasting.    There is a yawning chasm in most companies between what marketing and operations believe constitutes a good forecast. The sales force often heavily influences marketing forecasts. In many companies, this is the part of the organization that believes any number is a target to be beaten. Various kinds of deviant behavior result from this simple belief. If financial reward is linked to the achievement of targets, the rational salesperson will lowball the forecast to improve the chances of beating it. Such a systematic bias can lead to chronic supply problems and widespread customer dissatisfaction. Operations managers quite frequently compensate for this systematic bias by adjusting forecast volumes upward. Pressure from senior management, wedded to a desire to please customers, can lead to an opposite bias, with its associated overstocks and subsequent discounts to move excess inventory.

This problem has a two-stage solution although implementation may not be easy. First, managers in all functions have to be convinced that the critical forecasting goal is accuracy and that game playing is unacceptable.[2] Second, sales and marketing managers must understand that aggregate accuracy is not sufficient. Capacity scheduling, whether for airline seats or package sizes, requires disaggregated accuracy. Marketers are all too prone to believe that higher sales in one area balance out lower sales in another. Such a view does not help operations scheduling in the slightest. It is easy to see why forecasting models have consumed such enormous intellectual effort over the decades—they appear to offer relief from the organizational politics that so often surround human inputs. However, there are still a lot of problems to bear in mind.

Reducing Demand Swings.    Left to natural market forces, demand forecasting is inherently difficult and is becoming increasingly complex as environmental turbulence increases. What makes life even more difficult is artificial demand fluctuation caused by tactical marketing actions. The most common of these is price promotions. Periodic price promotions typically lead to wild demand swings as some customers increase consumption. Firms temporarily "buy" some customers from competitors, and other customers buy forward and place goods in inventory when prices are low, then reduce purchases when prices are "normal." If price promotions occur on a regular basis, however, the promotion itself may become the normal price, leading to even lower margins. Two problems arise from these demand swings. First, they make forecasting more difficult, hence the necessity of higher inventories or opportunity losses from forgone sales. Second, regardless of this increased uncertainty, the fluctuations in demand make for an inefficient operations/logistics system and higher costs.

## THE PRICE OF PRICE CUTS

Lucent Technologies' stock price dropped from a high of over $130 in late 1999 to under $20 about one year later. At least one of the reasons for this debacle was heavy price discounting and aggressive vendor financing in late 2000, as the firm struggled to reach revenue targets. A consequence of this action was the inability to forecast demand for 2001. The product development

> group simply had to guess what customers would buy. It guessed wrong. Lucent manufactured products that customers did not want. In fiscal 2000, revenues grew 12 percent but inventories increased 34 percent!*
>
> * *Fortune* (February 5, 2001), 143–148.

One way to deal with this problem is to move to "everyday low pricing" as have many firms such as Procter & Gamble. When well executed, the increased efficiency in the operations/logistics system that results from better forecasting and smoothed demand more than makes up for the loss in margin from reducing prices.

In other situations, competitive advantage may go to the company that learns how to manage such uncertainties and demand swings better than their competitors. To deal with the marketing/supply chain issue, strategic thinking is already moving on from supply chain efficiency (cutting costs as operations people always do) to the building of superior agility and responsiveness to market change (which is what marketing people are supposed to do). Some of the effects achieved by those who exploit other companies' inflexible operations and supply chain systems may be unusual.

## GUERRILLA MARKETING IN THE GROCERY BUSINESS

In the British supermarket grocery business, two of the dominant three players are Tesco and Asda/Wal-Mart. In the United Kingdom, Safeway is a much smaller company that has struggled to survive. Tesco and Asda both pursue value-pricing strategies; they have vowed to equal the price cuts of any player in the market, including each other.

New Safeway CEO, Carlos Criado-Perez, a former Wal-Mart executive, is pursuing a strategy of using local promotions to drive up sales and convert occasional Safeway shoppers into loyal Safeway customers. The difference in Safeway's approach is that it runs promotions on a localized store-by-store basis, largely driven by store managers. This approach is common in the United States, but anathema to rigidly centralized British and European retail chains. The strategy is based on the philosophy that retailing is essentially local, and the intent is to compete for consumer loyalty in specific local neighborhoods. At any point in time, Safeway has about 20 special price offers moving around the country. Its aim is to disorient competitors.

Rivals have pledged to match Safeway prices, and Criado-Perez says: "So, of course, we help them. We fill their car parks with Safeway advertisements so all *their* clients can benefit from *our* offers in *their* stores. They last about fifteen minutes—those offers do about six months of sales in one week so they don't have the supplies and have to take the banners down." Consumers then have to go to Safeway if they want the product in question because the Tesco and Asda stores are out of stock. Predictably, by the time the large companies' supply chains have recognized the stockout and flooded product into their stores, Safeway has moved the price promotion to another town, leaving its larger competitors heavily overstocked. One competitor, facing the supply chain disruption that ensues from Safeway's guerrilla tactics, concludes, "The man is a nightmare." Safeway continues its "hit and move" strategy, and has seen a remarkable recovery in its stock price.*

*Adapted from N. F. Piercy, *Market-Led Strategic Change: A Guide to Transforming the Process of Going to Market* (Oxford, England: Butterworth-Heinemann, 2002), 723–728.

## Changing the System

Improving the situation is better than nothing, but the real truth is that firms must discard the historical model and develop new approaches. There are several reasons for this.

First, driven by globalization, intense competition is causing significant structural change in established industries. Scarcely a day passes without the announcement of a megamerger or new strategic alliance, often between seemingly unlikely partners. The net result is that the competitive environment and the demand for products are much less stable.

### INTERNET FORECASTING PROBLEMS

Turbulence in Internet advertising has made revenue forecasting extremely difficult. The revenue of Yahoo!—one of the World Wide Web's more successful companies—derives mostly from advertising. On October 11, 2000, analysts' estimates of revenues for each of the four quarters in 2001 were $(millions) 330, 350, 370, 410. On March 6, 2001, they were $(millions) 230, 270, 310, 390. Two days later, on March 8, estimates were $(millions) 170, 185, 205, 230.*

*Estimates by Goldman Sachs and Bloomberg Financial Markets, *The New York Times* (March 11, 2001).

Second, as affluence rises in the United States, Europe, and Asia, the discretionary portion of the consumer dollar is rising even higher. Today in Britain, weekly food costs are less than the amount spent on leisure;[3] and a Virgin Group spokesperson has suggested that today's teenagers make decisions each weekend between buying CDs or topping up their prepaid cell-phone calls. Such intersectoral competition further reduces the predictability of consumer demand. One respected analyst believes the freedom of sophisticated consumers suggests that we should anticipate radical changes from historical patterns in consumer spending: For consumer goods companies, "Predictions of consumer behavior are being thrown into disarray by the chaos that this new freedom is causing."[4]

Finally, in the scramble to secure competitive advantage, the rate of innovation shows no prospect of slowing, but rather is increasing. While definite progress has been made in forecasting demand for established products, difficult forecasting problems arise for new products. The newer the product, the greater the difficulty—hence the greater the forecasting challenge.[5] Also, no matter how sophisticated our forecasting models, we must rethink the problem if those models are based on historical data, generated by a system that is undergoing rapid and unpredictable change.[6]

The only solution to many of today's operations problems is shifting to an approach equipped for twenty-first century realities. The long-term solution to many problems at the operations/marketing interface is to redesign that interface to deal with a turbulent and unpredictable world.

Shifting from Product Push to Customer Pull.   The essential factors in redesigning operations systems are flexibility and responsiveness, with shorter cycle and changeover times. Operations systems are shifting from the traditional "supplier push" approach to a "customer pull" philosophy. The traditional philosophy was discussed earlier—manufacture products, place them in inventory, then ship them when the orders arrive. In contrast, the customer pull philosophy says to identify demand, then make and ship the products as and when customers buy them.

The information revolution has vastly aided the shift to customer pull.[7] For example, in the traditional system, the supplier to a national supermarket chain manufactured product, then shipped it to regional warehouses. There it would be held until called for by the supermarket chain. Periodically, chain store managers assessed their product requirements and placed orders with their regional offices. Aggregated orders were then placed with the manufacturer, for delivery from its regional warehouse. In this system, very little information flowed between the supermarket and the manufacturer—just annual forecasts and, periodically, aggregated orders from several individual supermarkets (and none from the individual supermarket outlet).

Consider the possibilities in the new information economy. Bar-coding technology allows the supermarket to know, on a moment-by-moment basis, sales of a particular product at each outlet. Furthermore, the manufacturer, via extranet technology, can know this information simultaneously. Thus, the manufacturer knows actual product demand at the point of sale, in real time. In addition, the manufacturer has available similarly disaggregated data from previous years, together with data on such demand-affecting factors as competitive advertising, price promotions, the weather, and type of day (weekday, weekend, holiday).

Working with sophisticated forecasting models based on the data, the manufacturer can plan production. In addition, individual delivery bundles per supermarket can be prepared at the factory, eliminating the costs of bulk breaking within the distribution system. When combined with cross-docking, delivery time is greatly reduced and the entire system operates with significantly less inventory.

### MY COLA IS HOW OLD?

One study of the sheer waste and avoidable costs in traditional operations and logistics systems highlights the humble can of cola. In traditional manufacturing and logistics approaches, while processing the product and its package required only 3 hours, the finished product spent nearly 11 months in warehouse storage and on trucks. The British supermarket firm Tesco now operates a constant replenishment system to its stores, tightly integrated with suppliers' production and distribution systems. The can of cola on that company's shelves is now less than 2 weeks old, not 11 months.*

*J. P. Womack and D. T. Jones, *Lean Thinking: Banish Waste and Create Wealth in Your Corporation* (New York: Simon & Schuster, 1996).

Mass Customization and Segments of One.   Before the Industrial Revolution, most transactions were local, goods were made to order, and standardization was unknown. Substituting machines for human and animal power permitted large-scale production of standardized products (see Figure 7.1). For example, the development of handguns and rifles with standardized parts that could be mass-produced in a factory and replaced by

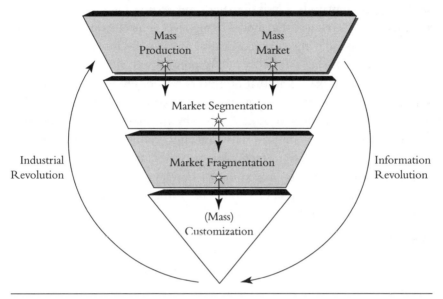

Figure 7.1   ECONOMIC EVOLUTION

the user fundamentally changed U.S. history in the nineteenth century. Prior to this, every firearm was handmade and had to be repaired by a craftsman; a weapon malfunction in the wilderness was seriously bad news. Combined with mechanization of transportation, centrally produced goods could be distributed to widely dispersed potential markets. Resultant low prices and inherent potential demand led to rapid growth.

However, mass production of standardized products ensures success only under conditions of relative scarcity. As customer power grew, mass markets increasingly broke up into segments and firms that attempted to satisfy customer needs with varied offers. The critical organizational trade-off concerned the granularity of segmentation. Fine-grained segmentation enhances the value delivered to customers, but at an increased cost of making, promoting, and distributing a wider variety of products. For much of the last part of the twentieth century, market segmentation was the watchword for strategy development as firms strived to resolve the customer value/cost trade-off.

The critical point is that advances in operations management have fundamentally changed this trade-off between customization and cost. In many industries, changeover times from making one product to another have dropped drastically. Until the 1980s, the received wisdom in the U.S. automobile industry was that model changeover time ranged between four and six hours—today the changeover time is measured in seconds! The increased manufacturing flexibility and responsiveness, along with the associated cost reductions, mean that producers can address ever finer-grained market segments or market fragments. Many believe the ultimate evolution will be "mass customization," whereby the economics of mass production are favorably combined with tailoring products to the individual.[8] This evolution in operations technology is well matched with today's demanding customers and improved model-building, data mining, and multivariate statistical techniques to divine the future structure of demand.

In a sense, with mass customization or so-called segments-of-one, the ongoing evolution of industrial economies has come full circle. Panasonic's custom-made bicycles and Levi's custom-made jeans were pioneers of this approach in the early 1990s, but the preeminent example is Dell Computer.

## THE DELL BUSINESS MODEL

Since the inception of his company, Michael Dell's basic approach has been to sell direct to customers—initially through print advertisements, catalogs, and over the telephone—and now through Dell's Web site. From the outset, Dell invested in operations technology to add customer value; for example, the firm focused on fast assembly capability, rather than on developing new product technology in-house. Although the direct response system cannot leverage the relationships and infrastructure of a conventional distribution system, such as that traditionally used by market leader Compaq and others, it offers several advantages over the conventional approach. First, Dell retains margins that would otherwise be paid to distributors. Second, when new products are developed and current products become obsolete, Dell does not have to deal with obsolete inventory. Third, Dell has minimal inventory because it only manufactures to order—the entire global operation runs on about six days' stock. Fourth, Dell receives payment before manufacturing the computer.

Think about it. When you order a computer, you pay by credit card, so Dell has your money before manufacturing the product. Your product is immediately scheduled for production, and the various parts required in assembly are ordered. Your computer is shipped to you a few days after you place the order. If you had a system like this, what would be the implications for the amount of working capital you need and for the cost of financing it?

The heart of Dell's business model is a rapid response operations system that Michael Dell has labeled "virtual integration." Dell is linked electronically to suppliers and to customers. Today, customers submit orders to Dell's Web site, and suppliers send constant flows of parts in response to these orders. In effect, information exchange is the substitute for Dell's raw material inventory, currently under two hours for many items. Dell's business model comprises five principles:

1. Price for performance (Dell mainly sells high-specification machines to business users).
2. Service and support (leveraged by superior customer knowledge).
3. Customized products (customers select component options to configure their own computers).
4. The latest technology (Dell now runs on about six days of supply in inventory and can be in the market one week after a technology innovation like a new chip, with no inventory markdowns).
5. Superior shareholder value.

These principles have been in place pretty much since the outset. The most significant difference made by the Internet is the third principle—customized products. Major customers—treated as partners—have their own "Premier Pages" through Dell's Extranet. Details of the Premier Pages are hammered out between Dell's key account managers and corporate procurement. When individual executives in one of Dell's partner companies want to purchase a computer, they simply go to Premier Pages. Here they are faced with design choices, for example, working memory, hard disc size, DVD slot. A price is generated for each of several configured computers. When the customer finds the desired configuration, the order is entered and the production process commences.

Not only does Dell enhance customer value by delivering exactly what the customer requires, it secures up-to-date information on customer needs and requirements. The power of the learning effects created by these technology-based customer connections gives Dell a continued edge over competitors. Michael Dell describes the boost to this business from the Web site as ". . . essentially rocket fuel for the direct-sell engine."

Since inception, Dell has persistently wrong-footed competitors. In 2001, Dell leveraged its low-cost system by reducing prices, placing significant pressure on competitors suffering from a downturn in PC demand. Dell's success underlines the message regarding the impact of supply chain design on customer value delivery. The Dell story is an amazing illustration of a strategy that achieves great shareholder value by creating superior customer value.

Superb design and management of the marketing/operations interface has been critical to Dell's success. Some of the most remarkable value-driving innovations occur when product design, operations system, logistics, and market strategy are integrated.

An important idea here is the order penetration point. An operations system is like a series of activities organized in the form of a vertical ladder. The farther up the ladder a customer's order must climb, the more likely it is that a response will be slow. Said another way, the closer to the customer the manufacture of the product can be placed (the lower down the ladder), the more rapid will be the response. The vertically integrated operations systems (starting with basic raw materials) that traditional integrated steel makers employ are at a significant response disadvantage compared with nimble arc furnaces that reprocess materials which have already had upstream processing. Outsourcing strategies implemented to offload risk and reduce operating leverage also speed customer response.

However, putting this principle into practice affects the design of the product and the location of physical facilities. If the product design has sufficient flexibility to allow assembling combinations of subassemblies or modules into different products for different customer needs, these requirements are easier to meet. This principle underlies Dell's process and was also behind the "Have It Your Way" program that Burger King, the world's second largest hamburger chain, ran in the United States. It also explains why most Chinese restaurants can feature large menus and fast service!

## COMPETING THROUGH CUSTOMIZATION

In 1980, Andersen Windows, a $1 billion private company, was a mass producer making standard windows in large batches. As customers increasingly requested custom windows, Andersen added custom options, but not only were its thick catalogs (from 1985 to 1991, Andersen's product line increased from 28,000 to 86,000) confusing to both distributors and customers, the calculation of price quotes could take a long time. By 1991, 20 percent of truckloads with Andersen windows contained at least one order discrepancy. Andersen then replaced its catalog with interactive software for its retailers and distributors that allowed customers to design their own windows and to generate a price quote. Orders are transmitted to Andersen's database and assigned a bar code for tracking. By 1995, Andersen offered 188,000 different products, but fewer than 1 in 200 vanloads contained an order discrepancy. More recently, Andersen has attacked the $15 billion replacement window market by making windows entirely to order.[a]

Canadian Pacific Hotels (CPH) decided to focus efforts on individual business travelers, a highly discerning and demanding customer group. For joining its frequent-guest club, CPH promised to provide customer requirements at every hotel stay. Canadian Pacific mapped the "guest experience" and prescribed service levels for each of dozens of events, based on what customers said they expected. It changed management structures and, at each hotel, appointed a champion with broad cross-functional authority to ensure that staff lived up to the expanded promise. In 1996, CPH's share of Canadian business travel jumped 16 percent in a market that expanded just 3 percent.[b]

Unilever's unique family planning aid, Persona, also illustrates customization at work. Over time, it synchronizes itself ever more closely to the user's fertile periods—truly a learning product.[c]

[a] *Fortune* (September 30, 1996).
[b] *Fortune* (July 21, 1997).
[c] Other companies offering individualized products include Reflect.com, Procter & Gamble's Web site for sales of cosmetics, and Nike for footwear products.

**So, What about Working Capital?**   There seems to be significant confusion, at least in the popular business press, as to whether working capital is a "good" thing or a "bad" thing. Working capital, defined as current assets less current liabilities, is a cost to the firm because positive working capital must be financed. The major current assets are cash and short-term securities, accounts receivable, and inventories; the major current liability is accounts payable. Setting aside cash and short-term securities that provide a cushion for actions the firm may wish to take, most of the discussion revolves around accounts receivable, inventory, and accounts payable.

Problems with reducing working capital occur when the firm makes changes to these elements of working capital without changing the business system that requires them. For example, tightening credit terms can reduce accounts receivable—but this may reduce sales. Inventories can be reduced—but this also may reduce sales because the product may not be available when the customer wants to buy. And paying suppliers late can increase accounts payable—but this may disrupt supplier/firm relationships and cause the supplier to stop supplying. In such a situation, reducing working capital by reducing one or more of these three constituent elements may negatively affect sales, profits, and shareholder value.

On the other hand, reducing working capital by introducing a new system may be highly positive. Dell's system reduces working capital but does so in a manner that is consistent within the business system. Accounts receivable are reduced because customers pay by credit card when ordering the product, and inventory is reduced because Dell has introduced sophisticated just-in-time processes.

**Don't Forget the Critical Elements of Infrastructure.** Efficient telecommunications and transportation systems are critical infrastructure elements that allow instantaneous transfer of information and efficient, timely movement of goods anywhere in the world. These elements enable rapid delivery of finished products to individual purchasers and vastly reduce pipeline inventories throughout the economy. They also permit manufacturers to reduce spare parts inventories and supporting facilities, thus increasing the efficient use of capital.[9]

However, a third, but vital, element of infrastructure is trust between buyer and seller. Less obvious than telecommunications and transportation, trust is essential to the management of high-level economies and to achieving the levels of logistical performance that should accompany them. The trade-off between buyer and seller is simple. The buyer provides detailed information about its own sales levels and internal operations to the seller; the seller must perform in such a way as to elicit a high level of trust from the buyer. On what other basis could a supermarket chain allow inventory to be taken out of the distribution system? How else could Dell Computer operate with parts inventory of two hours or less? Around the globe, today's buyers and sellers interact remotely, confident that transactions to which they are committed will be reliably and promptly consummated, with only rare exceptions. Sellers eager to retain their customers and enhance their reputations sometimes go to extraordinary lengths to achieve this goal.

### KEEPING SUPPLY CHAIN PROMISES

GKN is a major supplier of automotive components, and the world leader in constant velocity joints. As a supplier to the world's major automotive companies, GKN must adhere to tight just-in-time delivery schedules or run the risk of shutting down a customer's operations. On one occasion, an executive we know chartered a helicopter rather than miss a scheduled delivery. Would this sort of behavior be sanctioned in your company or would the executive be punished for incurring extra costs?

**Disintermediation and Reintermediation.** An important consideration for both marketing and operations concerns disintermediation (the removal of intermediaries) and reintermediation (the addition of intermediaries). Disintermediation may provide significant opportunities for securing margin advantages (margin that intermediaries would otherwise have earned).

### REMOVING TRADITIONAL INTERMEDIARIES

Ford has tested disintermediation options by taking over dealers in both the United States and Britain. In addition to gaining immediate margin advantages, the goal was to achieve significant growth and margin benefits by developing secure and long-lasting relationships with final customers. Examples such as Dell, and the problems it posed for competitors like Compaq with traditional distributor-based systems, illustrate the possibility of major changes in many other industries.

A difficult challenge for operations managers and marketers will be the management of new distribution alternatives, while retaining for as long as necessary their traditional channels. Such shifts have occurred before, for example, when chain supermarkets supplanted traditional corner grocery stores; but in those days the pace of change was slower. Further, because major channel shifts tend to be infrequent in most industries, many executives lack experience in managing them.

On the other hand, reintermediation occurs when a new intermediary places itself between supplier and customer. Successful new intermediaries add value to the customer and are able to extract profit margin from the previous direct relationship. Internet players like Amazon.com and Yahoo! provide examples of successful new intermediaries.

One of the firm's major problems is bringing supply and demand into balance. Methods are available for improving the traditional system, but increased environmental turbulence will make new models mandatory for those companies that hope to win in the twenty-first century. For companies to secure the marketing and financial benefits that flow from superb operations and logistics performance, the three Ts of infrastructure must coexist—telecommunications, transportation, and trust.

## OPERATIONAL ISSUES

### Quality

No discussion of the marketing/operations interface would be complete without a consideration of quality. The birth of the quality movement in Japan after World War II is well known. At that time, there was almost universal disdain in the West for the "Made in Japan" label. When quality was first introduced in the United States and Europe, it focused on statistical process control (SPC) and was concerned solely with operations.[10] Despite much educational effort, when U.S. manufacturers, particularly automakers, began to feel the heat of Japanese competition in the 1970s, it became clear that quality theory was not being practiced by the vast majority of non-Japanese corporations. Furthermore, even when SPC was practiced, the criteria were almost exclusively driven by technical functions, with little or no regard for the customer.

In those early days, the difference in the way Japanese and American firms conceived quality was dramatic. One of our U.S. clients conducted a benchmarking visit to Japan during the 1970s. We vividly recall that the firm's executives were astounded to hear that when their Japanese competitors had a quality problem, they shut down production. In contrast, when the U.S. firm had problems in production, it kept the line running and attempted to fix quality-impaired products later. With such behavior, the ensuing competitive problems for the United States and Europe were not surprising. As quality began to be taken more seriously in North America, the situation was not unlike the early days of the marketing concept. In a significant number of companies, the reaction boiled down to "That sounds like a good idea, let's hire someone to do it for us; then the rest of us can continue doing things the way we always have."[11] Little did they realize what was in store.

## Quality Function Deployment

According to researchers who have studied the subject, operations and marketing inhabit two different "thought worlds."[12] Even a moment's reflection would surely convince each party that it needs the other; otherwise the future would be bleak. Marketers need something to market and operations need orders to fulfill. One of the major barriers to effective cooperation has been the lack of a suitable language for communicating between the functions. Quality Function Deployment (QFD) provides the language, even though its implementation has been fraught with difficulty.

Although not a new concept, at its best QFD offers a way to systematically develop not only a product, but also a process and a plant around customer requirements instead of around the supplier—the traditional way. Used properly, QFD provides a vehicle for informed discussion between marketing and operations. It can link together an entire chain of activities starting from customers' preferences, all the way to production planning (Figure 7.2).[13]

## Quality Concerns May Matter More Than Sales and Market Share

A troubling aspect of the marketing/operations interface in some companies is the response of operations personnel to high-demand situations. Sometimes the pressure to meet or exceed production quotas is so strong that quality control systems designed to protect customers take a backseat

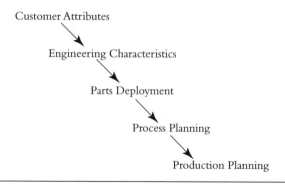

Figure 7.2   QUALITY FUNCTION DEPLOYMENT

to meeting volume targets. There have been many such incidents, but the Odwalla case is one of the more dramatic examples.

## REAL QUALITY ISSUES

In 1993, juice manufacturer *Odwalla* opened a new plant. Odwalla's juices had such high readings of general bacteria that a contractor warned in a memorandum that its "citrus-processing equipment was so poorly maintained that it was breeding bacteria in 'black rotten crud' and 'inoculating every drop of juice you make.'"* Following an outbreak of salmonella in orange juice served at Walt Disney World, the state of Florida, the major producer of citrus juices in the United States, introduced regulations prohibiting the use of split or decayed fruit, and required a two-step cleaning process with both an acid-based detergent and chlorine. Odwalla, located in California, did not adopt these measures.

Indeed, when Odwalla's quality assurance manager announced he was going to test for *Listeria,* a pathogen that can harm pregnant women, the senior VP who had decided not to implement the chlorine wash (because of a perceived aftertaste) forced him to back down. His major concern—the QA manager might collect a body of subpoenable data!

On October 7, 1996, despite the efforts of a quality control inspector, apple juice was made from loads with 25 percent to 30 percent defective fruit (i.e., high decay and worms). Not only did production personnel, striving to meet high production targets, fail to stop the line using the defective fruit, but they refused to provide additional sorters to pick out defective fruit. Juice produced on that day contained a deadly strain of *E. coli* bacteria. As a result of drinking the juice, a one-year-old girl died and some 70 people became sick; some were seriously ill and required many days of hospital treatment.

*C. Drew and P. Belluck, "Deadly Bacteria a New Threat to Fruit and Produce in U.S.," *The New York Times* (January 4, 1998).

## Keeping Operations Up to Speed

Benchmarking is an important tool for assisting operations in improving its performance. Benchmarking studies should be conducted periodically against best identifiable practice, whether in the industry or elsewhere (so-called best-of-class benchmarking). Too often, however, these exercises are very poorly performed. In many firms, "best practice" studies use only internal examples. Almost as bad is to benchmark second-rate organizations.

**MAKE SURE YOU COMPARE YOURSELF TO THE BEST**

As noted earlier, line changeovers from one model to another in the U.S. auto industry used to take four to six hours for all manufacturers. Only in the 1980s did the U.S. manufacturers discover that for Japanese automobile manufacturers the changeover time was just a few minutes. Faced with relatively low demand for many models, firms like Toyota and Nissan had developed methods to reduce changeover time. When they started exporting vehicles to the United States, this manufacturing advance significantly helped Japanese firms' competitiveness.

The moral of this example was that U.S. manufacturers were benchmarking the wrong competitors. Rather than focusing on those firms with "best in the world" operations, insular attitudes led them to concentrate on each other. Benchmarking is a valuable tool to help manufacturing managers improve their firm's competitiveness, but they must identify the right benchmarking target.

## THE LEAN ENTERPRISE AND THE IMPACT OF THE SUPPLY CHAIN REVOLUTION

It is worth thinking a little more about where supply chain management is taking the business. Earlier in this chapter, we discussed some of the problems with traditional manufacturing and logistics systems and introduced approaches to dealing with them. Certainly, these newer approaches improve the marketing/operations interface. However, something more profound is occurring, a total rethinking of supply chains. If you haven't yet been exposed to such changes, listen up, for they may be headed in your direction. The watchword is the *lean enterprise*. Lean enterprise thinking is starting to take hold in several industries and it raises many issues for the marketing/operations interface.

The term "lean enterprise" was coined to describe a new concept of business based on supply chain supremacy.[14] The underlying impact of the progenitors is captured in the phrase "from lean production to the lean enterprise." The focus is to redesign the organization around the supply chain, not to seek out minor improvements in logistics efficiency. The potential impact on the type and level of customer value provided is massive.

So far, we have hinted at the future—customer pull replacing supplier push, the fast responsiveness of integrated supply chains in meeting ever-escalating customer demands, and so on. However, these are really just the first signals of what managers should expect.

The supply chain movement is creating new types of organizations, new collaboration-based value chains, and new business models. These innovations will have a profound impact on the definition of customer value and on the practice of marketing. The days of beating engineers around the head with customer satisfaction reports are fast disappearing. In the lean enterprise of the future, built around supply chain unity, customer choice and value are increasingly being defined by those who operate the supply chain. They believe it is time to take marketers to task for brand proliferation, market disruption, wasted resources, and unnecessary advertising and promotion. Their worldview, developed in sectors like the automotive industry, holds, for example, that based on the number of autos on the road, the demand for replacement mufflers is totally predictable, so demand for all products should be inherently stable. Their model is based on tight collaboration between suppliers, manufacturers, and distributors, information sharing across organizations, and integrated processes throughout the supply chain. The aspiration is the seamless supply chain, where "all players act and think as one,"[15] The competitive impact of the supply chain is the central issue, because in the future, "It is supply chains that (will) compete not companies."[16]

Look at the preceding paragraph again. Based on our discussions with executives, we conclude that marketing has not even begun to take seriously the impact of these new business models, nor developed the necessary dialogue with operations and supply chain management.[17] While marketers have been obsessing about brands and advertising, a new type of organization is being created out of operations and supply chain strategy. It is critically important that marketers develop a dialogue with proponents of the lean enterprise, or they will surrender the role of managing customer value, and the promise of Total Integrated Marketing will remain unfulfilled.

## Efficient Consumer Response (ECR) as a Prototype

The ECR programs in the United States and Europe started in the grocery industry but are diffusing to areas like health care, airlines, and food processing. They represent prototypes for what lean thinking and the lean enterprise may mean for marketing. By 1995, almost 90 percent of firms in the U.S. grocery industry were applying ECR. Inefficiencies in the system were the key drivers that ushered in ECR:

- *Forward buying and diverting.* Retailers purchased products when manufacturer prices were low, then held inventory until prices rose, to show an internal profit. Or, retailers purchased in geographic areas where manufacturer prices were low and shipped to areas where prices were higher.
- *Excessive retailer inventory holding.* Commonly, retailers held over three months' supply.
- *Damaged and unsalable goods.* These were at unacceptably high levels.
- *Complex promotional deals and deductions from manufacturers to retailers.* In some cases, up to 80 percent of invoices had to be processed manually.
- *Excessive promotions and coupons.* One informed observer estimated that of 261 billion coupons issued in the United States in 1996, less than 2 percent were redeemed.
- *New product excesses.* About 22,400 new grocery products were launched in the United States in 1996, mostly "me-too" imitative brands; 90 percent were expected to last less than two years. Furthermore, the bottom 25 percent of brands stocked by supermarkets accounted for less than 1 percent of sales.[18]

Efficient consumer response has had a major impact on these excesses. To achieve a U.S. goal of taking $30 billion per annum of cost out of the supply chain, ECR focuses on managing flows of product, information, and cash in that chain. The key elements of ECR include:

- *Category management.* Collaborative planning by retailers and manufacturers, with responsibility frequently assigned to a leading manufacturer, has removed 20 percent of products from grocery shelves forever.
- *More efficient promotions.* There have been drastic reductions in couponing and special offers and the substitution of "value pricing."

- *Continuous replenishment.* This refers to the continual flow of product from manufacturers, with minimal inventory at retail and wholesale levels and direct store delivery. After three years of ECR in the United States, industry observers estimated that around 20 percent less inventory was in the system. For example, prior to ECR, a detergent packet from P&G typically reached the supermarket shelf in four to six weeks after manufacture; ECR reduced this time to seven days.
- *Electronic data interchange.* The computerization of ordering and payments systems has produced a paperless information flow.
- *Performance measures.* New ways of evaluating performance are based on logistics-related metrics.
- *Organizational change.* New ways of organizing include category management and key account management.

The implementation of ECR has led to a massive economic impact in what was a mature distribution channel. The euphoria about cost savings, however, may obscure some fundamental marketing issues regarding customer value. In 1997, Don Dufek, the ECR Operating Committee Chairman and a former Senior VP at Kroger told an American Marketing Association meeting that ECR is about increasing customer satisfaction and that "the real power is with the consumer." He then described how Kroger used ECR to drastically reduce the number of brands on the shelf and to lever the retail prices of other brands upward. Kroger's position raises some important questions:

- How do reduced choice and higher prices increase customer satisfaction?
- If every cent saved through ECR were passed on to the consumer in lower prices, would it pass the threshold of noticeability?
- Why should the length of time a manufactured product is on the shelf have any connection to customer satisfaction and customer value?
- Do we really believe that cooperative relationships among manufacturers and retailers will replace traditional conflicts? As one marketing executive remarked to us: "If your top five outlets say you are joining this club, or face the consequences . . . you join the club and pay your dues."

■ How will new products from manufacturers outside the "club" ever find their way onto supermarket shelves?

The ECR prototype of a leaner distribution channel raises some major issues for customer value and marketing strategy that have yet to enter the corporate dialogue. Perhaps this is hardly surprising in the face of highly seductive promises of significant cost savings. The critically important point is that these issues are not just about lean supply chains, they are about a new type of organization—the lean enterprise (Figure 7.3).

## Marketing and the Lean Enterprise

There are several important areas where marketing perspectives and the lean movement must come together to resolve some critical issues.

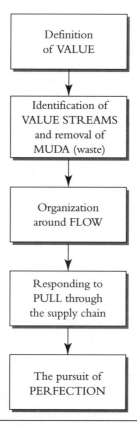

Figure 7.3   THE ELEMENTS OF LEAN SUPPLY CHAIN THINKING

Lean Thinking and Value.   One underlying principle of lean thinking focuses on the defining value in customer terms. Executives are challenged
to define customer value from the perspective of the whole product offering, and to set a target cost for the product on the basis that all identifiable
*muda* (waste) will be removed. At first sight, this looks like sound marketing principles! What marketing executive could disagree? The problem
arises in the interpretation of these principles and the assumptions underlying its implementation:

- Value can be conceived and measured in terms of product engineering and service.
- What creates value in customer terms is easily identifiable (mainly
  lower prices), stable, and predictable (again, mainly lower prices).
- What creates value is a constant factor that cannot be changed by
  intervention.
- What creates value will be essentially the same for all customers.

Value to the lean thinker is straightforward, but it ignores much of what
marketers know about the impact on value of brand intangibles and personal
interactions, market segmentation, market evolution, and value migration
over time (i.e., essentially, customers change their minds about what value
means to them).[19] We need to do some talking here and urgently.

Lean Thinking and Value Streams.   The lean enterprise is based on collaboration between suppliers and distributors to drive out non-value-creating
activities. All *muda* is removed from a product's value stream by eliminating all supply chain activities that do not create value for the end customer. What could be better from a marketing perspective? What would
be better would be:

- Recognizing that such an awesome achievement as reducing from
  11 months to a couple of weeks the time from manufacture to supermarket shelf for a can of Coke may do nothing to increase the
  value to the consumer.
- Realizing that a lean enterprise which does not consider new products and brand extensions as somehow "bad," and is not designed
  to drive them out may provide value to consumers.

An ideal model of a collaborative supply chain producing only a limited set of unbranded generic cola drinks because this is more "rational" sounds like the old-style production orientation. A mandate for incorporating marketing processes that protect consumer choice and brand equity in the supply chain-based enterprise is becoming apparent.

**Lean Thinking and Flow.** Instead of "batch and queue" production processes, the collaborative supply chain is organized around flow. This powerful concept can make an immense difference in the delivery of customer value, as the following examples illustrate.

### MANAGING FLOW FOR GREATER CUSTOMER VALUE

In typical house construction, it is not uncommon for five-sixths of the schedule to be taken up with waiting (for the next set of specialists to do their work) and rework (to correct work done incorrectly or out of sequence). Managing by flow can speed construction and significantly increase the time dimension of customer value.

In a customer service context, have you ever suffered the long lines and interminable delays when you visited another country? The lean thinkers' questions about air travel are incisive and particularly relevant to the post 9/11 world:

Why not a smart card, to be read electronically, with all your reservation details from start to end of trip—from bus to aircraft to rental car to hotel room? Immigration details could be scanned from the smart card at check-in so officials at the point of arrival can do their important thinking while the passenger is in transit, instead of serving as an irritating bottleneck for travelers.

There is a major opportunity for collaboration between marketing and supply chain designers to reinvent service delivery systems that focus on the preferences of customers rather than suppliers.

**Lean Thinking and Pull.** In the lean enterprise, firms upstream in the supply chain do not produce a good or service until the downstream customer requests ("pulls") it. This process eliminates large inventories and reduces customer waiting time—the now classic example is Toyota's Daily Ordering System for replacement auto parts in Japan. Recall as well, the description of the awesome business model developed by Dell around this principle. The trouble is the hidden assumption that end-use demand for a product is inherently stable, and that marketplace chaos results largely from marketing actions. The role of marketing in the lean enterprise seems to be flattening out demand to make the supply chain efficient. "Deals" and "sales" are out; collaboration and central planning for the supply chain are replacing competition. Our fear is that the pursuit of cost-efficiency is building supply chains with zero redundancy and with incredible vulnerability to disruption.

Lean Thinking and Kaizen.    The pursuit of perfection is praiseworthy. The issue, however, is perfection on whose terms? Substituting company and supply chain priorities for "irrational" consumer preferences does not seem to be a great prescription for enhancing real customer value. How do we ensure that activities regarded as *muda* by engineers are not the basis for current or future value delivery to customers? If a two-hour check-in at airports makes travelers feel more secure, is it *muda*? If loaner cars that customers don't drive anywhere make them feel comfortable while the garage fixes their own vehicles, is it irrational? Do mixed-gender hospital wards that ease bed allocation problems really enhance customer value, when customers (patients) hate them?

While the strategic relationship between marketing and operations processes has always been important, the lean enterprise revolution and the search for supply chain supremacy has changed things in significant ways. Companies need to evaluate extremely carefully what supply chain strategies mean for customer value (in all the infuriating ways that customers see value), for brand equity, for service delivery, for the role of marketing, and for long-term shareholder value. Many organizations urgently need this debate.

## Dangers in Leanness

In particular, that debate needs to confront two critical issues. If inventory reductions throughout the system can really secure the promised working capital reductions, such that products are available to customers when and where they want them, then supply chain initiatives are achieving their purpose and shareholder value should increase. However, suppose that they are not. We raised the first problem earlier—there are opportunity losses.

Opportunity Losses.   Opportunity losses occur when the customer wants the product right now and is prepared to pay, but the product is not in stock. As a result, the customer abandons the purchase totally or purchases an alternative product from a competitor. There is a pernicious and potentially deceptive character to opportunity losses. The costs that supply chain innovation is trying to reduce are obvious. For example, simple ratio analysis typically highlights excessive inventories and negative trends, and the associated charge for capital use quickly cuts into economic profit and shareholder returns. This is not the case for opportunity losses.

Customers whose buying ambitions are frustrated rarely enter the seller's information system. Right now as you read this page, you are probably losing sales, but you'll never know it. To achieve, simultaneously, the joint goals of lower working capital with high levels of customer service (fulfillment) should be the objective, but this is difficult to obtain.

Redundancy.   Potentially even more dangerous than opportunity losses is the lack of system redundancy in some systems. In the lean enterprise, suppliers, OEMs, and customers (intermediary and final) are sometimes so tightly coupled that minimal disruption can bring the entire system grinding to a halt. A factory that depends on receiving component shipments every half hour, can ill afford the traffic jams that now occasionally gridlock New York City, regularly paralyze the M25 (London's major ringroad), or daily bring the San Diego Freeway in Los Angeles grinding to a halt. Nor is traffic the only problem. Disturbances can come from severe weather, French lorry drivers and farmers who regularly close most English Channel ports, terrorists, utility failures, and earthquakes (such as the one that hit Taiwan in 1999 and affected the world supply of computer components). The tightly coupled interdependency and advanced specialization of developed economies and their industries have made them extremely vulnerable to disruption. There is good reason why automotive manufacturers now expect a voice in their suppliers' location decisions.

We are fast reaching the point where both customer service and security considerations mandate planning for higher levels of system redundancy.

Whenever the costs of failure are high, such planning is desirable. Today, your car, in addition to high levels of active safety though better brakes and road-holding, is also typically equipped with dual braking systems, seat-belts, airbags, and a collapsible structure designed to protect you in case of accident by avoiding invasion of driver and passenger space. Boeing engineers quadruple redundancy into aircraft control systems to help avoid potentially catastrophic failure.

Technology is beginning to facilitate some decentralization and thereby reduce some of the risks involved in our complex interdependent systems to produce a more healthy and diverse infrastructure. For example, computing power is widely decentralized compared with 20 years ago; telecommunications alternatives have sprouted as many monopolies have been dismembered; and even power generation is moving away from a few very large and expensive facilities toward cogeneration and CHP (combined heat and power systems) plants.

Companies today should be wary of the supply chains they are now constructing, especially as activities they once conducted in-house are increasingly being outsourced. At a minimum, good contingency planning for emergencies must be a required part of their planning efforts, while at the margin, redundancy considerations may dictate stepping back from some of the more extreme options in coupling systems too tightly.

## From Fragile Supply Chains to Agile Supply Chains

If our view of the awesome achievements of supply chain management in reducing costs and developing innovative business designs seems a tad cynical—it's not just us. The next generation of supply chain design focuses not on lean but agile. Think back to Safeway in the United Kingdom setting out to compete by disrupting its larger competitors' supply chains.

Importantly, in response to the impact of turbulent and volatile markets, companies are emphasizing the design of supply chains that are not lengthy, slow-moving pipelines, but are agile and responsive to market change.[20] Supply chain agility means using market knowledge and collaboration to respond to market volatility, whereas the lean approach seeks to remove waste and manage volatility out of the supply chain by leveling demand.[21] The agile supply chain specifically reserves capacity to cope with unpredictable demand. Whereas the lean supply chain requires long-term relationships with suppliers, the agile model mandates fluid and market-based relationships to enhance responsiveness and the capacity for rapid change. Agile supply chains emphasize customer satisfaction, not just meeting a more limited set of value criteria based on reduced costs.[22]

There are at least two ways that marketers can use this development in supply chain thinking and design. One approach is to laugh loudly and shout "I told you so . . . you got it wrong!" at operations colleagues as they attempt to rebuild flexibility in the supply chain. The second way is to seize this remarkable opportunity to integrate marketing issues and marketing processes into the new supply chain designs being developed. If there were ever a time when operations and supply chain colleagues would like marketers to buy in and help out, we suspect it is right now.

## TOTAL INTEGRATED MARKETING: THE CHALLENGE TO OPERATIONS

Environmental and competitive changes have profound implications for managers working in operations on logistics, and most importantly for their relationship with the marketing process. In many cases, operations managers are being forced to rethink how to match their systems with demanding, even spoiled, possibly tyrannical, customers. Correspondingly, managers of the marketing process must respond appropriately to the challenges and questions raised by the new collaborative supply chain models being created in sectors as diverse as automotive, grocery, and health care. In particular, they may have to balance the opportunities for cost reduction against truly improving customer value, and also against long-term strategic risks.

The amazing ascent of Dell, and the problems posed for traditional push systems by pull models, or the challenge to Barnes and Noble from Amazon.com and other Internet-based sellers are likely models of major change for other industries. A difficult challenge for both operations managers and marketers will be to manage the opening of new distribution alternatives while retaining their traditional channels as long as necessary—IBM has largely given up this struggle against Dell and entered a series of collaborations instead.

The challenge for marketers is a tough one, but the potential rewards in enhanced competitiveness are significant. Traditional logistics managers, who most likely honed their skills by making incremental improvements in existing systems, are now faced with the possibility of cataclysmic change. We expect to see aggressive cross-industry recruiting for both logistics and marketing managers who have proven experience in managing distribution changes. To avoid a high risk of losing customers, these two areas must form an effective partnership in the coming transition. The move from lean to agile in supply chain design is a major opportunity for integrating marketing mandates into supply chains and realizing the synergies we have been promised in the past.

A particular problem that will make the task of operations managers even more difficult is that established companies find themselves custodians of operations facilities designed to meet a demand structure that no longer exists. In a turbulent and unpredictable world, flexibility and agility become prerequisites for successful performance, and the design or redesign of operations facilities must reflect this reality.

### FLEXIBILITY IS A KEY TO RESPONSIVENESS

When the designer jean revolution occurred, one of the authors met with a senior executive at Burlington Industries, the large textile company. He was bemoaning that they were underutilizing their two newest, expensive facilities—they had been built to run large volumes of standard denim. Although their most fully loaded facility was much older, its inherent flexibility permitted shorter but, nonetheless, economical runs of the unique denim specifications then being requested by designers. State-of-the-art technology is not always superior—you may sacrifice flexibility for efficiency.

In a similar vein, a Boeing executive argued that the 737 became the world's best-selling commercial jet because of the operator flexibility it permitted. The now old—but identical—cockpit design in the aircraft's many versions enabled operators to switch planes around to accommodate unpredictable traffic patterns, without upsetting crew schedules.

In fact, the key to flexibility sometimes lies in labor, sometimes in capital. Certainly, designers who understand the demands of today's volatile market would be well advised to consider modular design concepts (or what, in automotive parlance, has become known as platform-based design) and a production process that can flex to accommodate such designs. Panasonic's customized bicycle production in Japan relies heavily on skilled manual workers. To further illustrate the importance of flexibility, the largest bacon factory in Europe supplies its product not only to European countries but also to the United States, Japan, Korea, and numerous other markets. The key to its success is production-line workers who are skilled in the cuts and standards required by these overseas markets and who can adjust their output to fluctuating demands.

Management must be able to match skill requirements, as well as designs and operations processes, to evolving market requirements. These requirements appear likely to demand increased flexibility rather than the rigidity that characterized many operations and logistics functions of the past century.

# MARKETING AND SALES

## SYNERGIZING STRATEGY AND SALES

O f all the functions that you might expect to work comfortably and closely with marketing, sales would seem to take pride of place. In fact, marketing departments came into existence mainly to better coordinate sales and advertising. So, you could reasonably presume that marketing and sales would know how to get along together. But in reality, the relationship is frequently unhappy and is characterized by rivalry. The expansion of sales into much of what we think of as operational marketing has intensified this rivalry. The potentially destructive misalignment between marketing and sales negatively affects value delivered to customers and is costly to shareholders. On the other hand, a high degree of cooperation and integration between marketing and sales can lead to a huge competitive advantage in the marketplace.

### DO YOU RECOGNIZE ANY OF THESE SIGNS OF SALES/MARKETING PROBLEMS?

- Your marketing strategies fail to affect sales operations, impeding effective implementation.
- Newly developed marketing strategies ignore customer and competitor insights developed by the sales force, perhaps because marketing has no system for securing these insights.
- Managers in other functions fundamentally misunderstand what sales can and should achieve. For example, do your financial controllers seem to think that the only reliable measures of sales effectiveness are increased sales calls and reduced telephone charges?

169

- Conflicts between sales and marketing managers frequently spill over into unproductive acrimony.
- You are experiencing serious salesperson retention problems and escalating replacement costs.
- There are significant mismatches between the tasks that salespeople must perform to implement your marketing strategy and the ways that they are organized, evaluated, and rewarded.
- Career paths for your salespeople take them away from customers and place them in management posts or other functions just when they have proved to be your best performers.
- You have noticed undercurrents of pervasive burnout and emotional exhaustion among your salespeople as they struggle to live with the ambiguous roles they must now play.
- Your firm offers little support for salespeople making transitions from one role to another, or you are seeing lower performance in the areas that matter most (even if the short-term numbers still look acceptable).
- Your salespeople are enraged to discover that their major competitor is their own company, possibly another sales force or a direct-selling Internet channel.
- Your customer relationships are weakening at a time when this loss is most damaging—generally speaking, this is not good for sales!

To examine these issues, we first clarify the relationship between sales, marketing, and management at the strategic level. Next, we explore the pivotal role that sales activities should play in the survival and growth of the enterprise as well as in the newly emerging models that promise to change the firm's relationships with customers. Then, we discuss the integration of sales and marketing plans and strategies, emphasizing the critical importance of sales strategy and execution in the delivery of value to customers.

This discussion sets the stage for examining operational considerations at the sales/marketing interface. The good news is that we can address many of the practical barriers to integrating sales operations with marketing strategy. However, more broadly, the traditional distinctions between sales and marketing are changing in important ways. The increased concentration of the traditional customer base in many industries has led to significant growth in key account management domestically, regionally, and globally. At the same time, the emergence of customer-based organizations is leading to a reallocation of tasks between sales and marketing departments. Although these reallocations afford potential benefits for both functions, they demand a different approach to the sales task. In many cases, this will result in changed criteria for sales-force recruitment, selection, and development. We conclude the chapter with our Total Integrated Marketing perspective to identify ways forward.

## STRATEGIC RELATIONSHIPS

It is not unusual for executives and companies to have difficulty distinguishing sales from marketing and vice versa. Historically, this was an issue in business-to-business markets, but changes in fast-moving consumer goods (FMCG) companies mean that firms whose end customers are consumers are also looking closely at the distinction.

At one level, the sales/marketing distinction doesn't seem to matter. Certainly, we have worked with companies that didn't know the difference and couldn't care less. What mattered to them was that the tasks traditionally associated with each function were performed well—who performed them, or what the performer's title might have been, worried them not one whit. We have also worked with companies that didn't know the difference, and it almost destroyed them. For this reason, we should recognize that what has traditionally been defined as the responsibility of sales departments and what has traditionally been defined as the responsibility of marketing are now in considerable flux.

### Why Doesn't Management Understand What Modern Sales Organizations Do?

Much of the drive behind Total Integrated Marketing is the need to build superior customer and shareholder value by improving the linkages between marketing processes and functional specializations. But, there is another wrinkle: Sometimes the issue is not just "marketing and . . ." but instead is about building more effective relationships among other functions to achieve superior value delivery. In any case, the goal may be to build better understanding and cooperation between the sales organization and managers in other functions inside the company. Marketing always has been a boundary-spanning process, but in many companies a key challenge seems to be bridging the gaps between the sales force and management. These gaps, which seem to be pervasive, are another result of the serious management problem of internal orientation.

### DOES THIS SOUND LIKE YOUR MANAGEMENT?

One of the authors addressed a senior management workshop at the prestigious Institute of Directors' facility on Pall Mall in London. More than 100 executives—mainly general managers and finance directors—were focused on how to leverage better productivity from their sales organizations. Participants were asked to clarify their goals. The resounding answer: "We have to stop salespeople wasting time, so they can make more sales calls and become more productive." We identified numerous examples of salespeople's scandalous "time-wasting":

✔ They make calls on customers and don't come back with orders.

✔ They spend hours on the phone to operations about deliveries instead of making more customer sales calls and getting more orders.

✔ They seem to spend their lives talking to our accounts department and customer service instead of being in the field.

✔ They keep writing reports about new product development instead of selling what we already make.

Contrast these perspectives with H. R. Challey's findings on what major corporate customers say makes a world-class sales organization.[1] This research suggests they apply the following criteria to judge sales quality: "Managing our satisfaction personally; understanding our business; recommending products and applications expertly; providing technical and training support; acting as a customer advocate in the supplier company; solving logistical and political problems for us; finding innovative solutions to our needs and solving problems we didn't know we had."

Do some senior managers deliberately set out to make it difficult, if not impossible, for the sales organization to do what customers say they value most? Are sales calls aimed at building and reinforcing customer relationships a bad thing? If the firm has not developed other processes for helping customers secure information and service, is it wasteful for salespeople to troubleshoot customer problems with internal departments, instead of letting them do it themselves? We do not think so. Senior managers need to get out of their comfortable offices and better understand what the sales organization does to build customer relationships and keep the firm's value promises.

## THE PROBLEM WITH "IVORY TOWER" MANAGEMENT

The top management team at a major publishing company became involved in executive education. They found out (actually somewhat late in the day) about relationship marketing and the balanced scorecard, and decided this was for them. They plunged the sales organization into customer relationship management and customer satisfaction surveys; development sessions on building customer relationships were mandatory for salespeople.

This sales force sold advertising space in annual publications, mainly to small and midsize businesses. For those customers, the following criteria were critical in placing advertisements in a directory once a year: Do it fast, get the design right first time, and make it cheaper! Their initial bemusement at salespeople now wanting to visit, chat, and take them to lunch quickly turned into hostility because of the time they were wasting. The result—unhappy salespeople being pushed by managers to do things customers did not want.

There's nothing wrong with rocket science, but managers don't need it to deduce that perhaps they should ask salespeople what value means to their customers, instead of assuming they already know the answer. Because of senior management's ill-conceived foray into executive education and its failure to understand what their salespeople actually did, and what drove value for customers, this firm now has to sort out plummeting sales-force morale and falling customer satisfaction. Apparently, some managers will go to amazing lengths to disrupt and incapacitate the sales operation (at least that is what they manage to achieve, whether they mean to or not).

## LEARNING TO TRUST THE SALESPEOPLE (BECAUSE THEY KNOW MORE THAN YOU DO)

We met with a disgruntled marketing VP from a sophisticated medical diagnostics firm. He was unhappy because he had discovered that members of the sales force were "in cahoots" with clinic customers to reduce prices and undermine product profitability. In reality, his firm's finance department had developed a complex pricing approach that led to high prices when demand was high (i.e., when hospitals had orders to test patients), and lower prices at other times (when much less testing was requisitioned). The practical result was that, because little testing was conducted over the weekend, prices were highest on Mondays and lowest on Fridays.

Because the firm's products deteriorated rapidly, standard products delivered on Friday would be unusable on Monday. As a result, salespeople were advising customers to order higher specification products on Fridays—these would also deteriorate but would still perform adequately on Mondays and, because of the vagaries of the pricing scheme, would be less expensive.

Ignore for now the dubious wisdom of devising pricing schemes that annoy customers, what we are describing is salespeople working with customers to enhance value and lock them in. We recall that someone suggested that this might be a good thing for salespeople to do!

## YET MORE WAYS TO SCREW UP THE SALES OPERATIONS

Consider Apple Computer's experience in its core education market. For years, Apple had addressed this market with a loosely organized group of third-party resellers, but in early 2000, the company decided that it would no longer outsource its sales activity but use its own sales force. As Steve Jobs tells it, "We were very straight forward and told these third-party salespeople that, 'Hey, in four months we're going to switch and you're going to be out of a job.' Obviously these folks did everything they could to sell as much as they could by June 30, when we let them go, and did absolutely nothing to build for sales in the July quarter. So when our folks got there, they found there was no pipeline work at all: They had to start from scratch. *And, duh, this was during the peak buying time for schools* [emphasis added]. It was just stupid on our part to do this then, and that was my decision. It was a train wreck and it was totally my fault."[a]

Then, look at what happened at Xerox. Incoming CEO Rick Thoman reorganized the Xerox sales force by industry. A single representative would now analyze a customer's entire business and identify the best way to manage the complex flows of data, images, and graphics. Nothing wrong with that, but Xerox did not retrain the sales force. That was a problem. And what about the switching of accounts among salespeople? Did the salesperson/customer relationships developed over many years have any value? And what if previously well-served accounts now did not know which salesperson to call for

> assistance? And suppose tight labor markets made it difficult to replace those salespeople who did not want to relocate? Were long-time Xerox customers dissatisfied? You'd better believe it! Did Xerox's competitors take advantage of this chaos? You'd better believe that also. Did Xerox's market value drop precipitously? And did Xerox's board of directors get uptight? They certainly did, and Thoman was unceremoniously fired.[b]
>
> [a] *Fortune* (May 14, 2001), 124.
> [b] *Fortune* (May 29, 2000), 42–43.

For those of you who sit atop your organizations: Misunderstanding what the sales force does can be dangerous to your career.

## The Changing Relationship between Sales and Marketing

Theodore Levitt explained the difference between sales and marketing many years ago. He said that sales attempts to get the customer to buy what the company happens to have, whereas marketing's job is to get the company to have what the customer wants to buy. This neat dichotomy suggests that each job is difficult, yet essential; but they are very different jobs.

Recognizing these differences was important in the traditional functionally organized company. It seemed logical that the task of persuading customers to buy was qualitatively different from identifying what customers would want to buy, then securing cooperation from the rest of the organization to produce it. In fact, the reality we are confronting today is radically different from these convenient functional differences that seemed to make sense in the past. As noted earlier, in some companies, persons with a sales title perform the marketing task; whereas those with a marketing title are preoccupied with achieving weekly or monthly sales targets.

Have you talked recently to a FMCG brand manager whose main role in life is to run sales promotions for retail customers to maintain share of shelf space and brand sales? Or, how about conversing with a key account salesperson just returned from a new product development committee meeting at a major customer's facility. Now who is selling existing products, and who is leading the effort to manufacture products tailored to specific customer requirements? Brand managers focused on sales figures, and key account salespeople driven to deliver new and exciting products— this is about more than poorly chosen job titles. This reversal underlines a fundamental change in the roles of marketing and sales, and consequently in the relationship between them.

Research sponsored by the Marketing Science Institute further highlights the significance of this change. In many industries, salespeople are the major influence on a buyer's motivation to continue a supplier relationship. Salespeople drive the firm/customer relationship by influencing the customer's perception of the shipper's reliability and the value received from the supplier's products and services (versus value offered by competitors). As a result, salespeople have a major impact on long-term sales to that customer.

This may help convince those executives who still view the sales organization entirely in tactical terms (promoting sales after the clever marketing people have devised a brilliant strategy) that they should talk to their customers about where the value truly resides. Would this conversation lead to more marketing hires or to better-quality salespeople? Perhaps these executives should sit down first, before customers tell them the simple truth: The salespeople are the brand! When we examine the role of the sales force in the inception and development of major business strategies, we should probably not be surprised that neat divisions of labor look better in textbooks than in the real world.

## THE VALUE OF AN ENTERPRISING SALES FORCE

Enterprise Rent-A-Car, the market-share leader in U.S. auto rental, now has a major international network. In 1957, Enterprise started leasing automobiles in a Cadillac dealership. Its 1964 entry into short-term rental was largely in response to customer requests to salespeople for temporary replacements while their own vehicles were off the road. Salespeople began calling on insurance companies and repair garages to prospect for temporary replacement deals. (They always carried doughnuts in the morning—that's how to get garage mechanics' attention really quickly!) Salespeople found that insurance offices and garages hated making rental arrangements for customers—it was extra, unpaid work and customers expected a ride to the car rental depot. Enterprise has built a multibillion-dollar auto rental business and a quarter century of uninterrupted profitability out of smart sales operators (and doughnuts).

Now, let's continue that interesting and insightful idea about marketing being strategy and sales being operations—because actually it may never have been true. It must be said and highlighted: Convenient assumptions that marketing is about strategy, and sales is about operations (sometimes called "marketing operations") just do not make sense any more. The urgent need for Total Integrated Marketing grows out of exactly this type of change as well as the conviction that those who cling to the past are in for a rude awakening in the none-too-distant future (about now, in fact).

It is still true that the firm's customers are the source of all revenues, and that sales is the only function charged with creating revenue flow. (Increasingly, direct channels may operate alongside the conventional sales force [e.g., the Web page as a sales medium], so that sales operations directly control only part of the revenue stream.) As Peter Drucker argued, all other activities in the business are costs.

The sales function must do its job very differently in the new environment. We might say that sales as a function is in a state of metamorphosis. Because the typical sales force is not managed strategically, many companies have simply failed to grasp the significance of what they are witnessing. Consider the following parable.

## A SALES PARABLE

In the beginning there was a sale, and the sale was good. But the sale was *transactional.* Yet, so was everything else, for the company measured its success by the number of these transactions, and its customers were unidentifiable. Yet, as the power of customers grew, they insisted that they be recognized and dealt with differently from others, for they had purchased many, many times. These customers wanted a *relationship* with the company. Later, as the relationship became stronger, the seller and buyer had greater trust in each other. The business of the seller became dependent on the customer, even as the seller became an ever more important supplier to the customer. Finally, they decided to form a true *partnership.*

Now you may think that this is the end of the parable, but as the partnership developed, it transpired that the supplier became more expert at its job, and the customer less so. One day, the buyer decided it wanted to *outsource* those operations that were the entire reason for purchasing from the supplier in the first place, and the symbiosis was complete. Selling as it was traditionally envisaged was no longer necessary. What remained was a vitally important customer liaison task, and a necessity to run the outsourced operation so that it was profitable for both the erstwhile supplier, and for the customer.

What we have just described is not just a parable. It is the reality in more and more cases. It used to be argued that if marketing did its job properly there would be no need for a sales force. Nowadays, we could argue that if sales is truly successful in its job, there should be no need for a sales force (at least not a conventional one). We may be exaggerating a little, but we are merely indicating the immense change occurring in our conception of sales and selling. As noted in Chapter 5, firms are increasingly viewing customer acquisition and customer retention as different strategies, and are beginning to organize their marketing and sales activities around them.[2] However, the way they are doing it contains some surprises.

For example, as a consequence of outsourcing, contract manufacturing is now one of the world's fastest growing industries.[3] The outsourcing of services traditionally supplied internally has contributed to the immense growth of companies such as Philadelphia's ARAMARK, a large and diversified service company. This shift from transactions to relationships to partnerships to outsourcing—and the corresponding deepening of customer/supplier relationships—has generated a shift from traditional sales force operations to key account management.

In the traditional selling model, buyer–seller interactions are conducted through a single point of contact on either side, typically salesperson to purchasing professional (sometimes called the "bow-tie" arrangement; see Figure 8.1). However, as the relationship deepens, restrictions on the interface open up and interactions between supplier and customer become multilevel and multifunctional (sometimes called the "diamond" arrangement). No longer does sales (for the seller) nor purchasing (for the buyer) have a "lock" on the relationship.

The key account model operates in many forms, but some broad generalizations are possible:

- Because of the importance of those customers chosen to be key accounts, higher quality and better-trained people typically take the lead interface role. These key account managers are not necessarily the best salespeople; they may come from other functions that help develop the skill set required for the high level of responsibility.
- Key account managers may operate within the context of the traditional sales force or in a separate organizational unit. Because traditional salespeople often conduct day-to-day customer contact in

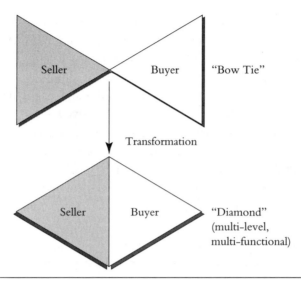

Figure 8.1   THE RELATIONSHIP TRANSFORMATION

dispersed locations, key account managers face a difficult coordination task when operating within the regular sales force.

- Although key account managers are responsible for managing the customer relationship, they do not generally conduct these activities alone. They are more likely to function as managers of teams charged with maintaining and developing the supplier firm/key account relationship. Team membership may include senior corporate executives and representatives from such functional areas as merchandising, customer service, technical service, logistics, production, and research and development. Team members most frequently interface with their opposite numbers at the customer account. In some cases, team members may report to the key account manager; in other cases, reporting relationships for team members remain within their functional specialties and they have a dotted line relationship to the key account manager.

As vertical partnerships are forged within traditional distribution channel systems, such teams will become more commonplace. In customer-focused firms, teams may consciously become the dominant organizational form for managing key accounts. Multinational organizations are beginning to develop global account management systems whereby global account managers (often multilingual) develop global account strategies that virtual teams implement around the world.[4] At this point, key account management merges with customer relationships and/or partnerships, and business plans are jointly developed in an interactive fashion.

Whereas moving to key (and global) account management creates a significant coordination task for both parties, it also makes the relationship far more difficult to break up.[5] As business and personal relationships broaden and deepen over time, and systems and processes are developed to link the two organizations, mutual dependency increases. Some companies that are committed to a key account management philosophy are interviewing prospective customers as if they were going to be employees. Conversely, some customers insist on selecting the supplier's key account manager from a previously developed short list.

In each case, the thinking is straightforward. Genuine partnership offers real benefits for both parties, yet supplier and customer want to raise the probabilities that the partnership will work and pay off. As the switching costs to exit a partnership rise significantly for both parties, there may be diminishing need for a sales force (at least not the conventional, transactional, order-taking sales force). Some partnered customers are starting to reject conventional sales calls as an unnecessary waste of their managers' time. Conversely, the sales organization becomes a coordinating mechanism for managing the multiple points of contact with customers. Certainly, someone has to ensure that everyone is hearing the same music when dancing with a major customer.

Moving beyond partnership to complete outsourcing of particular customer operations is the goal of many sales forces. BHP Steel (now OneSteel), the large Australian producer, long ago successfully sold numerous Australian appliance manufacturers on the concept of eliminating paint operations by switching to higher-value-added prepainted steel. Industrial gas companies and medical equipment manufacturers alike have taken complete responsibility for previously internally run operations. And Lou Gerstner made outsourcing customers' computer operations a cornerstone of his revival strategy for IBM, with early successes in securing business from such major organizations as Kodak, Xerox, and Du Pont.[6]

To convince the customer to entrust such important activities to an outside supplier involves creative selling of the highest level, far different from the traditional attitude of "bring in the order." Such agreements are typically long-term, and account management for successful contract renewal requires very different skills from those traditionally found in the sales force, or even in conventional partnership arrangements. Old-style salespeople often refer derogatorily to the exceptionally high service component of account management as the "farmer" role, whereas most of them seem inclined to view themselves testosterone-driven "hunters." Some scholars even argue that the "hunter-farmer" distinction is the best way to organize sales and service operations. Certainly, it reflects the different strategies discussed earlier. There seems little doubt that, as the emphasis on customer satisfaction and retention increases, traditional ways of organizing sales and service efforts will be subject to further scrutiny.

However, this ladder of sales achievement (for that is what it is) represents something far more striking—the beginning of a complete redefinition of the sales task. Instead of having the job of selling what the firm produces, sales increasingly must create mutually profitable long-term relationships with customers. This radically different perspective has important implications for the number and kinds of salespeople hired, how they are recruited, selected, trained, and retained, and perhaps most importantly, how they are supported in managing complicated relationships. Yet the process does not stop there, for the information revolution promises to shake traditional views of sales and marketing to their very roots.

## Sales and Marketing: A Revolution Brewing— Or One Already Bubbling?

Historically, marketing dealt, for the most part, with markets and groups of customers (market segments). Sales, by contrast, typically focused on individual customers. Yet, technological and structural change threatens to outdate the finesse that marketers have developed in segmentation and targeting. The fact of the matter is that all customers are individuals, and market segmentation was never anything more than a compromise between treating customers as though they were all alike (mass market) and treating them as individuals.[7] The advent of data-based marketing and mass customization has raised questions about the viability of segmentation at the consumer level. In distribution channels, the great increase in concentration has already made much conventional thinking about market segmentation obsolete; key account (or customer) management has replaced it.

These trends provide another nail in the coffin of the traditional distinction between sales and marketing. Just as we (and others) have suggested that traditional brand management may eventually give way to customer management,[8] so the marketing job may be transformed into a sales job. In the new world, perhaps every good salesperson should be a smart marketer, and every marketer much more of a salesperson.

But, does this mean that separate functions are no longer required for sales and marketing? Managers typically ask this organizational question when we raise these challenges, but it is not the truly important question. We have already pointed out that in some companies marketing does sales jobs and sales does marketing jobs. What really matters is that competent individuals perform these tasks effectively—the labels are much less important. The need for large, specialist marketing departments will probably diminish. As the sales job is upgraded in terms of its intellectual and skill requirements, the pressure on marketing jobs will likely increase. Nonetheless, there is a very important proviso.

Marketers are sometimes far too fond of emphasizing the long-term importance of the job they do. It is certainly true that strategic marketing makes a tremendous contribution to a business. Equally important, however, is short- and medium-term survival. Supporting the vital role of strategic marketing does not imply a diminution of the sales role. This is not an either/or situation; both functions are critically important. Yet, a word of warning is in order.

In many organizations, the short term drives out the long term; or stated somewhat differently, the sales job gets done at the expense of the marketing job. (This is especially true when both sales and marketing responsibilities rest on the shoulders of a single individual.) Although the distance between the sales and marketing functions is diminishing, we should beware of this tendency. Perhaps, in some cultures, the opposite problem can occur, for excessive patience may also be a fault. In Anglo cultures, however, a short-term bias is more likely.

If we accept that the marketing philosophy should drive the corporation as a whole, total integration of all business activities in the quest to acquire and retain customers will become the twenty-first century mantra. As the sales role expands to include operational marketing activities within a broader framework of customer management, and as senior management increasingly views innovation as the key to profitable growth and embraces the role of brand custodian, the outlook for traditional functional marketing becomes questionable. As companies reduce the number of brands they offer, megabrands will supersede individual product brands, and brand management responsibility will climb the hierarchy to general management. When this occurs, we may find a surplus of marketing people looking for "sales" jobs—a reversal of the historic pattern.

## Marketing Plans and Sales Budgets? What Nonsense!

If this subheading surprises you, it shouldn't. At least, not if you have read the first part of this chapter! If the job of sales is changing as described, then it's high time to stop thinking that sales activities don't need planning. Although you may not have considered it, many companies still go about their business in this manner. The conventional system implies that marketing (business) plans are the important drivers and that sales has secondary status. Sales budgets always should have been the consequence of careful planning, but in many companies, traditionally they were not. In many companies, even the sequence of planning and budgeting activities is illogical.

Do you recognize any of the following in your corporation?

- The finished marketing plan is delivered beyond end-of-period deadlines.
- The sales force commences its planning process well into the operating cycle and may finish before marketing plans are delivered.
- The sales force has no input into marketing objectives and strategies. Consequently, the marketing plan is irrelevant to the day-to-day concerns of the sales force, leading to its view of marketing as an ivory tower department.

To avoid these problems, developing the sales plan and strategy must be an essential element in the well-managed company's repertoire. To develop sales objectives and strategies appropriately, marketing plans must be near completion, if not finished, before the sales strategy development process commences. In the best processes, considerable interaction between marketing and senior sales management occurs as they hammer out objectives and priorities in a spirit of cooperation, instead of through political infighting and conflict. After all, those who are parties to developing strategy are more likely to implement it than those relegated to the observer role. This process is especially critical when, as is frequently the case, a general sales force sells a variety of products to several market segments. Here, the field sales strategy and sales force activities play an essential integrating role. To ensure that sales and marketing managers are present at the appropriate objective-setting and strategy-development meetings, some firms have developed market-sales coordinator positions.

In Chapter 5, we established that strategy, in general, involves the allocation of resources to achieve defined objectives. In this same spirit, sales strategy seeks to achieve sales objectives by assessing the appropriate level of sales resources. It then allocates those resources where needed, for example, across products, new versus current customers, and/or market segments. Whereas sales strategy deals with broad and general sales effort allocation, the sales program identifies specific required actions, typically comprising sales action plans for individual salespeople, supervisors, and managers.

The primary purpose of sales strategy is to integrate the market strategy, typically comprising multiple product/market segment strategies, and selling effort. If the firm sells a single product to a single customer or market segment, allocating sales-force effort by product and/or market segment is not an issue. More likely, however, the sales force is responsible for selling multiple products to multiple market segments and customers. How to allocate the firm's selling effort among these product/market segments and customers is at the heart of the sales strategy. These allocations are a critical determiner of the results the firm secures (e.g., sales, profit contribution, agreement to examine/test the product, favorable customer attitudes, and so forth). This is a far cry from just setting a sales budget as a target to be met, and taking the planning effort no further. Few companies actually developed sales strategies in the past. Thankfully, this is changing rapidly.

Typically, sales managers cannot quickly vary the overall level of sales resources available to them. However, they may be able to determine how and why salespersons have spent work hours, and change the focus. In their everyday roles, salespersons perform many tasks—traveling, gathering intelligence, checking inventory, providing customer service, receiving training/education, participating in meetings, communicating, keeping records, planning, merchandising, checking credit, and making collections. The presence and relative importance of each of these activities varies from firm to firm and depends on the type of business, line organization and in-place organizational systems and processes. Sales managers must decide how the sales force should divide its time among these activities and the proportion it should allocate to actual selling ("face time").

A second purpose of sales strategy is to specify how the firm should deal with customers and competitors. In particular, what specific customer and competitor targets should the firm choose? How should the sales force go about securing customer commitment to its products and services in the face of competitive challenges? Fulfilling this purpose requires translating the market strategy (Chapter 5) into a sales framework. Key elements in this translation task are:

- *Strategic and operational objectives.* Sales-force objectives should be a direct reflection of strategic and operational objectives in the market strategy. There must be specific market objectives for each product/market segment in which the sales force operates.
- *Strategic focus.* The focus of the selling effort should be directly related to the strategic alternatives in the market strategy. The sales task in developing new customers is quite different from that of attempting to cross-sell a broader product range to an existing customer.
- *Product line focus.* Product lines involve key relationships for multiproduct sales forces. Crucial decisions concern the allocation of selling effort across different products and often create significant conflicts. A similar situation occurs for market segment focus.
- *Positioning.* The customer focus and sales approach elements of the sales strategy flow directly from positioning decisions in the product/market segment strategies. The sales strategy reflects these choices of customer and competitor targets and core strategy but typically develops them in greater detail.
- *Supporting marketing mix.* From the perspective of the product/market strategy, the sales strategy is one of several elements in the marketing mix. As a result, the marketing mix specifies the general parameters within which the sales strategy is developed.

The final purpose of sales strategy is to identify the specific requirements needed for implementation. These include organizational arrangements, support activities, systems, and processes that firms employ for directing and managing the selling effort, and human resources for sales-force staffing.

Whenever a firm uses a general, as opposed to a specialist, sales force, the sales strategy has a much broader scope than the product/market segment strategy. Regardless, an intimate and direct relationship should exist between market and sales strategies. The sequencing failures with which we prefaced this discussion are one reason this sort of relationship does not occur. Another is a pervasive attitude in many institutions (not the least of which are leading graduate business schools) that tend to place marketing positions on a pedestal, and treat sales activities as much less important.

Our advice to sales managers and salespeople is to reject any sales targets or budgets that are not the result of a well-thought-out sales strategy and plan. Not only are these targets likely to be unrealistic, you probably won't get the support you need to attain them. Some of our salespeople friends and colleagues asked us to pass on these messages to management!

## MEMO FROM THE SALES FORCE TO MANAGEMENT

- Your market strategy tells me that you want to specialize selling effort by customer type. Could you please tell me why we are still organized geographically so that I have to call on all customer types in my territory?
- Much of my income comes from volume-related commission. That's just fine. But now you're telling me that "customer relationships," "customer satisfaction," and "customer value" are the priorities. You pay me incentive, I'll sell product. You want this other stuff—who's paying for it?
- Anyway, don't tell *me* about all this relationship stuff—tell my *manager!* The day managers stop being obsessed with the hard numbers (sales units, revenue, budgets) and pay anything more than lip service to this other stuff, then maybe I'll take it seriously, too!
- Why do you expect me to get excited about all this stuff coming out of marketing? My career path stops at Regional Manager, and I get there by outselling everyone else.

The changing role of sales, and the evolving relationship that sales has with marketing, is heady stuff for a new era of doing business. The problem right now is that many companies are stuck with sorting out operational issues between marketing and sales. Certainly, employees need to do a better job today so that there is a tomorrow to worry about. But how firms organize, reward, and develop career paths for salespeople has major implications for implementing marketing strategy.

## OPERATIONAL CONSIDERATIONS

In your firm, managers can greatly facilitate the sales/marketing interface by sorting out the relationships between marketing planning and strategy, and sales planning and strategy. We have just discussed these issues. However, you must also consider the following here-and-now matters.

### How Should We Organize the Firm's Efforts? The Growing Role of Market and Customer Management

Traditionally, marketing and sales have been organized in very different ways. For manufacturers, at least, marketing was organized around products or brands. By contrast, the dominant organization for sales was geographic. Under these conditions, mapping marketing strategies into sales strategies gets complicated. These mismatched organizational structures constitute a major impediment for achieving Total Integrated Marketing.

Typically, the sales force is a major, if not the primary, contributor to the successful implementation of market strategies. Business-to-business markets have always viewed it this way, but the major packaged goods companies, recognizing that working with trade customers is now a key determinant of success, increasingly take a similar perspective. If the sales function pursues its own independent course of action in the field, the chances that business or market strategies will achieve firm objectives drop close to zero.

### MATCHING SALES TO STRATEGY (OR NOT AS THE CASE MAY BE)

In the late 1990s, Lucent Technologies developed a structure of semiautonomous business units, each with its own salespeople, to achieve greater focus, push profit and loss responsibility further down the organization, and generate entrepreneurial behavior. It was difficult, however, to gain agreement or cooperation among the different units. One example was the "softswitch," a communications switch that outsiders could program. Lucent developed softswitches in each of several divisions—research, next-generation products, switching, internal new ventures, wireless, and optical, as well as from Excel, a 1999 Lucent acquisition. Salespeople for each group attempted to do their jobs. Said one customer, "I understand what Nortel is doing and I fully understand what Cisco is doing, but I'm confused on what Lucent is actually offering, because I've heard different descriptions of the same solution from different Lucent teams."[a] In fall 2000, when Lucent failed to meet its revenue targets and its market value plummeted, CEO Richard McGuinn was fired.

In the early 1990s, British Aerospace Regional Aircraft (BARA) formed its Asset Management Division to dispose of secondhand planes, secured when several large customers entered bankruptcy. This division competed vigorously with the new plane sales division, frequently driving down prices.[b]

[a] *The New York Times* (January 21, 2001).
[b] N. Capon and J. Hulbert, *Marketing Management in the 21st Century* (Upper Saddle River, NJ: Prentice Hall, 2001), 415.

As changes in the functions of sales and marketing occur, these integration problems should diminish (although others will no doubt arise to take their place). In many services companies, however, marketing is now organized around customers rather than around products. For example, Citigroup has developed an account management system in which parent account managers (PAMs) have global responsibility for individual customers. Cisco Systems, IBM, Hewlett-Packard, and other leading firms have developed, or are developing, similar structures. In some cases, these structures are matrixed with existing geographic organizations; in others, the geographic structures have been allowed to wither away as customer management becomes the dominant organizational approach to the market, at least for major customers. In these firms, integrating sales and marketing efforts is much less of a problem.

As companies reorganize along these lines, integration problems will still arise. However, they are more likely to involve such issues as the direction of product development, particularly when customer desires become more differentiated and major customers demand greater clout in these decisions. Regardless, in this world, sales and marketing should work together more effectively for, as noted, these functions may become less distinguishable from each other. For the time being, if marketing strategies fail to take into account the realities of the sales organization, they are unlikely to be successful. It's that obvious.

## Rewarding and Managing Salespeople

Perhaps the single most vexed question in managing sales organizations is how to reward salespeople. Traditionalists believe that incentive compensation is the critical tool for motivating salespeople to do their jobs. Many salespeople favor these schemes—particularly open-ended systems that, in theory at least, do not cap potential earnings. Many accountants also take a favorable view (though not to open-ended systems), because they link sales costs directly to sales results. Others suggest that fixed salaries are the most effective way to reward salespeople since they provide for security and certainty of income. From the firm's perspective, sales costs increase less rapidly than sales revenue when times are good, and fixed salary provides the right to more closely direct working activities. The issue is complex and highly contentious, and each school of thought is probably right in specific circumstances.[9]

The most important question is, How does the salesperson incentive system link to the sales and marketing strategies? If you believe that predominantly variable compensation is the way to go, incentives should support implementing these strategies. If, on the other hand, your firm is wedded to a fixed salary structure, you must identify what motivates your salespeople, and use the resulting insights to drive implementation of your strategy. Whichever approach you use, you simply cannot ignore the factors that shape the behavior of those individuals who are implementing a major part of your strategy. Many executives operate in ignorance, then act surprised when salespeople continue doing what they have always done, instead of doing what seems to be in the firm's best interest.

Over and above matters of salesperson compensation, another critical issue is often hidden away inside the sales organization, and as a result, marketers largely ignore it. How do line managers direct salespeople's efforts and activities? The answer, in part, relates to how they, themselves, are evaluated and rewarded. In traditional sales organizations, field sales managers are basically "commanders and scorekeepers"; they rely on financial incentives to direct salespeople to the most effective activities. They focus on salesperson outcomes—sales (units and dollars), profits, market share against targets, and costs against budget forecasts. If the line manager is only interested in short-term numbers, a salesperson would have to be quite remarkable (or perhaps plain stupid) to care about anything else. In contrast, modern sales organizations are transforming line managers into coaches and facilitators. These sales managers do not focus simply on salesperson outcomes, although they know these are important. They try to secure salesperson behavior that drives critical long-term results. These sales managers monitor, direct, evaluate, and reward on this basis.[10] Making the traditional-to-modern transition has been problematic for many sales forces, not least because traditional sales managers typically do not know how to be coaches and need development support to achieve this competence.

Marketers often have little influence on the makeup of the sales force. Although they may believe that one kind of sales force is better than another, they must operate with the sales-force hand they have been dealt. They must, therefore, make it their business to understand the goals and priorities of sales managers, for those goals and priorities have more impact on salespeople than great marketing strategy presentations. Marketers may not be able to transition sales managers from commanders/scorekeepers to coaches, but they must account for sales managers' impact on implementing marketing strategy. Street-smart sales managers can be the marketer's greatest allies in changing how the company does business with its customers. What marketers must not do is ignore the impact of sales managers on what salespeople actually do. For marketers to ignore sales managers invites sales managers and their salespeople to ignore marketers in return.

## Salesperson Planning

When the supplier embraces key account or customer management strategies, the importance of planning for individual customers rises dramatically because the stakes are so high. Nonetheless, even for firms implementing traditional strategies with dispersed customer bases in conventional organization structures, good planning by individual salespersons can ensure strategy implementation. This is not the place to develop planning templates, but marketers must recognize that individual salesperson plans are an essential component for integrating business and market plans with this vital selling resource.

## Frequent Interaction

Unbelievable as it may seem, in far too many companies, sales and marketing interact rarely, if at all. Not only does this separation breed misunderstanding or, even worse, active dislike, it is self-defeating for managers charged with implementing marketing strategies. Can you imagine one of your executives saying, after listening to a presentation by a senior sales manager: "That's the first intelligent sales type I've encountered." One of us heard exactly that. The comment speaks volumes more about the speaker than about the sales manager.

Discriminatory recruiting and development patterns frequently have fostered the damaging gulf that separates marketing and sales in many companies. But it isn't always so. Many years ago, when one of us consulted for Marion Laboratories (now part of Hoechst Marion Roussel), there was frequent and regular interaction between sales and marketing, and continuous movement of individuals between the two departments. Because Marion had no R&D department, and relied on licensed products (mainly from overseas), it was more than usually dependent on sales and marketing prowess. Marion's excellence in these areas, unmatched by most competitors, was a key contributor to its success. We also referred earlier to Jack Welch's concept of a boundaryless corporation—the last place a boundary should be permitted is between sales and marketing. All too often, this is where we find one. If your sales/marketing boundary has not yet been demolished, you'd better get started!

Improving patterns of socialization and communication may even dispel the classic myth—when salespeople grow up, they become marketing executives. Nothing but misplaced corporate logic would support the idea that individuals who have proved their worth as salespeople and/or line sales managers can only advance in the company by moving into marketing management. Yet, this seems to be the pattern in many corporations. There is a critical need for better career planning to retain talent in the sales organization and secure maximum corporate payoff from experience in managing customer relationships. If this means promoting the best salespeople to vice president while they continue to work as salespeople, so be it. Remember: Sales brings in the revenues, everything else is cost!

## TOTAL INTEGRATED MARKETING: FORGING THE SALES/MARKETING LINK[11]

For companies that are traditionally organized around products or facilities, integration of marketing and sales activities will continue to be a critical issue for making Total Integrated Marketing real. Nevertheless, you can increase your chances of business success by heeding the following suggestions:

- Make sales management a party to developing business and market strategies at an early stage. We prefer team-based strategy development, but if this is not possible, sales management must at least receive critical information from marketing before submitting required sales budgets.
- Recognize that sales budgets are not sales strategies. Without a well-thought-through plan for achieving the sales budget, those numbers mean little.
- Implement an explicit reconciliation process such that business, market, and sales strategies are consistent and coherent.

The distinctions between sales and marketing are becoming fuzzy. Direct marketing is leading marketers away from imprecision toward models of measurement, prediction, and control, and from targeting broad segments in mass markets to focusing on narrow niches. Advances in information technology increasingly allow individualization of the marketing effort. Concurrently, powerful forces are concentrating the firm's revenues with fewer customers, raising the ante for the firm at each customer, and driving a need for more and more sophisticated coordination of customer relationships.

Securing positive long-term relationships with shrinking numbers of customers is a serious challenge. Firms that address it head-on must improve and upgrade the often-uneasy relationship between marketing and sales. As the relationship management model takes hold, customer retention and development will rise in importance relative to customer acquisition.

Coordinating multilevel multifunctional interfaces requires a different set of skills than those of traditional salespeople. To keep pace with this evolution, sales-force skills must be enhanced. In the future, these skills will be more akin to those of the general manager than the traditional salesperson. Salespeople with doctoral degrees are less rare than several years ago, and as globalization takes hold, language abilities will become increasingly important. Of course, because firms will concentrate their efforts on fewer and more important customers, sales-force numbers will go down.

The sales/marketing interface as one of the most important in the firm. Changes in marketplace and competitive strategies emphasize the validity of this viewpoint. Together with technology, they are bringing about a convergence between the two traditional functions. Companies that fail to appreciate how these roles are changing will undoubtedly lose marketplace opportunities to their more progressive competitors. Genuine partnership between marketing and sales is a key prerequisite for effecting Total Integrated Marketing.

# MARKETING AND R&D

## INSPIRING AND INITIATING
## INNOVATION IMPERATIVES

The turbulent business environment, with its enhanced customer requirements and heightened competitive pressures, is putting almost all
firms under pressure to bring new products and services to market. As
previously noted, companies earn superior profits and enhance shareholder
wealth by providing value to customers that is not available from competitors. To accomplish this, firms must either improve existing products and
services or develop radically new offerings—with ever-reducing cycle
times. Innovation is an imperative for the survival of firms in the twenty-
first century.

A major problem for large corporations is that many of them have been
better at refining and exploiting existing technologies than at taking advantage of new technologies. Even worse, the global consolidation of
companies is likely to generate even more bureaucratic organizations that
stifle creativity and innovation.

In fact, companies that don't intend to make most of their present product lines obsolete within the next five to seven years are probably already
in trouble. Microsoft plans to turn over its entire product line every four
years; and at 3M, 30 percent of sales come from products less than five years
old, 10 percent from products less than 12 months old.[1] Jack Welch's exhor-
tation to General Electric management—"destroyyourbusiness.com."—has
an underlying message: The information revolution has produced a whole

different ball game. If you don't cannibalize your own business, someone else will take it away from you.[2] In many situations, the capability to develop and market innovations faster and better (but particularly faster) than the competition will be a critical factor in survival.

## DRIVING CORPORATE STRATEGY WITH R&D AND MARKETING

Pharmaceutical giant, GlaxoSmithKline (GSK) was created from the merger of European pharmaceuticals groups Glaxo Wellcome and SmithKline Beecham. With sales of $25 billion and over 7 percent of the global pharmaceuticals business, GSK's annual R&D budget is more than $4 billion. Although its product pipeline is superior to that of any competitor, keeping the R&D bureaucracy nimble and market focused is a substantial challenge. The key to the strategy is sustaining R&D superiority.* Sheer R&D spending alone, however, will not establish competitive superiority; not only must the product pipeline produce more innovations, it must also commercialize products better than competitors do. Until R&D is linked to a customer through effective marketing processes, it is worth nothing.

*M. Flanagan, "R&D the Key to the Merger of the Century," *The Scotsman* (February 2, 1998); and "The Global Leader in Pharmaceuticals," Press Release (January 17, 2000).

There is sound evidence that new product development effectiveness may hinge on the quality of the relationship between marketing and R&D.[3] That relationship, however, is often unsatisfactory. In many companies, management has believed that R&D was their "engine for growth," only to be disappointed by the poor profits of products in the marketplace.[4] Jan Leschly, architect of the GSK merger, points out that in the last 15 years of the twentieth century the entire worldwide R&D-intensive pharmaceuticals industry brought only 137 products successfully to market, whereas thousands of others failed despite the investment of billions of dollars in their development.[5] The Dutch multinational, Philips, employs no less than 1,500 creative research staff, with a budget of $300 million a year, and owns 65,000 patents, but it has regularly failed miserably in commercializing its inventions. One commentator suggests that "the company's research establishment has been inward-looking and arrogant," and the company has simply failed to link its researchers to the marketplace.[6]

So, it is essential to find better ways to link marketing processes to R&D. However, it gets more complicated than this.

## IS THE REAL ISSUE "MARKETING AND R&D" OR "MARKETING AND TECHNOLOGY"?

This particular set of issues is bigger and more pervasive than sorting out strained relationships between marketing departments and R&D divisions. In the past, the prevailing model for developing innovative products was through the firm's internal research and development efforts. For many companies, those days are long gone.

### COLLABORATIVE R&D ALLIANCES

One of the fastest growing products in the home entertainment market is the DVD player. The DVD (digital versatile disk) format provides vastly superior quality in viewing movies and other products through the television set or the personal computer, and is expected to replace traditional formats like videotape. Nine companies, including Sony, Panasonic, and Toshiba, jointly developed the DVD format in the mid-1990s. Collaboration pools R&D expertise and shares risks, but importantly it avoids the damaging competition between different formats that characterized the launch of home videocassette recorders (VCRs).

Fewer and fewer firms that are serious about enhancing shareholder value will be able to cling to the "not-invented-here" (NIH) syndrome. Firms seeking leadership positions will have to secure new products and services from wherever they can get them, not just from internal R&D technology. Even companies that focus on internal research and development, with large R&D budgets, will need to develop relationships with other organizations. To gain access to technology, they may outsource R&D, set up R&D partnerships with other organizations, take equity positions in R&D-focused organizations, make technology purchases or license agreements, or acquire other firms (or parts of firms). Since small start-ups actually pioneer more innovations than do the R&D departments of megacorporations, a critical factor in the long-run success of large businesses is likely to be keeping up with new developments, either directly or through relationships with venture capital firms.

## THE NEW WAYS OF THE WORLD OF TECHNOLOGY

World-leading computer chip manufacturer, Intel, conducts extensive internal R&D, yet is one of the leading corporate investors in venture capital start-ups. In 2000, Intel invested $1.3 billion in 330 deals. Other leading investors in start-ups are General Electric, Microsoft, and Dell Computer.[a]

Forest Laboratories licenses, develops, and sells drugs from small, often European, pharmaceutical companies. Research focuses on bringing drugs to market, not on basic molecular research. Forest has an impressive drug portfolio including Aerobid (asthma), Celexa (depression), Infasurf (respiratory distress syndrome in premature babies), and Tiazac (angina and hypertension).[b]

Procter & Gamble (P&G) has formed a new Global Business Development division to seek joint ventures, spin off companies, and license more technology. In particular, P&G has teamed up with Whirlpool to develop Personal Valet, a product that will take out wrinkles and deodorize clothes in 20 to 30 minutes.[c]

[a] *The Wall Street Journal* (February 22, 2001).
[b] *Fortune* (September 4, 2001), 126.
[c] *The New York Times* (March 16, 2001).

As well as thinking about better ways to handle the marketing/R&D interface inside the company, management needs to address the broader issues of technology strategy: [7]

- Whether to develop technology inside the organization or secure it from outside.
- Whether to produce products and services based on this technology or make arrangements for other entities to develop those markets. (A separate issue concerns the manufacture of these products and services.)

In addition to better functional coordination between marketing and R&D, the challenge is partnering marketing processes effectively with innovation imperatives. These include managing intrafirm interfaces (across divisions), interfirm relationships (between independent firms operating in alliance), and research networks (where R&D is a collaborative venture between partnered organizations). Not least is the challenge to be fast to market.

## SPEED TO MARKET CAN BE A CRITICAL SUCCESS FACTOR, OR IT CAN KILL A COMPANY

More and more often, leading companies tend to work strategically with several combinations of technological development options. Time is a critical issue. In the mid-1990s, a McKinsey study on high-technology products showed that new market offerings that were on budget but six months late, earned 33 percent less profit over five years than projects that were on time and within budget. By comparison, projects that were on time but 50 percent over budget, earned 4 percent less profit. Recognizing that speed-to-market is critical, firms such as 3M, Microsoft, and Cisco Systems actively pursue acquisitions for their technology portfolios.

### BUILDING THE TECHNOLOGY PORTFOLIO

Between 1993 and 2000, using its then high stock price, Cisco acquired more than 70, mostly small, companies for its technology portfolio. At Cisco, acquisitions are a business process, run by a 60-person group. To retain staff in these firms, Cisco provides lots of opportunities and freedom, believing they are the most significant assets it has acquired.

It is telling that these are not the megamergers and acquisitions that grab the headlines—they are smaller, technological fill-in acquisitions. Also, in each of these examples, the acquiring firm has a consistent high level of internal R&D spending as well. Megamergers/acquisitions have a pathetic success rate; less than 40 percent are value enhancing for the acquiring firm's shareholders. This suggests that critical analysis about finding and/or keeping customers for the newly merged entity plays too small a role in some of the decisions.

## DO WE REALLY UNDERSTAND WHAT FAST CHANGE MEANS?

At a board meeting in a well-known technology company, one author observed the following. The head of R&D unveiled the outcome of an extremely expensive project, which promised a significant performance improvement over existing and competitor products. He "guaranteed" that they had a two-year lead over competitors. When marketing and sales pressed hard, he conceded that perhaps the competition might catch up in 18 months. They believed him. In the event, the main competitor caught up less than 90 days after the product launch. The competitive advantage had lasted less than three months.

So, how can being faster to market than competitors possibly kill a business? The risk is that in industries characterized by a fast rate of innovation, the lack of tight, effective integration between marketing and R&D may destroy customer loyalty and undermine long-term profits. See if the following scenario seems familiar. When the firm develops something new, management pressure is to get it on the market quickly before the competition gets there first. This pressure may overwhelm commercialization processes and the readiness of the technology. Commitment of large investment to the innovation turns marketing into a hard sell to move the product, while quality and service (as customers perceive it) take a back seat. Customers may buy the innovation, but in the absence of superior quality and service, they are likely to migrate to the next supplier, with the next "big idea," and the cycle starts again.[8]

Integrating marketing processes and technology strategy is a high priority in managing the relationship between the functional groupings inside the company as well as collaborators and technology-drivers beyond the corporate boundaries.

## STRATEGIC RELATIONSHIPS

Managing fractious interfaces between different functions is the key challenge to achieving Total Integrated Marketing. For successful commercialization of innovation, it is critical to bridge the gap between the cultures of marketing and R&D. Managers have to harness all the firm's organizational resources to develop new products and services for customers. This integration must also occur across the corporation, possibly in other countries with different cultures, as well as with business development groups seeking acquisitions and alliances. Yet more difficult to manage will be interorganizational interfaces. For example, the firm may work with a customer or customers to hammer out requirements and, at the same time, with a network of suppliers and codevelopers of solutions, to bring innovative products to market.

> ## DON'T COPY THIS ...
>
> Xerox is in trouble. Technological and financial problems have beset the once proud developer and monopoly supplier of products based on xerography technology. At least one reason has been its failure to commercialize innovations developed at its Palo Alto Research Center (PARC). Breakthrough product concepts like the first personal computer and the graphical interface were developed at PARC. But Xerox did not commercialize them.

The marketing/R&D interface is an important focus for management attention in Total Integrated Marketing. But, broader issues encompass more than the development of new products and services for current customers. After all, Drucker said that the firm had two, and only two, major functions—marketing and innovation. He didn't say develop new products and services solely to serve current customers.

## Sustaining and Disruptive Technology

In one of the most important management books of the 1990s, Clayton Christensen described the danger of concentrating innovation effort only on current customers.[9] Christensen recognized the critical distinction between *sustaining* and *disruptive* technologies, and what they mean for company strategy.

Sustaining technologies are responsive to the needs of current customers, but disruptive technologies satisfy the needs of a different customer group, at least initially. It follows that current suppliers usually develop sustaining technology innovations, but new entrants frequently pioneer disruptive technologies. The devastating effect of disruptive technology comes from three related factors:

- Initially, the disruptive technology usually has inferior performance on the attributes that matter most to the existing customers for the current technology—it simply is not as good as what they already have.

- Existing suppliers have low expectations of volume and margin in the disruptive technology—it does not look like a good investment to better serve current customers. Why would they want something that is not as good as what they already get, and say they like?
- It follows almost inevitably that resource allocation processes within the current suppliers underfund R&D in the new technology.

But time and time again, although the disruptive technology is inferior at the start—it gets better. Then, its cost advantage combined with performance that is equal or better than the existing suppliers' technology puts those suppliers out of business. Meantime, conventional marketing has been running customer satisfaction surveys and telling managers that their best and most profitable existing customers do not want the innovation. Ultimately, your business can get beaten up by an innovation that you did not take seriously because (1) it was inferior, (2) conventional marketing claimed it was not a serious threat, and (3) your customers told you was not for them—until they changed their minds and adopted it. This casts a somewhat different light on the requirements for an effective relationship between marketing and R&D.

## DISRUPTIVE TECHNOLOGY CHANGES INDUSTRIES

In the computer disk drive product, 14-inch Winchester and 2.5-inch drives were sustaining innovations for mainframe and laptop computers, respectively. Existing disk drive suppliers had pioneered them. By contrast, 8.5-inch, 5.25-inch, 3.5-inch, and 1.8-inch drives were all disruptive technologies that initially satisfied the needs of different customer groups—manufacturers of minicomputers, desktop personal computers, laptop computers, and portable heart-monitoring devices, respectively. Different firms manufactured most of them. In addition, new entrants pioneered flash memory (a further disruptive technology used for palmtop computers, electronic clipboards, cash registers, and electronic cameras).*

* Other examples of the damage wrought by disruptive technologies on incumbents are hand-held calculators on slide rule manufacturers, overnight package delivery (e.g., Federal Express) on freight forwarders, TV on radio, CDs on long-playing records, jet aircraft on turbo-props and ocean liners.

Companies with both sustaining and disruptive technologies are more likely to successfully ride the waves of competitive challenge and continually changing customer needs and expectations. These technologies should not necessarily be developed in-house, and it may not be possible to develop them in-house. In a world of scarce resources, it is only by broadening the technological search beyond internal R&D that companies can hope to continually rejuvenate their product lines to stay ahead of competition. In fact, the challenge for managers may be to protect disruptive technologies from destruction by the sustaining technologies within their own companies.

### NURTURING THE NEXT BIG IDEA

In the past, IBM has missed out on new technologies and opportunities. The company has changed the way it identifies and pursues promising new ideas that may conflict with existing business units or fall between established organizational boundaries. They are managed as "Horizon Three" businesses separate from the rest of the organization. (Horizon One businesses are mature businesses like mainframe computers, and Horizon Two businesses are current growth businesses.) Horizon Three businesses are located in separate organizational units, with dedicated teams of managers. They are insulated from the company's established management methods and performance yardsticks, and they get personal sponsorship from a senior executive to ensure that there is no organizational "push-back" against disruptive innovations.[a] By late 2001, IBM also was operating 59 separate strategic software alliances, mainly with small third-party software houses, to bring "the hot, the cool, the fast, where IBM needs it."[b]

[a] R. Waters, "Never Forget to Nurture the Next Big Idea," *The Financial Times* (May 15, 2001).

[b] M. Schifrin, "Partner or Perish," *Forbes* (May 21, 2001), 26–28. The three horizons concept is described in M. Baghai, S. Coley, and D. White, *The Alchemy of Growth: Practical Insights for Building the Enduring Enterprise* (Cambridge, MA: Perseus Books, 1999).

Part of what makes the challenge of disruptive technology so difficult is that it is difficult to identify developing technologies as either disruptive or sustaining. And, what is a disruptive technology for one company may be a sustaining technology for another. Many companies would view the Internet as a disruptive technology. For Dell, however, the Internet is a powerful sustaining technology that enhances Dell's ability to implement its direct model.

## Get Your Organization's Act Together for the Market!

Innovation management is becoming a pressing issue. Many management thinkers have addressed this question and concluded that incremental innovation requires completely different management organization from discontinuous innovation.[10] We have allowed our organizations to become unbelievably complex, and poor management of this complexity often leaves massive gaps between environmental opportunities or threats, and the organization's attempts to address them. The information economy is making these mismatches painfully obvious for many large and traditional firms. We need to understand why mismatches occur, and why they have such important implications for the marketing/technology interface.

Although describing the many ways of constructing organizational archetypes may generate insight into the problems of managing innovation,[11] it may also add complexity and confusion! A critical area, however, is the relationship between the stage of development in the company's markets, and the way management organizes the company's capabilities. This is always a crucial consideration at the business level and, unless the firm is heavily diversified, also at the corporate level.[12] Each situation suggests a different set or configuration of skills, resources, people, and organizational culture. In this way, managers can link product/market and organizational innovation, and see what it tells them about the challenges for their own companies.

## Market Entry Strategies and Innovation Management

In the short term, firms should select entry policies that make the most of their own skills and resources, and existing marketplace demands. However, a current lack of corporate resources should not necessarily prohibit an organization from addressing a particular opportunity. There has been much talk about core competencies in recent years, and focus on core competencies underpins many corporate pruning campaigns. However, if the choice is between (1) an attractive market opportunity and little core competence, or (2) a poor market opportunity and significant core competence, most companies would be better off going with the better market opportunity. Jeff Bezos, CEO of the most innovative (if not yet profitable) B2C Internet business, had little in the way of core competence for running a dot-com retailer when he started Amazon.com; nor did the originators of eBay, the most consistently profitable B2C Internet business.

Market entry strategies can be grouped into four areas: pioneer, follow-the-leader, segmenter, and me-too.

**Pioneers.** Because they are developing new products and technologies, pioneers do not enter existing markets; instead, they must develop them. The innovations they bring to these markets typically result from consistent and extensive R&D spending. They build long-term success, not on a single innovation, but on a continuous stream of innovative products. Because their drive to enhance shareholder value rests on technological development, these firms must develop in-house the R&D skills and organizational commitment to produce genuinely new products and services. Most importantly, pioneers must possess marketing skills that enable them to introduce these products into the uncharted waters of new markets.[13]

The risk-taking internal corporate culture of pioneer firms enables them to be consistently successful. This culture can accept the inevitable failures that accompany innovation. Typically, such companies have enough "organizational slack" to commit the necessary human and hardware resources when newly developing markets require them. In addition, they need the financial resources to support heavy and consistent R&D expenditures, the purchase of equity stakes or technologies, and the frequently steep costs of market development.[14]

Pioneering is a high-cost option, and governments typically recognize the unique contributions of these firms (and individuals) through patent law. Successful pioneers often can secure limited monopolies for their discoveries and enjoy the resulting high margins. To gain this advantage, many pioneers employ armies of patent lawyers intent on protecting the firm's intellectual property. However, even in the absence of patent protection, significant advantage often accrues to the successful "first mover."[15] Companies that have frequently pioneered new products based on their own R&D efforts include Du Pont, 3M, Intel, Sony, and major pharmaceutical firms.

A simplistic view of marketing suggests that marketers should determine customer needs, then seek to develop products and services that satisfy those needs. For potential pioneers, what current customers believe they require is irrelevant and potentially even harmful![16] Yet some of these new technologies ultimately spawn products and services that yield substantial profits, even though pioneering is a journey into the unknown with high degrees of uncertainty. The firm's mission should set broad parameters on the scope of research effort but beyond that, there should be relatively few constraints. Pioneering research requires a portfolio of many projects that may result in just a few successes.

## INNOVATING OUT OF THE BUREAUCRACY

At 3M, company scientists spend most of their time on company-approved projects. However, they may also spend up to 15 percent of their time on individually designed projects, not subject to the corporate R&D bureaucracy. The most famous result of this process has been Art Fry's development of Post-it notes, a multimillion-dollar product for 3M.

As researchers make progress, and R&D shifts from fundamental insights toward potential products, the guiding hand of the business unit mission is no longer sufficient. Without constraints, R&D departments tend to pursue their own agendas and ignore shareholder value. Lacking a serious market-oriented review, research projects can gain a life of their own. Research for its own sake may keep scientists happy, but it often does little for shareholders. This can be a notable problem with large R&D departments whose bureaucratic processes and procedures place all sorts of roadblocks to getting potentially successful new products out the door. To deal with this difficulty, several major chemical companies now make R&D budget approval dependent on preparation of a satisfactory marketing document. Personnel from R&D prepare these documents (to standardized guidelines developed by marketing), and the review panels include marketing executives. In effect, the technology development group has to make the argument and supply evidence that a market really does exist if the R&D project is successful. This project-proving stage is critical.

As projects get closer to developing commercial products, product and market test results feed back customer responses to R&D for product modification prior to launch. Marketing considerations must play a major role in decisions about timing (e.g., the pros and cons of launching a less than perfect product early versus waiting for a better entry yet losing time and possibly first-mover advantages).

**Follow-the-Leader.** Rather than pioneer new markets, companies can also achieve early entry by waiting for a competitor to innovate, then following its lead as quickly as possible. Companies using this approach avoid the high-risk financial outlays for projects that fail. They assume the risk of allowing the pioneer to gain first-mover advantage or even patent protection. A follow-the-leader strategy can be a viable option when a company deliberately selects it. In reality, however, many risk-averse companies with weak innovation capabilities follow this course by default, not by design. In either case, this strategy requires a different organization.

The major driver for follow-the-leader firms is competition. For firms pursuing this entry strategy, competitive intelligence is crucial. Sophisticated competitive intelligence may identify competitor's R&D projects before launch, and if the R&D department is geared to take fast action, a follow-the-leader firm may even launch before the pioneer. Such firms focus on development rather than research. Either the development occurs in-house or the firm seeks to acquire products/entire companies in developing markets. Theodore Levitt described this as a "used apple" policy. Let someone else take first bite of the apple—if it looks okay, go ahead; if the apple is wormy, stop! Follow-the-leader firms allow pioneers to spend the research investment to develop new products and services, then enter as soon as possible with a focus on development. Success requires being able to react quickly when it becomes clear that the pioneer has developed a potentially successful product or service. In addition to competitive intelligence, important capabilities are versatile development engineers, who can design products based on the pioneer's R&D efforts, and "can do" patent lawyers, who search out weak spots in the pioneer's patent filings.[17]

Follow-the-leader firms also need financial resources, both to maintain high levels of development spending until they can match the pioneer in customer benefits and to invest in a market where the pioneer has started developing first-mover advantages. Successful examples include Matsushita, which followed Sony into the VCR market, and the Ethicon division of Johnson & Johnson, which consistently and successfully followed U.S. Surgical's (now Tyco) medical device innovations some 18 months later with lower prices. Another example of a battle between pioneer and follow-the-leader is the competitive struggle between Netscape and Microsoft in the Internet browser market, in which the follow-the-leader firm appears to have emerged victorious.

It is also worth remembering that, pre-Starbucks, few Americans would have paid a premium for high-quality coffee, but now many coffee bars get the benefit of Starbucks' education of the consumer. When Toyota entered the U.S. compact automobile market, it had the advantage of being able to interview Volkswagen owners (the leading small car producer at the time) to identify their preferences, whereas Volkswagen had entered the market without such information.

Time is critical in many phases of business, but nowhere is it more important than for follow-the-leader firms. First-mover advantage is very real: Awareness, name recognition, customer loyalty, customer switching costs, access to preferred distribution channels, and market knowledge are all potential prizes for the pioneer. The longer the delay before the follower enters, the greater the pioneer's ability to secure and cement these advantages. Follow-the-leader firms must therefore exhibit both speed and flexibility to capitalize on actionable information. Overcoming the pioneer's first-mover advantages probably will require a superior offer, but followers have potential access to data that the pioneer lacked at the time of entry—actual customer use under real-world conditions. These data can help a motivated development group design offers that will overcome the pioneer's advantage. Sometimes, the pioneer's strengths in technology become its Achilles' heel. They ignore customer intelligence because they are tied to the existing offer or are trying to recover their R&D investment, apparently failing to understand that it is a "sunk" cost.

Segmenter.   As markets develop, product/market information becomes more generally available and competitors enter. Supplier options increase and power shifts from supplier to customer. Customers become more knowledgeable and accomplished in using the products, and competitors are more astute in responding to customers' emerging needs. As market growth slows and overcapacity becomes the norm, customer requirements typically become more specific creating segments across the market.

Since the market has by now grown significantly, segments can be very large. Segmenters often seize the advantage by offering products and services that more nearly satisfy the needs of one or more segments than do those of the early entrants. Segmenters again need different capabilities. At this stage of market development, technological expertise is no longer the driving force. Instead, the firm's critical requirements are marketing research to understand customers and identify potential market segments, and the ability to successfully address narrow market niches.

By the time segmenters enter the market, technological superiority is much less relevant. Segmenters succeed to the extent that their marketers understand the fine-grained needs of customers, can develop groups of customers with similar needs (segments), and can construct offers that satisfy those needs. For the segmenter, the traditional tools of market research are most likely to improve the prospects of commercial success for the innovation.[18] To address several segments simultaneously, the company should have a modular design philosophy and flexible but cost-effective operating systems. Early entrants are often encumbered with inflexible and relatively costly operations systems ill-suited to this stage of market development. Success for the segmenter depends on developing close working relationships among marketing, R&D, and operations. This is often a considerable challenge for traditional functional organizations.

In the automobile industry, Chrysler's highly successful introduction of the minivan into the mature automobile market was a segmenter innovation that all major automobile manufacturers ultimately copied. Mazda resuscitated the long-dormant sports car segment with the much-imitated Miata (MX-5). New entrants into the portable computer video projector market are taking what began as a business presentation product into the consumer market as a way to display digital photographs and videos.

In this information-intensive world, segment boundaries are continually changing. Firms must keep searching for new segment opportunities, and R&D must respond with product variations that satisfy their requirements. Sheer technological horsepower in R&D is much less important than flexibility and the ability to work closely with marketing.

Me-Too. Some firms may enter a market even though it is fully developed and growing slowly at best. At this stage of market development, price sensitivity typically increases, and more customers are willing to choose among equally acceptable competitors on the basis of cost.

Overcapacity and intense price competition typically characterize this market. To create shareholder value, me-too competitors with essentially similar offers must achieve a low-cost position. They need aggressive procurement operations and a significant capability to reduce costs through value engineering. They must also be able to manage efficient high-volume operations with low overhead.

Me-too companies typically have limited product lines and are often leaders in process innovation. Their strategies can play havoc in segmented markets where several competitors make value-added offers. Companies that appear to have adopted a me-too approach include AMD and Cyrix. These companies allow Intel to pioneer new processor generations, then follow with lower-price alternatives. In the pharmaceutical industry, firms such as Novopharm and Patiopharm focus on producing low-cost generic versions of existing drugs rather than pioneering new ones. Airlines such as Southwest and JetBlue, in the United States, and EasyJet and Ryanair, in Europe, provide similar examples in commercial aviation. Although they have been innovative in constructing and managing their operations, they are late entrants whose success depends primarily on their low-cost position.

## Organizing for Innovation

Some readers may find this title oxymoronic.[19] Creativity and innovation are not normally identified with organized processes or entities. Given a broad view of innovation, and different market entry options and capabilities, it follows that there is no best way of organizing for innovation.

The four growth strategies are in mutual conflict. Whereas a large firm may conceivably pursue them simultaneously in its different businesses, this is not only unlikely, but even dangerous, within an individual business. A successful pioneer must spend heavily on both R&D and market development. In the most striking contrast, the critical issue for the me-too entrant is to develop a low-cost position. The different entry strategies impose conflicting demands on the business's capabilities. A much-publicized example of the difficulty in managing more than one of these entry strategies was Merck's decision to build a separate facility to enter the generic pharmaceutical business, and its subsequent pullout before even commencing operations. Likewise, British Airways elected to float off its low-cost airline, Go, only a few years after it commenced operations.

Firms choosing the earlier (in time) market-entry strategies must be continually concerned with potential competition from firms embracing the later market-entry archetypes. Pioneers must watch for firms adopting follow-the-leader strategies; pioneers and follow-the-leaders must be concerned about segmenters; and pioneers, follow-the-leaders, and segmenters must all defend against me-too entrants.

Not only should management formulate an entry policy for any operating business, it must set the stage for nurturing the appropriate capabilities needed later in the cycle. For example, a firm may excel as a pioneer. But the technological superiority that brings profits and growth early in the cycle matter much less when segmenters and me-too entrants are pursuing their entry strategies. Failure to manage transitions associated with changing market conditions that spur other firms to enter with new strategies has caused the demise of many businesses. Since these transitions now occur more quickly than in the past, they pose formidable challenges for incumbents.[20] Instead of attempting to build internal capabilities, which may take years, a firm may choose to form an alliance or outsource to others. However, alliances can lead to leakage of ideas and the dilution of any profits from innovations. Similarly, contracting out can lead to reneging or poor performance by partners.[21]

## OPERATIONAL CONSIDERATIONS

Management theorists argue persuasively that different kinds of innovation demand very different organizational arrangements. Whereas incremental innovation can be managed successfully within the existing organizational structure and system, discontinuous innovation cannot. The failure to heed this advice explains what Richard Foster described as the attacker's advantage.[22] Historically, discontinuous change in technology has often heralded a shift in industry leadership.

It follows that there can be no single way of managing the interface between technology and marketing. For example, me-too entrants succeed by cutting costs to the bone and securing business based on price. These firms collapse the barriers between segments by offering good value on the fundamental benefits that customers seek. Instead of paying a premium for additional fine-grained benefits, customers are prepared to forgo the benefits to obtain low prices. The challenge for marketers is to identify those product features that really matter to customers and those that do not. The interaction with R&D is about designing these basic products, but also about doing it inexpensively.

The issue is really about developing innovation management systems that fit the overall strategy of the business. Within this process, the role of marketing should change depending on the business strategy. Each market-entry strategy underlines the need to coordinate marketing and R&D, both when determining the marketing capabilities that can exploit innovation opportunities and when planning the operational execution of a given project.

An interesting question is, How widespread is such an approach? Think about your own experience: How many companies have you known where marketing supports general management with analysis and recommendations on such issues? In our experience, precious few match up. Too many marketers rush around trying to improve this month's or this quarter's sales or market share. Too few marketers are securing future sales and market share, or engaging in the appropriate interactions with their R&D colleagues.

Certainly, the erosion of high-level marketing positions in many companies, as discussed earlier, is one cause of this failure. On the other hand, if these positions had added significant value, they would not have disappeared in the first place. One way or another, marketers must bear some responsibility for the frequent mismatches between organizational capabilities and marketplace needs. It is this failure of marketers to adequately perform the strategic part of their job that leads to the oft-expressed frustration of R&D people.

Most R&D personnel are well aware that their products take too long to flow from the laboratory to the market, and many try hard to change this pattern. Marketing must be able to look sufficiently far ahead to offer guidance to the R&D effort. But the problem is not only with R&D and marketing personnel; senior management not only should nurture such a dialogue, but also should modify human resource selection, development, and reward systems accordingly.

All technological development must start with ideas. To a large extent, R&D develops these ideas into products, yet the potential sources of these ideas are widespread. Management should encourage input from anyone who might generate useful ideas for new technological developments. Innovative ideas may emerge from marketing executives, suppliers, developments in basic research or applied technology, or the firm's broader environment, as well as customers. However, no matter where the ideas were initially generated, marketing skills and capabilities are critical to successful commercialization.

For many years, companies have run suggestion systems, but Internet technology has greatly enhanced the ability to make these systems all encompassing. Some companies are developing deliberate processes to sidestep the R&D bureaucracy.

### GETTING NEW IDEAS

In 1996, Shell's Exploration and Production division set up a GameChanger panel with the authority to allocate $20 million to unconventional business ideas from anywhere in the division. In three years, the process generated 300 ideas, some for entirely new businesses, most of which had never surfaced in the conventional management system.

In 1997, Procter & Gamble (P&G) formed a Corporate New Ventures group funded with $250 million seed money, reporting only to top management. Using a corporate collaboration network, My Idea, employees throughout the firm funnel ideas to an innovation panel. Go-ahead projects may tap into P&G's entire global resource base. By late 1999, the company had launched 58 new products. Swiffer, a new cleaning product, was launched in 10 months, half the normal time.

The Swiffer example is a reminder that, the costs of delay in market entry may be immense, and the rewards for fast movement through the process enormous. In this area, zeal for short-term profit may inhibit the creation of shareholder value. The mantras of efficiency and budgetary control, typically driven by accounting and finance professionals, may come into direct conflict with the creation of shareholder value. Top management must resist this pressure.

On one issue concerning new ideas, we are adamant. We reject out-of-hand the facile notion that the only source of good new product ideas is the customer. This policy may lead to the development of sustaining technologies, but not disruptive technologies.

Don't customers have good ideas of new products and services? Of course! Don't customers have an important role to play in helping to shape and define product and service concepts? You bet! Shouldn't customers be involved in the product development and testing process? Certainly! And shouldn't marketing play the key interface role with customers? Right on! But should customers be the sole drivers of this process? Absolutely not!

Smart marketers are aware that new product ideas don't just originate from customers and market research—if only life were that simple. The touch-sensitive computer screen was a neat gadget for making the screen bleep until it found its applications—just about every retail location and hand-held computer. The MP3 recorder that downloads music from the Internet was an interesting curiosity—but has subsequently revolutionized the recorded music business. Both originated from R&D, not from market research questionnaires that asked people what they wanted.

Some go further in underlining the damage a simplistic belief in market research can cause for radical product innovation. A pioneer of consumer product innovation, Harry Drnec, then CEO of the European beverage company Maison Caurette, admits to this problem:

> My biggest mistake was in allowing market research to dictate one of my major decisions. . . . Where I went wrong was in allowing a system to dictate my decision. Now I know why I hate market research. . . . If you know your business well enough, you ought to be willing to take a chance on a product that you believe in.[23]

Customers can play a major role in the development process. During development of the Lexus, Toyota attempted to establish U.S. market requirements for a luxury sedan by having its chief engineer live in the United States with the "natives" for several months before beginning the design process. In the service arena, frequent business travelers assisted Marriott Hotels in conceptualizing the ideal budget business accommodation that subsequently became Courtyard by Marriott. Said the manager who sponsored this project, "In designing the actual product, the research allowed management to focus on the items customers wanted; we avoided focusing on things important to management but not important to the customer."[24]

In organizational terms, the emphasis may be on freeing innovation from the constraints of conventional structures and systems (e.g., the Horizon Three business concept at IBM). An interesting development has been the establishment of fluid, team-based processes for exploiting innovation quickly and effectively.

## VENTURE MARKETING ORGANIZATIONS

Some companies have established venture marketing organizations (VMOs) to apply the principles of venture capitalism to identifying opportunities for innovation and concentrating resources on the best. Starbucks has a VMO approach to innovation.

Starbucks approaches new opportunities by assembling teams whose leaders come from the functional areas most critical to success, possibly the originator of the idea (if qualified). If the right skills are not in the company, the team goes outside. To lead its "Store of the Future" project, Starbucks hired a senior executive with retail experience from Universal Studios, and to develop its lunch service concept, it chose an executive from Marriott. After the company launches the new product, some team members may stay to manage the venture, whereas others are deployed to new opportunity teams or return to line management.

Teamwork extends to partner organizations. Because Starbucks lacked in-house packaging and channel management skills for a new ice cream project, it teamed with Dreyer's to get the product to market in half the normal time.

Opportunity ideas can come from anywhere in the organization; originators use a one-page form to send the idea to a top management team. The team rates new ideas against impacts on company revenue growth and effects on the complexity of the retail store.

In the product's first year, Starbucks' Frappucino, a cold coffee drink, contributed 11 percent of total company sales. The idea originated with a front-line manager in May 1994, gaining high priority status from the top management team in June. The new VMO developed marketing, packaging, and channel approaches in July. A joint-venture arrangement with PepsiCo was in place by August. The first product rollout was in October, with full national launch in May 1995.*

*N. A. Aufreiter, T. L. Lawver, and C. D. Lun, "A New Way to Market," *The McKinsey Quarterly,* 2 (2000), 52–61; N. Aufreiter and T. Lawver, "Winning the Race for New Market Opportunities," *Ivey Business Journal,* 65 (September/October 2000), 14–16.

## Building Bridges between R&D and Marketing Cultures

The basis for culture clashes between marketing and R&D is easy to understand. Marketers are typically impatient for action, results–oriented, imprecise, and often impulsive. Although creative insight plays an important role in research, the typical researcher is likely to be patient, precise, methodical, and trained to be wary of inspirations. Differences in education often heighten conflicts: Marketers tend toward liberal arts and business majors with little scientific background, and R&D personnel generally have limited training in marketing processes.

Because the "thought-worlds" of researchers and marketers are often far apart, coordinating R&D and marketing personnel may pose enormous problems. Researchers are often suspicious of what they perceive to be the technological incompetence of marketers, whereas marketers may well view researchers as commercially naïve. This problem is difficult enough if the researchers and marketers work for the same company; it is more difficult if they come from different national cultures; and it becomes even more complex—perhaps with serious consequences—if R&D becomes a networked activity involving partners and brokers.[25] Notwithstanding these potential culture clashes, companies can develop systems to cope with the problem.

## OLIVETTI'S MULTIMEDIA R&D

The Italian company Olivetti has faced the challenges of reinventing itself twice: from a typewriter business to a personal computer company, then from a PC company to a multimedia business. In the idea generation phase of the move into multimedia technology, Olivetti set up its own pattern of multinational R&D collaboration agreements among companies and research institutions. Olivetti subsequently launched Europe's first multimedia sales kiosks with videophones as an electronic delivery channel for financial services.*

*P. Zagnoli and C. Cardini, "Patterns of International R&D Cooperation for New Product Development: The Olivetti Multimedia Product," *R&D Management,* 24 (January 1994), 3–15.

In a comprehensive study, A. D. Little found that a few companies had established a small marketing group within R&D, whose mission was "to provide a long-term marketing perspective to help R&D choose what technologies or ideas it should be pursuing."[26] However, a substantial minority of sample companies did not encourage direct contact between R&D personnel and customers.

The culture problem often has simple roots. Because marketing people just do not know R&D people, marketing/R&D interactions are between virtual strangers. Often their organizational homes are geographically disparate, and there is no possibility of developing and cementing bonds at the watercooler. Although developing integrated career tracks might reduce culture problems between sales and marketing, it is rare for R&D personnel to spend time in a marketing function and still rarer for a marketing executive to spend time in R&D. One ray of hope comes from technologies such as e-mail and chat rooms that enhance communication through company intranets. Research with project teams shows that improving communication enhances team integration.

In some high-technology businesses, the link between R&D and customer-facing personnel is changing as R&D becomes a major component of relationship marketing. This is especially true in account management situations where R&D personnel may be members of a key account team. In this role, they learn to work on technology innovation directly with customers (and suppliers). Their involvement becomes a defining part of the buyer–seller relationship that may improve the firm's marketing capability and provide differential advantage.[27]

Key members of the R&D team may become important assets at launch time, when they can offer much needed credibility to customers who may be facing significant technological and economic risk. A major reason for EMI's initial success with the CT Scanner was the role played by Nobel Prize winner, Sir Godfrey Hounsfield, the driving force behind the technological development. Hounsfield made many speeches and visited key potential customers in a successful effort to develop demand for a very expensive technological innovation. In the pharmaceutical industry, Sir James Black attained similar iconic status for his innovative discoveries.

Internal R&D is just one avenue for generating new products and services. Technology purchase, joint-venture technology agreements, and equity stakes in start-ups are alternative paths for securing new products. It follows that the firm may not directly market the products and services that derive from its own technological advances. Not only must the firm be able to create value for customers, it must have (or develop) the processes for delivering that value. Although the new technology development may match the firm's R&D skills and competencies, marketing the products developed from the technology may not. If some other organization has better skills at exploiting a particular technology, the firm might want to sell or license that technology. It can then direct its own marketing efforts in areas where it is better positioned; or perhaps the firm may choose to sell itself in its entirety.

## Why Isn't Creating Value the Same as Making Profits?

This may seem a curious question if you equate value with profit; in fact, they are sometimes far apart. Nowhere does the distinction between value and profit come into focus more clearly than when examining innovation and R&D. Virtually all new ventures show losses in their early stages. As such, they must be protected from the blind application of EVA calculations, and from those who believe that short-term profit is the sole measure of business performance. This seems obvious—but if it is so obvious, why do managers frequently fail to understand R&D's contribution to value creation? This misunderstanding leads to some very bad decisions.

Although researchers may be heavily capitalized with research equipment, it is the researchers themselves who represent the crucial scarce resource in R&D effort. Companies preoccupied with reporting quarter-to-quarter profit increases often forget this simple fact. Because the R&D effort is typically driven by highly skilled human resources, acting either as individuals or as team members, consistency of spending on R&D is essential to productive research efforts. Adjusting R&D budgets to meet short-term profit goals is disastrous to research productivity. Sometimes the order to cut R&D comes from top management, but R&D managers themselves have been known to halt research efforts because the department has reached an annual budget limit, without making any attempt to quantify the opportunity costs. The costs of delay can be staggering.

### THE COSTS OF BEING SLOW

Pharma Company is developing a new drug with sales potential of $1 billion. These days, such drugs are not at all unusual. Assume a variable (contribution) margin of 90 percent (also not at all unusual in this industry). Each day of delay in the research process represents an opportunity loss of $1 billion × 90 percent/365—almost $2.5 million a day!

We often dramatize this issue by asking executives to predict the stock price of a major pharmaceutical company if the R&D budget were cut to zero. Assuming an R&D budget of $1 billion (a conservative figure), there would be an immediate and significant increase in profits. Yet, without exception, managers tell us that the stock price would drop, despite the profit increase. Stock prices reflect investors' expectations about future earnings—the future earnings stream of a pharmaceutical company that ceases to spend on R&D would be strongly affected.

Research has demonstrated the financial benefit of R&D spending,[28] yet only recently have financial analysts recognized this important relationship. In the hypercompetitive world of the twenty-first century, companies must regenerate competitive advantage ever more rapidly. If they are to prosper in this environment, R&D efforts must rise in commensurate fashion.

## Managing the Development Process

The speed with which the firm moves through the new product development process has become crucial to competitive success. In the past, companies often paid too little attention to the opportunity cost of being late to market. As the pace of market development has intensified and competition has spawned faster rates of imitation and innovation, there have been frantic efforts to speed up development. The drive for speed-to-market sometimes tempts firms to skip stages in the development process, but this is foolish. The "shoot first, aim later" philosophy more often than not leads to disaster. Empirical research suggests that completing all stages in the development process is a significant predictor of success—54.8 percent of new product successes undertook nine or more documented stages in the development process, compared with 38.2 percent of new product failures.[29] Instead of skipping stages, a far more sensible approach is, first, to eliminate unproductive time lags by reengineering the process and, second, to ensure efficiency by using the best possible technology.

Reengineering the development process involves a careful review of activities to reduce the length of the critical path. Such scrutiny may reveal opportunities to conduct activities in parallel that personnel previously performed sequentially. Technology may also facilitate efficient operations. The CAD systems have drastically reduced design time in many industries while Rapid Prototyping Systems (RPS) enable many companies to develop full-scale prototypes much more quickly. In other cases, using virtual reality to supersede reality has led to significant timesavings.

### SAVING TIME IN R&D

In the drug industry, researchers test potentially therapeutic new compounds on populations of virtual patients; while Boeing used a combination of CAD and virtual reality to bring the 777 from concept to reality faster than any commercial jet in history.

## Interpersonal Factors in the Marketing/R&D Interface

The effectiveness of the marketing/R&D interface depends in large part on the people involved. However, it is not at all certain that marketers are well suited for the role of working with a team to develop radically new technology. One observer has opined:

> [S]ince the average MBA program concentrates on developing skills in consumer behavior measurement, market research, advertising and marketing planning, it is difficult for marketers to appreciate how technology can create new and superior products.[30]

Some have suggested that the onus should be on R&D managers to do a better job of educating marketers. This suggests they should try to develop personal relationships, and inform and convince marketers of technological changes that may create new business opportunities or threaten existing products.[31] Although this is good advice (for effective innovators will always try to remove or reduce impediments to their success), the problem is more deep-seated.

First, companies serious about competing via innovation must recognize that the educational task is multidirectional; urging R&D to educate marketing but not vice versa is a mistake. Not only must marketing and R&D talk to each other, finance, operations, and human resources—all the functions—must also be involved. Second, in most companies, marketers are technologically deprived. Training can address this problem, but recruitment, selection, and career path strategy can also be helpful. Finally, managers must make special efforts to identify marketers who are interested in the strategic (versus operational) part of the marketing job. Marketing inputs should play a role in the development and commercialization of advanced product technology; marketing staff in many companies lack the necessary knowledge and competence.

A critical interpersonal problem is the functional allocation of tasks across the marketing/R&D interface.[32] Such allocation often impedes the cross-pollination of experience and ideas. In many cases, although marketing and R&D personnel talk to each other, they attempt to dictate to one another and do a poor job of building on each other's ideas. The traditional dominance of one or the other function in the company's culture exacerbates this problem, but in general, marketing falls short in providing strategic, long-term guidance.

Many researchers who study company interface problems believe that overcoming them requires concerted management effort. One consultant argued that "to sustain innovation, management needs to continuously integrate the contributions of different functions into coherent strategies and plans."[33] He advocated process coaches and a drastic rethinking by management, with an emphasis on process mapping. In addition, in accord with our theme of Total Integrated Marketing, the core message is that firms must "customerize" technology by introducing a customer dimension into all technology development and deployment.[34]

Interpersonal factors are extremely important both within and across functions. But, in an era when innovation is more and more central to the success of the firm, there is probably no more critical interface than that between R&D and marketing. Get this one wrong, and there may be no redemption.

## CONCLUSION

There is little doubt that marketing can add substantial value to incremental innovation—the extensions and modifications that tend to be the stuff of innovation in most established markets. The case for discontinuous or, even more so, thoroughly disruptive innovation is perhaps less clear-cut. The profitable commercialization of any innovation requires substantial marketing nous. When launching products with radically new technologies, or with properties far removed from existing products, the necessary marketing skills are usually of the highest order. However, marketing theory and practice with radical innovation are lacking. The need has arguably never been greater, but there remains a huge gap between the need and the reality. What then can practicing managers do to improve new product performance?

The extreme or "pure" research—the really big "R"—is essentially serendipitous. Few companies engage in this type of research; but other than attempting to divine the future evolution of human society and providing the broadest possible guidance, marketing concepts can add little. In virtually every other case, however, strong arguments can be made for Total Integrated Marketing.

Strategic marketing inputs, can guide basic research. Further, creating opportunities for R&D personnel to interact with customers can increase the chances of successfully commercializing innovations. Much commercial innovation is incremental, and imbuing the whole team with a customer-driven marketing philosophy is vital. That teamwork is critical to new product success is beyond dispute, yet so often companies fail in this endeavor. Technologies such as QFD provide powerful tools for facilitating such teamwork (Chapter 7), but their adoption requires the courage and conviction of strong leadership.

Most worrying is that some marketers still have a naïve belief that focusing on the customer can allow them to divine all wants and needs, while they continue to deny that technology may potentially create new wants or needs. Further, and equally unsettling, if the firm segregates all R&D into separate organizational units following the recommendations of some theorists, a pure "technology push" approach may result. Somewhere between these two extremes, there has to be a better approach. Better strategic management of the marketing/R&D relationship may help you to discover that middle way in your organization, and contribute to realizing the benefits of Total Integrated Marketing.

# MARKETING AND CUSTOMER SERVICE

## CONCENTRATING ON THE CRUNCH WHEN THE CUSTOMER MEETS THE COMPANY

It seems strange that although most managers claim to be "market oriented" and "customer focused," many organizations underfund customer service, manage it poorly, and focus on the wrong things. This is especially difficult to understand because it is blindingly obvious that the contact between the customer and the customer service organization frequently is where the customer actually decides whether the company provides value. There is overwhelming evidence that well-designed and executed customer service—whether provided before or after purchase—is a significant source of competitive advantage. Customer service superiority is also a more quickly accessible competitive weapon than many others; you may not be able to hike product quality overnight, but surely you can leverage customer service.

Superior customer service does not mean pandering to customers with servility and obsequiousness. It means providing the kind of support to the company's product that adds value in the customer's eyes. This simple fact seems to have escaped the attention of all too many managers. One of our colleagues recently observed: "If corporate functions were characters from Dickens, marketing would be Uriah Heep: unctuous, ubiquitous, unbearable. . . . Whatever people may desire of their products and services, they adamantly do not want kowtowing from the companies that market to them. They do not want us to prostrate ourselves in front of them and promise to love them, till death do us part."[1]

The costs of getting this wrong may be substantial, and no one is immune.

## WAL-MART'S GERMAN CAMPAIGN

Wal-Mart is the world's largest and most customer-service-conscious retailer. In January 1998, Wal-Mart arrived in Germany with sweeping price-cuts and its U.S. business model of high-level customer service—the "10-foot rule." If a customer comes within 10 feet of an employee, the latter must smile and offer to help; this rule includes greeters, checkout clerks, and bag-packers. The prevailing rule in German retailing seems to be "the grumpier the better," and what is more, German consumers seem to prefer it that way. They have been suspicious, infuriated, and offended by Wal-Mart's assertive customer service policies. In late 2000, Wal-Mart's German losses were approaching $200 million, the company had the lowest rating of all retailers in a national customer satisfaction survey, and Wal-Mart postponed its German expansion plans.*

*T. Helm, "Service with a Smile Frowned on by German People," *Daily Telegraph* (October 28, 2000); T. Major, "Wal-Mart Shrinks Plan for German Expansion," *The Financial Times* (April 24, 2001).

The trouble is that managers make assumptions. Supply chain managers assume that the secret of service and value superiority is offering the product faster and cheaper. But why is it, then, that customers appear to have placed such high value on certain new car models (such as Mazda Miatas or the new Mini), Harley-Davidson motorcycles, De Beers diamonds, or Harry Potter books—even though they had to wait to get their hands on them?

Accountants and operations managers assume that value means getting the price down. But when Starbucks charges us $5 for 25 cents' worth of coffee, why do we come back for more? Salespeople assume that better deals mean better value. And some marketing people assume that giving customers a plastic loyalty card will win their hearts and souls.

Look for similar faulty assumptions in your company because they can fundamentally undermine the delivery of real customer value and can divert customer service into expensive areas that create no value for customers.

There is only one useful definition of high-quality customer service—
it adds value to a product or service for a particular type of customer.

Those who realize that customer service is only high quality if it increases customer value may have a substantial competitive edge. Superior
customer service (i.e., it provides the services that matter to customers)
has major payoffs. These include higher levels of customer satisfaction,
faster adoption of innovations, significant repurchase levels, and positive
word-of-mouth recommendations to other buyers. There are few areas
where Total Integrated Marketing can have greater impact than in customer service—but the effects are not always obvious. This takes us back
to where we started: Customer service is only superior if it delivers benefits that customer's value.

### CUSTOMER SERVICE THAT DRIVES CUSTOMER VALUE

The marketing VP of a major U.S. health insurance organization told us that
one of his company's proudest boasts had always been that it could process
claims faster than any competitor. Major investments in technology, total
quality management, and training underpinned this claim.

When the VP implemented customer care events, he discovered that his
corporate customers found little value in fast claims processing (their own
systems were not as fast, so the paperwork just sat in a batch awaiting attention). What really bugged them, however, was finding errors (because
they cost time and money to sort out). The customers were telling him: We
don't care if it means slowing down—just get it right!

To invest in, and brag about, services that do not create customer value
is expensive and wasteful. It can also make the company vulnerable to
competitors who figure out what services do drive customer value. Diagnostic tools to evaluate service delivery systems are in widespread use—
but they must focus on the services that create competitive advantage or
they will lead management seriously astray. There is another point about
our health care example. Many people in the company already knew that
errors mattered more to customers than speed of processing. No one ever
bothered to listen to them. The company demanded and rewarded speed,
so that is what they got.

Figuring out what services really matter to customers and focusing resources on those services, even if it means dropping other things that might seem important, has incredible power potential.

## THE PRICE OF A GOOD NIGHT'S SLEEP

In the mid-1980s, the French budget hotel market was struggling with low growth, low occupancy rates, and poor profitability. Accor launched its Formula 1 hotel chain on the premise that what budget travelers actually value is a good night's sleep. They reasoned that low price was what attracted people to one-star hotels, and what caused them to trade up to a two-star hotel was the sleeping environment: One-star hotels generally were noisy, dirty, and had poor beds. They figured all the other services and amenities of the two-star hotels were largely irrelevant to customers. Formula 1 offers clean, quiet rooms with comfortable beds, just like the two-star hotels, but at the price of a one-star hotel (because they have omitted all the other two-star hotel services). By 1999, Formula 1 had a market share larger than the sum of the next five competitors. They not only had taken business from traditional hotels, but also had grown the market—more people were willing to stay over for a night if they could get a good night's rest.*

*W. Chan Kim and R. Mauborgne, "Finding Rooms for Manoeuvre," *The Financial Times* (May 27, 1999).

Sometimes customers appear positively perverse in what satisfies them. People in the leisure business assume that most of us do not like waiting in line. Standing in line at the theme park is therefore a bad thing, to be reduced. Most of us are familiar with the entertainers at places like Disneyland and Walt Disney World, who try to distract customers while they are waiting in line for the "big" rides. The huge Alton Towers theme park in Britain, however, has customer satisfaction data indicating that pleasure in their rides increases with waiting time (up to a point). Partly because it is relaxing and partly because of the street entertainers working with the lines of customers, effective service for them seems to involve optimizing waiting time, not reducing it to a minimum. So much for "rationality" in customer service!

Examples like this contribute to our mixed feelings about the changes that many companies have made in their customer service philosophy over the past few years. It is certainly both important and appropriate that customer service has been moved out of the managerial basement after so many years of languishing there. This department directly affects customer value perceptions and is a rich source of information about those customers. In the rush of enthusiasm to embrace its importance, however, some companies are viewing customer service as the automatic solution to all marketing problems, or even equating customer service with marketing itself. This is a major mistake that can lead to management disenchantment with service performance, loss of value to customers, and frustrated customer service employees.

Karl Albrecht, joint author of *Service America!* (1985), powerfully summarizes an alternative view: "Customers seek value, not 'service.' We've abandoned the obsolete term 'customer service,' which connotes the trivial, be-nice, smiley-faced attempt to pacify customers."[2]

As noted, some spectacular marketing successes of the twenty-first century seem to illustrate the exact reverse of conventional customer service and care, suggesting that we should positively "torment" customers.[3] Creating outstanding customer value may require far more creative and paradoxical strategies than training employees to say, "Have a nice day," to customers (especially if the employee's eyes actually say, "Believe me, I don't care whether you have a nice day."

### THE REAL WIZARDRY OF HARRY POTTER

The Harry Potter books by J. K. Rowling[a] and the first blockbuster Harry Potter movie have gained spectacular worldwide attention. They captured consumers' imaginations and created enormous anticipatory excitement. Both books and movie have been exceptionally successful. But Scholastic's campaign for Harry Potter was not conventional. Instead, it relied on exclusivity—you may want it now, but you have to wait because we say so. It was based on secrecy—a complete blackout on advance information, except for a few key facts, such as the death of a key character and Harry Potter's sexual awakening, strategically leaked to the eager press. Printers and distributors were tied in to strict confidentiality agreements. A rigorous embargo controlled booksellers, although some were allowed to tease consumers by displaying the book in a locked cage before "Harry Potter Day" (July 8, 2000). Interestingly, a Wal-Mart in West Virginia mysteriously and "accidentally" sold several advance copies, and coincidentally, the fortunate young purchasers were featured on the front pages of newspapers across the world.

> Scholastic also dropped heavy hints that there would not be enough copies to go around (though there were), and frantic queues of desperate buyers formed at bookshops on the appointed day.[b]
>
> [a] See for example, J. K. Rowling, *Harry Potter and the Philosopher's Stone* (New York: A. A. Levine Books, 1998).
>
> [b] See note 1. See also, S. Brown, *Marketing: The Retro Revolution* (London: Sage, 2001).

We want to examine both the benefits and limitations of customer service as well as underline its unique contributions to company performance. Service is not only a major defensive weapon for retaining customers, but also an offensive weapon and a resource for gaining insights into customer priorities and preferences. Poor customer service can create an involuntary demarketing effort, while alienated service employees in turn can jeopardize customer relationships, even changing customers into "terrorists."[4]

## STRATEGIC RELATIONSHIPS

For too many years, the customer service department was a stepchild of the firm. Tacked on, apparently as an afterthought, its organizational position was unclear, its staffing often mediocre, and its career paths nonexistent. In many companies, a posting to customer service was the corporate equivalent of being sent to Siberia. Most executives operating abroad insist that this is still the pattern for customer service in many countries. In most U.S. companies today, however, these conditions no longer prevail, which raises the question: What is responsible for the change?

Four interrelated factors seem to be significant. First is the growth of what is usually called relationship marketing. Driven by enormous improvements in costs and performance of information technology, it has become feasible for companies to identify customers and conduct longitudinal studies of the factors that influence their decisions. This has led to a much clearer understanding of the strategic role of customer service. Second, the refocusing of the quality movement on customer-driven definitions of quality has highlighted the role of service in delivering customer satisfaction. Third, in many companies the 80/20 rule operates, and managers recognize that unless key customers receive the right service, 80 percent of revenues may disappear. Finally, the increase in competitive intensity has led firms to concentrate on getting all aspects of their offer right. As core products reach competitive parity, the emphasis often shifts to competing on customer service levels.

But all is still not well in the world of customer service. Despite these powerful pressures, companies still try to foist "relationships" on customers who don't want them; pursue "quality" as measured by engineers instead of basing it on what customers value; and differentiate service levels and types that no one actually seems to want. Aggrieved customers are going public with their complaints on the Internet. With little effort but sometimes much ingenuity, customers exasperated by poor service can post their stories on a bulletin board or set up a Web site. Some firms have departments of "Web watchers" to monitor these public corporate humiliations and try to resolve problems. The watchers also look for complaints about competitors to avoid making the same mistakes. However, the sad truth is that many firms still don't get it!

Customer Relationship Management (CRM) systems are currently the best-selling IT (information technology) systems across the world and represent a management belief that if you just spend enough on IT, then the troubles with customers will go away.

In fact, relationship marketing, quality, and service-based competitive strategies all share the danger of creating customer expectations that the company simply cannot fulfill. As noted in Chapter 5, false promises destroy the credibility of a market strategy and are a great way to learn just how long customers' memories can be. They may forget a firm's advertising in 10 seconds, but they remember the disappointing service encounter for years. The gap between customer expectations and service delivery has become the basis of a powerful way of managing customer service.[5] Its importance has become more central as the service activities have changed.

Rather than being a stepchild, with at best a secondary position in management thinking, customer service is now likely to be playing an important strategic role. There is no better illustration of this point than the outpouring of books over the past 10 to 15 years as consultants and academics alike have offered prolific advice.[6] Underlying this flood of reading matter has been a formidable amount of academic research shedding new light on the subject.[7]

## Customer Service as Offensive Strategy[8]

Some companies have used service superiority either as the main plank of their business strategy, or at least as a key element. British Airways, which had been a poorly managed state-owned airline, relied on superiority in customer service to achieve global impact and high profitability as the "World's Favourite Airline." Unfortunately, when the company subsequently entered a phase of cost-cutting and outsourcing, it lost that service edge, culminating in significant operating losses. Nonetheless, superiority in customer service has been key to the success of many outstanding firms including Singapore Airlines, Four Seasons, FedEx, Kwik-Fit, Nordstrom, and Fidelity.

Even now, many managers still believe that they can only build sustainable competitive advantage on the basis of technology—preferably technology legally protected by patents. We take a broader view of technology than most, but we do not believe that the typical supporter of such a view would include superior service systems in their definition of technology.

There is good evidence that with appropriate effort, service-based advantages may be sustainable for long periods. Singapore Airlines has stayed at the top of the airline rankings for many years, despite vastly improved service levels from its competitors. FedEx's domestic service reliability has been renowned and unbeaten since the company's founding.

In many cases, service-based advantages rest on unique behavioral systems that typically reflect a carefully designed combination of recruitment, training, development, and rewards. They provide a secure competitive advantage because they are extraordinarily difficult for competitors to emulate.[9] Perhaps this is another manifestation of an issue discussed in Chapter 11—that the ultimate source of all competitive advantage is the human resource. Richard Branson, the British billionaire entrepreneur, rates employee satisfaction above customer satisfaction, arguing that only if employees are happy can a service business satisfy its customers.

## Customer Service as Defensive Strategy

Realistically, most traditional manufacturing companies still do not see service as the core of their offensive strategy. Many of them may find it difficult to understand how firms compete this way, because they cling to the belief that product superiority is the only route to competitive success.

Yet, even if companies are unprepared to use customer service as the cutting edge, they are starting to recognize the crucial role of customer service in defensive strategy. The growth of relationship marketing has encouraged more companies to explore the economics of relationships with their customers. Typically, it costs so much to acquire customers that it is irresponsible to lose them, at least when retention costs are relatively small. In that situation, customer service plays a vital role in defensive strategy, because it is the prime tool for customer retention. In some companies, it has even been renamed "retention marketing."

However, it is not always easy to explore the economics of these customer service decisions. Although many studies have purported to show the benefits of retention marketing, they often are based on customers' self-reports of what their behavior was or would be. These studies may provide some useful insights, but they also may be seriously misleading.

It is often argued that customer retrieval through outstanding company efforts to solve a service problem is likely to produce an enthusiastic advocate for the seller. For this reason, supplying positive responses to customers' complaints should provide a major opportunity. However, only two longitudinal studies have isolated what customers actually do, as opposed to what they say they will do. Both studies suggest that customers with a history of service problems defect at a higher rate than customers who have not experienced a problem, even when they claim to have been satisfied with the resolution of their problem at the time.[10]

In retrospect, this finding should not be surprising. Total quality management (TQM) would certainly focus on elimination of the causes of problems, not just their speedy resolution once they have occurred. Elementary consumer insight should lead to the same conclusion: Instead of having responsive service when something goes wrong with my car or airline flight, I would much prefer not to have a problem in the first place. The mythology of service recovery benefits has even led some managers to recommend introducing preplanned service difficulties to demonstrate their firm's responsiveness. Such devious strategies are singularly unwise.

## Customer Service as Learning Strategy

Although firms frequently ignore this benefit, customer service is a potential hot spot for listening to customers and learning more about their changing priorities. Because customer service is a critical point where customers meet the company (often for the first time if they have bought products through intermediaries), it is an amazingly productive source of lessons for managers about what really drives customer value.

This may seem to be stating the obvious. If so, look at your own operations and ask when the customer service people were last asked for input during the development of marketing strategy. Ask when the VP of Marketing last did a shift on the telephones or the help desk; made a service visit to a customer's facilities; or tried to report a problem via telephone and got lost in a maze of automated choices! Ask what methods your company has in place to channel the insights and customer knowledge of service personnel back into market strategy development. All too often, managers ignore this awesome resource for understanding what customers have to say when they meet the company. Why is it that apparently smart executives prefer to send another large chunk of their shareholders' money to a market research agency, instead of listening to their own customer service people?

Some years ago, *The Wall Street Journal* published "war stories" from the customer service department of a major computer manufacturer. These stories were basically concerned with the inadequacies and stupidity of their customers:

- The customer who could not get the computer "foot pedal" to work, and had to be told that the computer was not like a sewing machine, and please take the mouse off the floor.
- The people who feed floppy disks through a manual typewriter to type nice neat labels on them, thus breaking the disks.
- People who phone to complain that their software says "press any key," but the keyboard has no key marked "Any," so there must be something wrong with the keyboard.

These cases are recorded in customer service reports as "advice given = RTFM" (clean translation being "Read the Flaming Manual").

## URBAN MYTHS ABOUT CUSTOMER SERVICE ARROGANCE

This story was circulated by e-mail in 2001. Its source is unknown:

This is a true story from the (software manufacturer) helpline that was transcribed from a recording monitoring the customer care department. Needless to say, the Help Desk employee was fired; however, he or she is currently suing the (software manufacturer) organization for "Termination without Cause." Actual dialogue of a former Customer Support employee:

"Computer assistance; may I help you?"

"Yes, well, I'm having trouble with your software."

"What sort of trouble?"

"Well, I was just typing along, and all of a sudden the words went away."

"Went away?"

"They disappeared."

"Hmm. So what does your screen look like now?"

"Nothing."

"Nothing?"

"It's blank; it won't accept anything when I type."

"Are you still in the package, or did you get out?"

"How do I tell?"

"Can you see the C: prompt on the screen?"

"What's a sea-prompt?"

"Never mind, can you move your cursor around the screen?"

"There isn't any cursor: I told you, it won't accept anything I type."

"Does your monitor have a power indicator?"

"What's a monitor?"

"It's the thing with the screen on it that looks like a TV. Does it have a little light that tells you when it's on?"

"I don't know."

"Well, then look on the back of the monitor and find where the power cord goes into it. Can you see that?"

"Yes, I think so."

"Great. Follow the cord to the plug, and tell me if it's plugged into the wall."

"Yes, it is."

"When you were behind the monitor, did you notice that there were two cables plugged into the back of it, not just one?"

"No."

"Well, there are. I need you to look back there again and find the other cable."

"Okay, here it is."

"Follow it for me, and tell me if it's plugged securely into the back of your computer."

"I can't reach."

"Uh huh. Well, can you see if it is?"

"No."

"Even if you maybe put your knee on something and lean way over?"

"Oh, it's not because I don't have the right angle—it's because it's dark."

"Dark?"

"Yes—the office light is off, and the only light I have is coming in from the window."

"Well, turn on the office light then."

"I can't."

"No? Why not?"

"Because there's a power failure."

"A power . . . A power failure? Aha, Okay, we've got it licked now.

"Do you still have the boxes and manuals and packing stuff your computer came in?"

"Well, yes, I keep them in the closet."

"Good. Go get them, and unplug your system and pack it up just like it was when you got it. Then take it back to the store you bought it from."

"Really? Is it that bad?"

"Yes, I'm afraid it is."

"Well, all right then, I suppose. What do I tell them?"

"Tell them you're too **** stupid to own a computer."

Computer-literate readers can dwell for a second on the inherent stupidity of their fellow beings and then consider the following lessons: (1) Even sophisticated company spokespeople can be arrogant, smug, and offensive to their paying customers, and their customers know it; and (2) they simply do not know how to listen. The preceding stories underscore the appalling quality of the manuals sent out with the equipment and software. Customers who study the tortured, jargon-loaded directions often cannot understand the basics of using the products they have bought. The other issue is that people on helplines have attitude problems of their own.

Contrast the attitudes and ineptness of these companies with the superb design of the "opening the box experience" by Hewlett-Packard. Consider the obsession of Intuit with listening to customer problems and service needs and then designing genuinely user-friendly software like Quicken (which even your authors can operate without resorting to the smug advice of the nearest 12-year-old computer nerd). The payoff from treating the customer service encounter as a learning event can be enormous, and no company can afford to ignore it.

## Customer Service and Customer Relationship Management

In these early years of the twenty-first century, customer relationship management (CRM) is proving to be the hottest thing around. Global expenditures are estimated to have built from $2.8 billion in 1998 to $9 billion in 2002.[11] These systems attempt to integrate data from all points of customer contact into a single data pool. Advocates claim that CRM is a "customer-responsive strategy" that can gain competitive advantage by personalizing company-customer interactions; demonstrating trustworthiness; tightening connections with customers; and coordinating complex company capabilities (functions, resources) around the customer.[12]

Early promises are that CRM can enhance customer retention, focusing resources on the "best" customers, while reducing service levels for others, or even "firing" unprofitable customers. Because the technology provides a basis for individualized responses to customer queries, it may also take companies closer to adaptive, "one-to-one," or dialogue marketing. Some experts foresee new positions, such as chief relationship officer or customer officer, to oversee company efforts in managing customer relationships.

Yet, despite massive expenditures and great promises, companies that see CRM as a substitute for a customer service strategy almost certainly will have problems. Building databases and warehouses is likely to achieve very little unless a company has a strategy and processes to use the information; otherwise, CRM will represent no more than the ability to annoy more customers faster than ever before.[13]

At the strategic level, three major issues are surfacing already. First, companies need to be extremely cautious when using CRM data to withdraw service from, or even to cease trading with, unprofitable customers. Management should be certain that they are not dumping customers who could become highly profitable in the future, when currently profitable customers cease to be so. They also must be confident that their measures of customer profitability are the right ones—as discussed earlier, using inappropriate financial measures can destroy a business.

Second, think ahead a few years. Once Siebel, Oracle, and SAP have become extremely rich (because we all have CRM technology), then where does the promised competitive advantage come from? Because everyone has the same systems, CRM ends up as a cost of being in the business, not a source of advantage. Today's advantages typically become tomorrow's prerequisites.

Third, CRM provides a mass of data about existing customers. It captures nothing about customers who are not yet in the market and little about customers who have rejected the company in favor of competitors. Companies in fast-changing markets with disruptive technologies on the near horizon can create a huge strategic vulnerability if they pay attention only to their existing customers.

Finally, although CRM is still in its early stages, the impact on customer service is too important to be left to the IT people. Total Integrated Marketing demands that managers look at customer service efforts as strategic investments to build and sustain a long-term market position, not as purely tactical spends that they can switch around in response to financial calculations. Long-term advantage depends on developing customer service capabilities that focus on changing service priorities in changing markets, not clinging slavishly to the demands of existing customers. Customer service priorities should reflect clear market strategy goals, not moribund management assumptions based on the past. The learning capabilities of the customer service organization have probably never been more important than at a time when CRM is dominating management thinking in many companies.

## OPERATIONAL CONSIDERATIONS

The confusion of customer service with marketing is one of the most common and frustrating service misunderstandings and is the source of considerable operational problems.

In the rush of enthusiasm to embrace customer service, many companies seem to have lost sight of the difference between marketing and customer service. The risk of that confusion is that they will fail to perform some essential marketing tasks to ensure their future. Although most companies compete in a world where service is becoming increasingly important, there is much more to marketing than customer service alone.

Some companies have spent large sums to teach employees how to help disgruntled customers instead of addressing the root causes of dissatisfaction.

Regardless of how well you treat customers, if your company's products are unreliable, you are probably going to have unhappy customers. The challenge is to improve delivery of the perceived values customers are seeking and to build the next generation of value drivers.

## Service Segmentation

Another important consideration is that different customers buy different values.[14] It follows that they will have different service needs. Choosing the appropriate level and type of service is a major challenge and may require special segmentation for that purpose.[15]

Consider tired business travelers, boarding an evening flight from New York to Europe, who know that they have to work the next day. Do they really want to be kept awake for as long as three or even four hours while an elaborate meal is served, or would they rather try to get some rest? Typically, the airlines do not even ask, even though a $6,000–$8,000 purchase decision is involved. One of the biggest U.S. airlines promotes an all-on-one tray executive platter, but when one of the authors requested this recently, he was told that only one such platter was on board the flight! Contrast that weary, semicomatose business traveler with the vacationers in nearby seats, who want every drink, movie, foodstuff, magazine, snack, and meal they can get, because they are too excited to sleep and the trip is a treat. Airline travelers value different things. Smart operators like Virgin Atlantic provide "Do Not Disturb" stickers for passengers who want to sleep without cabin crew interruptions, and even supply nicotine patches for smokers to ease them through their flights.

The appropriate matching of service type and level can simultaneously increase both effectiveness and efficiency. Under the right conditions, customers often will happily coproduce a service that saves them time and frustration, and probably cut costs for the supplier. Eating lunch in a fast-food restaurant on a workday provides a ready example, for most people then find self-service acceptable. The widespread preference for automatic teller machines over human tellers for simple banking tasks is another illustration of customer willingness to coproduce in the right circumstances. When discussing business with a prospective customer or seeking financial planning advice, however, the very same customer may find these options highly inappropriate.

Despite poor results, many service providers are inflexible and try to force standardized policies on their customers in a manner reminiscent of Henry Ford's Model T production line. No wonder new service companies like Virgin seen to achieve a high success rate! When Colin Marshall was CEO of British Airways, he was fond of pointing out that management will never eliminate all service problems no matter how hard they try. It is therefore crucial that service personnel have the wit, imagination, and empowered confidence to respond appropriately when the unexpected problem occurs.

## More than Anything Else, Beware of Success!

Few traits are more irritating than the tendency of service providers to treat the customer's time as valueless, and the supplier's time as invaluable. It is a blatant, and distressingly common, example of inward orientation. Market power is a good predictor of these problems. Government, being a monopoly supplier of most of its services, has typically had an appalling record in this regard. How many people have wasted countless hours waiting in line for driver's license renewal, customs and immigration, visas and passports? Yet worse, how many have even waited in line to pay local taxes, or received insensitive and inconsiderate service (alright, let's just say it, and guarantee that we get audited—plain rude, obnoxious, and obstructive service) from tax authorities whose salaries are paid through those same taxes? It is true that some politicians are belatedly realizing that such experiences may actually cause resentment among voters, but attempts at improvement have frequently met with little success.[16] Privatization and outsourcing of government-supplied services have become increasingly common responses to service failures among governments of virtually all political complexions.

As governments in many countries have introduced competition into transportation, telecommunications, and basic utility supply, a detectable shift in service attitudes typically has occurred. Offices that were only open at the seller's convenience are now likely to be open when the customer needs them. Representatives who previously had to "talk to a supervisor" suddenly seem to be empowered to resolve difficulties, and the general level of courtesy shows remarkable improvement. Truly, customer choice is the most powerful driver of market focus and customer orientation that we have ever experienced.

In marketing terms, monopoly means reaching the ultimate market share. The moral for all companies in the preceding examples is that the seeds of company failure are most often sown during good times. This is when firms typically make unwise acquisitions at premium prices, diversify into businesses they know too little about, and build the overheads that bring bankruptcy in recession.

At Columbia Business School, we run what is arguably the single most successful executive program in marketing in the world. For many years, we have been auditing groups of managers, asking them to fill out a market-focus questionnaire for their companies prior to coming to the program. During the expansion of the earlier part of the 1990s, there was a significant rise in these companies' customer focus scores—no doubt a lagged effect of the late 1980s/early 1990s recession. By late 1995/early 1996, however, the tide turned, and the scores began to trend downward. There is nothing like success to build arrogance toward customers, and the full order books of the late 1990s led many companies to become less customer-responsive. Such companies inevitably will suffer in the inevitable slower growth period that has followed such an expansion.

This problem was summarized with chilling eloquence in *The Financial Times:*

> If there is a long-term threat to Microsoft and Intel, it will come in the first instance from within. Just at the moment their dominance seems most assured, the curse of monopoly will be gradually eating away at the company's success. The desire to preserve compatibility with previous products at all costs; the belief in a divine right to market share; a profound trust of the bona fides of competitors—these are the penalties that the gift of monopoly brings.[17]

## Watch All Points of Contact—They Are Watching You

Companies that developed first-class customer-service organizations may be forgiven for assuming that they had taken care of their service problems. However, Jan Carlzon, president of SAS, coined the phrase "moments of truth" to emphasize that each service provider/customer interaction is an opportunity for either customer satisfaction or dissatisfaction.[18] Telephonists, delivery personnel, and credit departments often can create or lose a customer forever. Consider the experience one of the authors had with a well-known travel service card company.[19] It illustrates how to lose a customer forever.

### YOU SHOULDN'T HAVE MADE ME ANGRY, PEOPLE . . .

Arriving in the office one morning, this particular author received several pink telephone message slips from the floor receptionist. One of these was a request to call an "800" phone number. On calling the number, the first statement he heard was, "Gimme your card number." Since he had no idea to whom he was talking, he promptly hung up. On reflection, however, it occurred to him that since he carried no credit cards, and only a few rarely used gas company cards, this was probably the travel service card company with which he had maintained a perfect payment record for almost 20 years. He therefore called the company back, and this time a service person politely answered with the company's name. After discussion with this person, he determined that the company had not received that month's payments. Two checks, personal and business, were involved, and after giving the company the numbers and dates of the checks, the service person advised waiting until the following Monday and calling back to see if the checks had been found. On the following Monday, they had still not arrived, and after some discussion, the author agreed to reissue checks. Since one check was small, but the other large, the company's service person recommended that he call his bank and stop payment on the larger check, which he promptly did.

About 10 days later, he received a message on his home answering machine telling him to call the company's credit department between the hours of 9 A.M. and 5 P.M. (Customer service was a 24-hour operation; credit clearly wasn't!) On returning the call, he was grilled as to why his check had "bounced." This occurred although the account was fully paid for the month. The record subsequently showed that the company had cashed (or, at least attempted to cash) four checks in the same month (two each for identical amounts). The customer service person who had assured the author that the history of the decisions had been entered into the company's information system either misled him, or—more likely—the credit department hadn't checked.

Not long after this episode, two events occurred right after each other. First, the CEO was replaced, a move long overdue, and pleasing to the embittered author, for it was clear to shareholders and observers alike that the CEO was more interested in the social scene than in running the company. Then the bill with the next annual membership fee arrived. The highest level of membership was expensive, and premium credit cards were matching the service at lower cost. The author, who had been charging over $50,000 a year on this card, decided not to renew because he had been treated rudely and without consideration of his record. He did so by writing a personal letter to the new CEO, welcoming him to the job. He also explained why he was not renewing his membership and pointed out that the reasons were indicative of the task the CEO faced. Along with the letter went the final payments, again in the form of two checks. Not only did the author not receive a reply to the letter, but, about a week later, his wife received a phone call from a person who claimed to be one of the new CEO's assistants. This caller became quite rude and abusive when it transpired that they had lost the final payment checks! One can only assume that she opened the envelope, read the letter and carelessly threw the envelope, assumed to be empty, away along with the bill and the checks. Once again, the checks had to be reissued.

The author immediately started using a credit card issued by Citibank (now part of Citigroup) and has received exemplary service. The new CEO of the travel service card company eventually succeeded in reinvigorating the firm, though the company never again achieved its previous preeminent position. The net present value of Citicorp's gain from the author's switching was considerable, but the loss to the other company was largely the result of the actions of the credit department, not customer service. The subsequent treatment by the CEO's assistant, however, served to completely remove any doubts that might have surfaced after the decision.

Oh, are business school professors customers from hell, or what? They don't just tell 20 people about bad customer experiences—they try to tell every executive and MBA participant in the world![20]

In addition to judgments customers make about their own interactions with company personnel, they also may observe interactions between the company and other customers. For many manufacturers, much customer contact, and hence perception of service, occurs not with their own employees, but with employees of other firms such as their distributors. This makes the management of customer service an even greater challenge. Globally, auto manufacturers are fighting to update and control their moribund dealer channels before direct marketers and the Internet have major impact with offers to customers that traditional distributors cannot emulate.

To complicate matters yet further, other customers and their behavior are often a critical factor in the service experience. Many services occur in group settings so that the nature, dress, and behavior of fellow customers affects service perception. For many passengers, the perception of the airline travel experience is closely correlated with the number of young children in close proximity. Some airlines make strenuous efforts to separate business-class travelers from tourists even before check-in and certainly afterward, not least because some businesspeople have issues with the diminutive persons' predilection for making contact between their half-eaten candies and half-drunk sodas and the businessperson's apparel. Similarly, the enjoyment of a cruise or resort holiday may be critically dependent on other guests.[21]

Rarely are goods producers concerned that sales to certain customers (or customer types) will have a negative impact (although they may refuse sales because of postpurchase service considerations).[22] In contrast, this is a critical issue for many service providers who put in place systems for refusing to deal with some customers who want to purchase their services, but whom they do not want to serve. Examples include nightclub bouncers, admission departments of educational institutions, and maitre d's in certain restaurants.

Despite the general dictum of marketing practitioners that "the customer is always right," in many settings—especially when other customers are present—service delivery personnel must be empowered to ignore this blanket rule. This may seem to be the ultimate in the targeting of customers, but the implications go further. The drunken airline passenger, the rowdy soccer fan, the sleeping MBA student in a finance class, the baseball fan behind home plate shouting out the home-team pitcher's upcoming pitches,[23] and the abusive and/or uncooperative customer not only may find the service unsatisfactory, but also may destroy service value for all customers—and the company must take this seriously. The advice to watch all points of contact includes contacts among customers as well as between the company and the customer.

## Changing Communication Vehicles: Managing the Old and the New

Internet-based business has already had a major effect on how suppliers and customers communicate with each other. It has also empowered consumers, who not only have moved from primarily passive to active and interactive capability, but for the first time have acquired a modicum of broadcast capability.[24] Internet communication is proving to be an efficient and effective way to deal with many customer service problems, as well as becoming a powerful tool for remarketing to the existing customer base. Dell is leveraging its Internet capabilities to move from customer service to "e-service," so that the computer phones home to Dell to describe the problem, and the two systems sort it out between themselves, before the user gets involved.

When difficult problems arise, the telephone usually becomes the key contact, and for many companies this is likely to be the case for some time to come. Yet, in developing their phone systems, many companies still seem focused on cost reduction instead of customer service. How many times have you been assigned to telephone automation hell? No surer way to lose customers can be invented than to trap them in an infinite "do" loop. In comparison, although it may seem a small issue, we are still staggered at how poorly some companies manage their central switchboards, and how the basics of telephone etiquette do not seem to be part of their training arsenal. Existing customers, particularly those with an ongoing working relationship with the company, are likely to have direct extension connections. Central numbers, however, disproportionately receive calls from two important kinds of customers: new prospects who don't have a direct number to call, and customers in trouble, who for one reason or another, don't have a direct extension number. These are acquisition and retention opportunities, but poorly trained switchboard operators are unlikely to recognize them as such.

The hours of operation of the corporate switchboard are also a symbolic but real customer service signal. It is patently obvious that in a global world, a global company is conducting business somewhere or other 24 hours a day, seven days a week. This simple observation has not appeared to cross the minds of some of those persons responsible for staffing switchboards. Even worse, such a trivial matter as staffing for longer telephone hours can be important to a firm operating nationally or regionally. A couple of years ago, at 4:35 P.M. on a Tuesday afternoon, one of the authors telephoned the headquarters of a New Jersey-based multinational with $7 billion annual revenue. His purpose was to reconfirm a meeting early the next morning. He received the following message: "This is the world headquarters of [name omitted]. Our office hours are 9:30 A.M. until 4:30 P.M. If this is an emergency, call security on . . ."

If a large company finds it difficult to staff locally for extended hours, technology also has an answer, for calls can be easily switched from office to office in different time zones to provide continuous seamless service to customers, no matter at what hour they call. Call centers are increasingly located in areas of the world where there is a surplus of trained labor at low cost, India being one of the major suppliers of personnel.

## HOW TO DO IT RIGHT

One of the authors was in Europe and called late at night to reconfirm a flight. The British Airways (BA) line answered immediately: "One moment please while your call is switched to New York." A pleasant American voice promptly answered and dealt with the reconfirmation. The caller then asked what the weather was like, to which the customer service representative asked why he would want to know the weather in Dallas when he was going to New York!*

*This example is from the halcyon days of British Airways under Colin Marshall.

Apart from the minor, but humorous, snafu at the end of the interaction, this is a great illustration of the concept of Total Integrated Marketing. Strange as this may sound to American ears, at the time of this experience, many European airlines had restricted hours on their reservations lines. Not only did BA provide the service, they were clever enough to add a little message to tell customers that their call was being switched to the United States. Thus, besides providing a service, the airline, with a simple phrase, communicated to customers how much it cared for them and their call, and did so in a way that distinguished BA from its competitors.

The new medium of the Internet and e-mail needs to refine many of the same customer service principles. Although improvements are occurring, many Web sites are not yet customer friendly. As large and small companies have joined the rush to the Web, they have not always asked themselves some obvious customer-oriented questions. Navigating around some sites is still inordinately difficult; and a user who has previously registered on a site, but has now forgotten a password or username, can find it painfully difficult to reenter—even though this is a common problem. Perhaps more fundamental than faulty Web site design, however, are the annoying attempts by some companies to shore up distribution relationships and discriminatory pricing practices by preventing customers from ordering over the Web. The shipping point and crediting of an order is irrelevant to most customers, but the unwillingness to accept an order is likely to send the customer clicking off to a more broad-minded competitor, or even—dread of dreads—to a new Internet-based start-up. Nitpickers may argue this is a distribution issue, not a customer service issue. We say, get your head out from the sand. The customer doesn't compartmentalize that way, and neither should you. Where I want it, when I want it is the new mantra!

For many purposes, e-mail is a great means of communication. It's economical; it avoids error-producing intermediaries like receptionists, assistants, and secretaries (but so does voice mail); and it leaves a trail that can sometimes be helpful in tricky service situations. However, customer service principles still apply. Prompt and polite responses should be the goal. It is worth remembering that there are times when a personal touch can work wonders, and the telephone call will pay dividends. We can't give blanket advice on when to shift modes, but properly trained service personnel should be empowered to make these decisions.

## TOTAL INTEGRATED MARKETING: MANAGING THE CUSTOMER SERVICE/MARKETING INTERFACE

The major challenge facing a company that wants to develop competitive advantage through customer service is its dependency on humans. This is inevitable in most service delivery systems. Some companies try to deal with this problem by automating as much of their service systems as possible. Banks have been leading proponents of this approach, which can work well for routine activities. Advances in artificial intelligence, expert systems, voice recognition, and information technology promise to expand the range of service problems amenable to automation significantly as the twenty-first century progresses.

Other companies, however, have concluded that since some firms find it difficult to deliver superior service through human resources, automation might provide a relatively nonimitable competitive advantage. Leading hotels and airlines use this approach. Although automation works well for routine service delivery, in special or crisis situations, human intervention is almost always necessary.

For automation partisans, these problematic requests for service have serious potential for alienating and losing customers. Careful attention to the design of the service system, and to selection, training, and reward systems can play a key role in achieving service superiority. Even in competitive markets, high levels of service can earn correspondingly high customer loyalty over significant periods of time, and therein lies the opportunity. The economics of relationship marketing are now well enough understood that we can be confident about the rewards from ensuring customer loyalty.

Managers committed to Total Integrated Marketing face a complex and demanding task in the customer service area. Customers' points of contact with the company (moments of truth) are not limited to superbly trained customer service staff. As noted, their most frequent direct contact is often over the telephone, but in addition to switchboard operators, these customers may well interact with truck drivers (owned or outsourced delivery services), production schedulers and shipping departments, and the dreaded credit department. The trend toward outsourcing will multiply the difficulties of implementing consistent, high-quality customer service. It is difficult enough to achieve these service goals with the company's own employees, but it becomes much more complicated in an extended network, outsourced business environment (a virtual organization). Specialists in different aspects of the total service function (e.g., FedEx) will undoubtedly emerge, but managing a total system with many outsourced contributors will remain a challenging coordination task.

Within your firm, after outsourcing reaches its culmination, there is no substitute for imbuing the whole organization with the precepts and values of customer orientation. We address this and other topics more fully in Chapter 12.

Over the next few years, the customer service function will probably undergo a difficult and politically awkward transition. Again, the driver is likely to be the information-technology-driven shift to what we have called the relationship marketing model. As noted in Chapter 8, this change has resulted in a rethinking of the relationship between marketing and sales, and in many cases a redefinition and even reorganization of the activities of both functions. Parallel changes seem in prospect for customer service. We have worked with companies where customer service reported to departments as diverse as finance, operations, and the commercial function. Its natural home in a functional organization is in marketing, but where that is not the case, marketers committed to Total Integrated Marketing must take the lead in working across boundaries to ensure that customer service is part of the market strategy. Their long-term task should be to remove internal boundaries by educating other functions about relationship marketing and the central role that customer service should play in the economic strategy. Until the boundaries are removed, a significant challenge will remain.

It is perhaps an ironic coincidence that concern for the customer has led to misplaced emphasis on service in some firms. We are enthusiastic advocates of customer service, and there are substantial opportunities to add value—but only if companies focus service efforts on the areas that matter to customers.

Responsive service will not compensate for basic deficiencies in the core product. Nor is the undifferentiated "just give them more of whatever we happen to have on hand" approach likely to be any more successful in the area of service than it is elsewhere. Companies must match service in type and level to the occasion and the customer. The saving grace is that many important services involve personal delivery. Although this may lead to the classic control-of-quality difficulties often quoted in the service literature, the potential remains to deliver customized, responsive service through a superbly flexible operations system—the human resource. When the inevitable problems occur, management must aim for flexibility and responsiveness and this is where the organization's human resources are a key competitive advantage.

# MARKETING AND HUMAN RESOURCES

## PARTNERSHIPS AROUND PEOPLE

Personnel departments have long had a poor reputation. That would change if HR professionals were to behave more like business executives.
Michael Skapinker[1]

How do you run an organization without people? The answer, of course, is that you can't. Nevertheless, it appears to be the goal of some of today's chief executives. Even dot-coms can't operate without people. The sensible reduction of overstaffing to become a more competitive, leaner, and profitable business is an unavoidable management responsibility. It reflects the impact of technology on systems, internal efficiencies, and variations in service levels necessary to deliver marketing offers to customers. It is a rational and reasonable procedure.

On the other hand, to wastefully squander a firm's stock of knowledge, needlessly ruin personal lives, and quite possibly advantage a competitor is somewhat less rational. This may sound patronizing and simplistic. If that is your reaction, try explaining why talented individuals leave major companies, only to become key contributors for a competitor or even to become the new competitor. When competition relied primarily on the acquisition and exploitation of tangible assets, perhaps the human factor did not weigh so heavily. In the new world of twenty-first-century competition, however, knowledge and intellectual capital will be the determining factors. This mandates a different approach to the organization's human resources.

This is the age of networks and strategic alliances, of outsourcing, of downsizing, of completely new organizational forms. Notwithstanding

**249**

these miracles of modern business, a simple and unavoidable truth remains. It is people who buy products, sell products, and deliver service. It is people who determine how customers feel about the experience of buying from the company. It is people who have ideas about how to do things better. These truths are so blindingly obvious that some companies appear to have forgotten about them.

It gets better. In fact, the emerging business era does not just mean that people are as important as they always were. It signifies that companies must depend on the learning skills, enhanced capabilities, superior commitment, and total engagement of their people more than ever before. Pine and Gilmore describe the transition to an "experience economy," where the goal is not simply selling goods and services, but creating experiences that engage customers in a highly personal and memorable way.[2] The essence of their view of the future is that ingenuity, innovation, and renewal precede sustained revenue growth. They describe the Minneapolis computer installation and repair company that calls itself the Geek Squad; its "special agents" dress as geeks, drive old cars, and turn a boring activity into such a memorable experience that customers buy T-shirts and lapel pins from the company's Web site. They describe the spectacular Rainforest Café, where mist rises from rocks to stimulate the senses, jungle noises pervade the background, and the mundane host announcement "Your table is ready" has been replaced with "Your adventure is about to begin . . ." Underpinning the creation of customer experiences to tap into new sources of value is the commitment and capability of our people to design and deliver these positive and memorable customer experiences. If "work is theatre" and "every business a stage," you need to worry about how good your "actors" are and how well you look after them.

Although most managers know about managing hierarchy and systems, the new imperative is to manage talent—possibly the most important competitive resource of all. It is also generally in short supply. Microsoft's Bill Gates may be one of the richest men in the world—feted by presidents and prime ministers wherever he goes—but he also sees no activity as more important than meeting superior employment candidates to convince them they should join Microsoft.[3] New economy visionaries Ridderstrale and Nordstrom, with their "funky business" philosophy, believe that a company's only unique asset is the brains of its employees. In that sense, employees' ideas and imagination are the company, and that is how executives must manage.[4] In many ways, the critical issue for companies has become "competing for talent." One manager describes the change required: "We must think of our companies less in product-market terms, and more as collectors of great people."[5]

This said, some managers are going to have to learn to bite their tongues and keep quiet when faced with the new demands of talented people who know about competitiveness and the shortages of skills. Required employee benefits may now extend to minding the baby, walking the dog, doing the marketing, planning vacations in "lifestyle management" packages, or providing "napping rooms" at work. One U.S. company recently found itself exhuming an employee's dead dog to move it to his new address as part of a relocation package.[6] It may seem ridiculous, but such demands are really not a trivial matter.

Some companies have already been driven to appoint chief morale officers to manage talent retention. In that context, the average tenure for chief executives of the Fortune 1000 companies in the United States (and the FT 100 in Great Britain) is under four years and falling![7]

In this chapter, we explore the significance of a firm's human resources as the key source of long-term competitive advantage. This is truly a corporate-level issue. We also explore the rapidly changing role of the oft-maligned human resources department. As firms restructure to compete in the marketplace, their reorganizations, flattening of structures, and expanded use of teams have put great stress on a function not typically hailed for its effectiveness. Change management has become a necessity for many large companies, yet most have found it to be a difficult task.

Finally, the fundamental changes taking place in marketing indicate the urgent need for heavy revisions in traditional recruitment and development practices, as well as the contract between the company and its employees. Direct marketers and service companies have so far been on the leading edge of these changes, but the power of database marketing and the Internet strongly suggest that virtually no company will remain unaffected. The human resource function will be critical to maintaining business competitiveness and could be the most important of all the traditional functions of the firm in achieving the changes described in this book.

In many companies, the time is ripe for building positive and value-creating relationships between executives who deal with customers (often in marketing departments at present) and executives who deal with employees (often in human resources departments at present). Human resource management grew out of old-style personnel management in the 1980s, reflecting the attempt to integrate people-problems with line management. These departments often use the term "strategic human resource management" to describe their expanded role. It is nearly a decade since management experts proposed the full-scale integration of marketing and personnel functions,[8] and maybe this idea is finally coming of age. Unlike traditional approaches to personnel management, strategic human resource management fits perfectly with Total Integrated Marketing.

# STRATEGIC RELATIONSHIPS

We began our quest for Total Integrated Marketing by stating our commitment to shareholder value, then linking this to customer value. However, value is created for neither shareholders nor customers, without people. Human resources are the ultimate source of competitive advantage, and in the following pages we explore the implications of Total Integrated Marketing for the strategic management of this asset. Consequently, we consider what this means for the relationship between marketing and human resource management. The following capabilities are usually described as sources of competitive advantage.

## Research and Development

Much quoted as a source of competitive advantage, unexpired patents can certainly be a key resource for many companies. They might not view the intellectual property in patents as a human resource. However, the ability to enhance product and service value results from past human endeavor, which the firm probably paid for. To ensure future advantage, moreover, the firm must have productive researchers in place and working. Management's recognition and support of the research team's efforts are key to ongoing success. Reducing funding for such efforts means that individuals are likely to leave the team, and the consequences may set back an effort by many months, years, or even indefinitely.

When President Carter canceled development of the B1 bomber, Rockwell management recognized that there was a strong possibility that a subsequent Republican president might reinstate the program. They took a step that seemed remarkable at the time. In the defense industry, notorious for hiring and firing, they developed a strategy for retaining the B1 engineering team. They temporarily set up a "rent-an-engineer" program that allowed Rockwell to keep the necessary human resources in place to permit quickly restarting the program. The election of Ronald Reagan confirmed its judgment, and the program, once revived, moved to completion much faster than would otherwise have been possible. Rockwell understood that in R&D the key resource is the human resource. We examined the marketing/R&D relationship in Chapter 9, but we must vigorously underline the hidden role of human resource management in nurturing that relationship.

## Sales Force

Another familiar source of advantage is the company's sales capability. It takes little insight to conclude that salespeople and the skills they possess are essential to marketing success. The devastation that companies typically experience when competitors recruit a group of their key salespersons provides ample evidence for this view. Indeed, the growing role of key account management places salespeople and their skills at the heart of the firm's relationship with its most important customers, as discussed in Chapter 8.

## Distribution System

Although distribution arrangements may be grounded in commercial law, their effectiveness depends on the strength of the relationships created over time. The opportunity for mutual profit must be present, but the human factor is also likely to be crucial. Marketing executives are fond of drawing charts picturing their distribution channels and highlighting channel shares and dominance. This is a complete illusion, unless they remember that the ties of personal relationships hold those channel systems together.

## Customer Service

As stressed in Chapter 10, people are central to customer service, in offensive, defensive, and learning modes. They are especially critical in crisis situations, which are "make-or-break" opportunities for customer retention.

## Operations

Despite the high levels of automation in many factories today, management of the manufacturing process, as well as a significant percentage of its operations, depends on human resources. The quality movement, contrary to many people's understanding, is largely about people—how they are deployed and how they work together. It was not until executives recognized this that the quality process began to work. As described in Chapter 7, the extension of traditional operations systems into integrated supply chains reinforces the importance of the relationship with marketing, and once more emphasizes that human resource management plays a hidden role in brokering that relationship.

We could continue with these examples for pages. It is difficult to think of any competitive marketing advantage that does not fundamentally depend on people. In fact, that is the whole point of Total Integrated Marketing—when you get down to it, in the effective organization, everybody markets.

If you need more convincing, consider the observation of a somewhat contrarian friend of ours that it is certainly possible to view the source of all competitive *dis*-advantage as the human factor. This reinforces our view of the pivotal importance of human resources and perhaps also underlines that these resources are often poorly managed.

One of the most productive things managers can do is to review the company's relative human resource strengths across its different functions compared with the competition. As a manager, you should ask, Where do we have strengths that we are not fully exploiting, and where are we losing out because a competitor has attracted, developed, and retained people with superior abilities? The results may change your priorities.

## Knowledge, People, and Competitive Advantage

Back in the mid-1980s when Peter Drucker urged managers to recognize the emergence of knowledge as the key to business success in the future economy, we are absolutely sure that he did not equate knowledge solely with the installation of sophisticated information systems. Powerful though they may be when successfully implemented, they are only part of the story. When James Brian Quinn wrote *The Intelligent Enterprise*,[9] we are equally sure that he understood that most of a firm's knowledge resided in the heads of its people, not in its formal information systems.

This recognition has only belatedly arrived in the heads of senior executives, and even then in relatively few firms. Anyone who has worked with a company that has unselectively "opened the window" to lose people will recognize the facts. The most mobile and marketable individuals are often the ones who depart, and large-scale layoffs may leave the firm without crucial skills. It is not at all uncommon to find such firms hiring back laid-off employees and executives as consultants, at even higher cost.

We do not denigrate the often-brave and usually painful actions that senior managers may have to undertake to align employment levels and types with company needs. Many firms accumulate fat in good times, and such cutbacks become necessary. When technologies and market demands change, companies sometimes have to adjust the number and available skills of employees in their workforce.

Nonetheless, the way that managers take these actions reveals that often they lack insight into their companies' real sources of long-term strategic advantage. In some cases, cost-cutting managers do not even achieve their short-term goals. The authors have experienced more than one case where temporary employees hired after cutbacks actually exceeded the number originally laid off. Without the excessive moralizing that characterizes consultants with 20:20 hindsight, we need to point out that it is those who permitted payrolls to bloat in the first place who are the root cause of these problems. Often, though, these executives are long departed, and others pay the cost of their decisions, as they run the salvage operation and endure the vilification (often public) that accompanies their efforts.

A company's need for all types of people ultimately depends on its market position—and on its marketing actions to hold and improve that market position over the long term. The marketing/human resource management interface cuts both ways, which is why it matters more than most.

There are positive indications that some firms can and do nurture and develop sources of people-based competitive advantage by strategic human resources management. An inventory of human resources capabilities should place priorities on these areas of advantage, and the people who work in them. The capabilities of crucial individuals should be marshaled, nurtured, and developed. Scenario analysis, envisaging the implications of the departure of key individuals should help management determine whether to offer specific service contracts. At least in our experience, senior managers often have such contracts, but key specialists rarely do, which seems the exact reverse of what would be advisable.

Companies that recognize a hierarchy of knowledge are also attempting to codify the knowledge of their employees. The hype surrounding the concept of the "learning organization" sometimes reaches amusing heights (and even really irritating ones). A memory is necessary to learn, and there is little collective memory in any organization we have worked with (though interestingly some firms are now working on developing one). Yet, unless companies change their ways, their information systems will do little more than record accounting results; they will miss the invaluable "soft data" in the heads of not only executives, but skilled machine operators and others throughout the organization.

It is often surprising how much employees know about things like customers and how much senior managers can learn from that source. Kimberly-Clark's solution to the problem of extending the customer lifetime value of wearers of disposable diapers did not come from technological innovation from R&D nor from the marketing department. It came from young employees who would talk with young customers and tell stories. From these stories came the Huggies training pant (looks like pants, but is actually a diaper), to please parents—not babies. Learning is not about rocket science: It is about people. Recognizing that fact debunks much of the hype about learning organizations and puts learning people center stage.

Not least among the imperatives for Total Integrated Marketing is the challenge to manage company talent and capabilities for maximum advantage, instead of obsessing with structure, status, and functional demarcation lines. One of the authors had the somewhat depressing experience of spending a day with a group of senior managers from the financial services industry to evaluate the impact of technology on their business. The reason for his depression was that, by the end of the day, the discussion had become stuck on the question, "Should we give the salespeople laptop computers?" This was less surprising than it might have been because the room was filled with middle-age males wearing business suits, whose status as company general managers established their right to be there. Reflection suggests that we might have had greater success in putting our minds around the technology revolution in financial services by inviting their secretaries or teenage children instead. Being the boss does not mean that you know more than other people in the company, but it should indicate that you are more prepared to learn. Too often, it does not.

## Managing Change

Effectively managing major organizational change remains one of the most difficult tasks for managers of established corporations; to a great extent this is a human resources issue. To accomplish change, either the present employees must develop new perspectives or new employees must join the organization. Both options represent a significant challenge, but environmental pressures mandate these changes in many companies. The sources of resistance are many and varied. The following problems are contributing factors.

Fixed Investment in Plant and Equipment.   Firms are frequently unwilling to scrap "in-the-ground" assets even when the market shifts against them and they fail to satisfy evolving customer needs. Faced with writing off a perfectly serviceable plant, many firms opt to continue with the status quo. Management may attempt to persuade customers that their current products and services are optimal or may refuse to believe market signals suggesting changed requirements. Managers responsible for publishing *Encyclopaedia Britannica* were told that the CD-ROM would change their business, but they refused to accept that the market was changing and continued printing books. Only a few years later, the company's sales force was disbanded, and the encyclopedia was made available free on the Internet, generating revenues from advertising and hot links for its new Swiss owner.

Rigidities in the Line Organization.   Although task specialization makes bureaucracy an efficient organizational tool for completing repetitive tasks, it becomes a dead weight when markets change. As corporations grow, the bureaucratic model leads to functional specialization, and rules and behaviors become embedded, often reinforced by day-to-day work pressures. Specialization can be important in developing the expertise to perform effectively. But frequently, specialization lacks mechanisms for encouraging lateral communication and cooperation across different specializations. As a result, the organizational units operate as functional silos, and the organization responds to change poorly and slowly, if at all. Lou Gerstner's turnaround strategy for IBM in the 1990s stressed the need to break free from the culture and power base of the traditional geographic sales organization.

**Short-Term Pressures for Efficiency, Cost Reduction, and Profit Maximization.** Specialization brings with it expectations about the efficiency of organizational subunits. For example, manufacturing strives to reduce unit costs, and sales attempts to maximize sales. A single-minded drive for efficiency by individual subunits rarely results in effective behavior for the whole organization. Instead, it generates destructive conflict resolved by internally focused compromise to the benefit of competitors and the detriment of shareholders. Ineffective goal-setting or reward systems can aggravate these pressures. One problem with total quality management in operations was that it frequently became more important to prevent internal customers (other departments) from complaining, than to worry about value to the paying external customer.

**Presence of a Dominant Culture.** All organizations have cultures that guide the everyday behavior patterns of their members. Organizational cultures typically develop over long periods and may be highly resistant to change. One or more functional areas often dominate organizational decision making. A culture in which operations personnel are dominant is likely to favor actions that improve operating efficiency[10]; a culture in which CEOs consistently are selected from the sales force is likely to follow actions favoring a sales orientation, and so forth.[11] Marks & Spencer, the once-mighty British retailer, was outpaced by competitors it did not take seriously. Now it is struggling to modify a strong, inwardly focused culture, where most senior executives have worked their way up through the business. By the end of the 1990s, there was a slow realization that recovery would depend on recruiting new leadership from outside the company and removing a blockade of middle-management culture carriers. Cultures can be changed, but the process may not be pretty.

**Social Fabric of Institutions.** Individuals in organizations know, and interact with, each other on a day-by-day basis, year in and year out. Sometimes, they may treat customers, competitors, and suppliers as intruders to dispose of before resuming the real business of the workday. This attitude is especially damaging when it occurs among front-line employees in service organizations. One employer attempted to address this problem with the following admonition:

> The customer is the most important person in our business. The customer is not dependent on us; we are dependent on him. The customer is not an interruption of our work; he is the purpose of it. A customer does us a favor when he comes to see us; we aren't doing him a favor by waiting on him. A customer is part of our business, not an outsider. He is not just money in the cash register; he is a human being with feelings like our own. He comes to us with his needs and wants, it's our job to fill them. A customer deserves the most courteous attention we can give him. He is the life-blood of this and every business. He pays your salary. Without him we would have to close our doors. Don't ever forget it.[12]

Reward Systems.    By and large, people in organizations do what is "inspected" rather than what is "expected." They tend to pursue results that produce rewards, and to a degree, they would be irrational to do otherwise. Goal setting and reward systems that reinforce internal perspectives encourage behavior consistent with those perspectives. Operations managers who are rewarded for driving down costs are likely to resist broadening the product line by adding new products. Conversely, sales managers rewarded for sales volume are unlikely to take kindly to trimming the product line. And engineers anxious to produce new products will not want to wait for market research or worry about the firm's ability to produce their designs at reasonable cost.

### YOU GET WHAT YOU PAY FOR—EVEN IF IT IS NOT WHAT YOU WANT

One of the authors addressed a workshop of senior auto distributor managers. All agreed that their key issue was customer relationship management to build repeat business and referrals. All pay their managers and salespeople volume-based commission. None pay additional bonus or commission for repeat sales to the same customer or for customer referral business. They were shocked that the speaker would even suggest such a thing and thought the idea was absurd. Unsurprisingly, most report frustration that their people persistently ignore relationship marketing strategies and go for one-off sales transactions. The speaker's unanswered question: Why would their salespeople care about relationships, when they are rewarded solely for volume?

**Resistance to Change.** Most large organizations need some predictability to function effectively. This requirement sometimes results in rigidity through programmed "standard operating procedures," creating an entrenched preference for the status quo that is a powerful barrier to change.[13] Furthermore, many managers prefer "a quiet life": It is much more comfortable to continue current practices than to undertake the new and different behavior mandated by external change. To be philosophical, organizational change is a drama that creates its dramatic tension out of the conflict between the natural human desire for stability and the apprehension created by change.[14] (Of course, in companies where "change" is a synonym for "downsizing," and everyone knows it, why would people welcome "change"?) The practical point is that this tension may be destructive.[15] Resolving the tension created by the need to change is one of the hallmarks of a successful leader.

**Information Systems.** Many firms' systems do not produce data that assist in early or correct diagnosis of problems (or, indeed, opportunities). As a result, even if management identifies the problem and finds an effective solution, the firm may have insufficient time to implement the necessary actions. Time and time again, companies make huge investments to record the historical past more precisely, but reject the crude indicators that suggest what is going wrong, with potential repercussions on the future. These information systems reinforce and legitimize the stranglehold of the "competitive box" that managers put around their familiar competitors and technologies, and leave them wrong-footed when new competitors and innovative business models attack. The massive impact of no-frills air carriers in the lucrative internal European flight market (e.g., Ryanair and easyJet) was highly predictable, but the conventional air carriers largely discounted it, leading to a weak, imitative response of attempting to launch their own no-frills operations.[16]

Largely because of difficulties like these, senior managers are turning to their human resources professionals to guide the change process. In some cases, this is explicit—Eagle Star, a Swiss-owned insurance company, was the first we know of to have a senior executive whose visiting card actually read "Change Manager." Her brief as an HR specialist was to provide support and assistance to managers throughout the business in building and managing their change programs.

The restructuring accompanying globalization and other strategic changes driven by the marketplace has led to a potentially serious problem. The recognition that change is needed does not automatically mean that firms know what they wish to become. As noted in Chapter 4, these choices represent extremely difficult and challenging corporate strategy decisions. Yet in the past several years, so-called change management experts have arrived on the scene who seem more preoccupied with the change process than with the desired outcome.

Since each firm is unique, we are not foolish enough to suggest standardizing the content of change programs. What we can do is to emphasize the argument that underpins the whole of our book. As markets globalize and information becomes cheaper and more easily available, all our marketplaces will become more competitive. To succeed in such markets, firms must widen and deepen their marketing capabilities. This means much more than being customer-focused (you may want to reread Chapter 1 to remind yourself how narrow conceptions of marketing can lead companies astray). Elsewhere, we have used the term "External Orientation" to summarize the general direction of change.[17] Table 11.1 highlights the contrast between the internal orientations that provide a starting point for many firms, and the external orientation that will likely be necessary to prosper in the twenty-first century. Successfully accomplishing a shift from an internal to an external orientation requires that the firm's human resources internalize the new imperatives and act accordingly.

| | *Internal* | *External* |
|---|---|---|
| Focus | Products | Markets |
| Know-how | Inherent in patents, machiner | Inherent in people, processes |
| Process | Mass production | Mass customization |
| Communications | Mass media | Tailored |
| Priorities | Efficiency and Productivity | Flexibility and responsiveness |
| Measurement | Profit, margin, volume | Value, satisfaction, retention |
| Customer perspective | Transactional | Relational |
| Organizational philosophy | Bureaucracy | Adhocracy |

Table 11.1  GENERAL CHARACTERISTICS OF INTERNAL AND EXTERNAL ORIENTATIONS. Adapted from S. H. Haeckel, "Adaptive Enterprise: The Sense and Respond Model," *Planning Review*, 42. (May/June 1995), 7–13. For a more expansive explanation, see S. H. Haeckel, *Adaptive Enterprise: Creating and Leading Sense-and-Respond Organizations* (Boston: Harvard Business School Press, 1999).

The key is recognizing that the outcome of the change, no matter what it is labeled, must be an organization that retains significant capacity for self-regeneration. It has to be capable of learning and of changing. In a static environment, this would not be necessary, but there are no static environments left—just managers who think there are and behave accordingly until they permanently damage their companies.

One of our distinguished colleagues who teaches organizational behavior is fond of representing the change process by drawing a simple diagram **A → B,** where **A** represents the starting point of the organization, → denotes the change process, and **B** is the ending point. This is a deceptive way of presenting the problem, for it fails to highlight that in a changing environment, **B** must be capable of renewal or change. One of the reasons that organizational change proves to be such a problem for many companies is that they have accepted the palpably false premise that change is the unusual event, and that lack of change is the norm. In times past, this might have been the case; it is not so any more. The term "Adhocracy" was coined solely to capture the need for the capability to adjust to new challenges and opportunities—to recognize that change is the natural state of affairs and lack of change is the exception.

A view of the change process as a drama in three acts is both simple and effective: (1) Recognizing the Need for Revitalization, (2) Creating a New Vision, and (3) Institutionalizing Change.[18] Although this model is obviously simplified, it provides a useful and helpful perspective. A few particular pointers may be in order, especially with respect to the marketing perspective on change.

Recognizing the Need for Revitalization.   Internally oriented organizations are almost inevitably late in recognizing the need for change. Although important, not all indicators of the need to change will arise from customers and competitors. The truly externally oriented company will actively scan all parts of its environment—political, regulatory, technological, and so forth—looking for lead indicators. Our observations of many companies have led us to conclude that real leadership is often about getting people in organizations to accept the need for change before it becomes obvious. By the time the need for change is self-evident, there is too little time left to make the necessary changes. When discontinuities, or even worse, disruptions occur, this type of company is poorly prepared and usually attempts to apply its existing procedures more rigorously, often accentuating the problems.[19] Good leaders may, in fact, heighten the perception of problems prematurely, merely to motivate employees to join in the change process. Ways to encourage an open and external orientation include bringing in outsiders or "gadflies," benchmarking not just within but also outside the industry, and encouraging employees to engage in a variety of external activities. Some senior managers object—they say we are simply encouraging their people to "rediscover the wheel," which is a waste of time as long as important people at headquarters know that things have to change. Our contention is that important people preaching the need for change usually changes nothing. Insightful leaders create ways for their people to discover the need for change for themselves[20]—they may be rediscovering the wheel, but then they own the wheel.

Creating a New Vision.    This is a shorthand way of saying that managers have to rethink their approach to business and actively engage their people in making the vision a reality. In today's environment, fundamental changes may be necessary. Yet, in a world where one Finnish forestry company can become the world's leading mobile phone manufacturer (Nokia) and another (Raisio) can invent and market (albeit with partners) an innovative cholesterol-lowering margarine, much is possible! Many senior executive teams fail to realize that to make change happen, people throughout the organization must embrace the new visions, missions, values, goals, objectives, strategies, and action programs. Many well-meaning senior managers have mistakenly spent hours creating statements to be printed on plastic cards, when they would have been wiser to spend the time engaging the hearts and minds of a broad group of employees in such a process. Creating a new vision is a vital part of Total Integrated Marketing. In Chapter 12, we explore this critical issue in depth. Our final comments for the moment are that any new contribution to the vision et al. arsenal should be externally oriented; and it should say, or at least imply, something about the firm's commitment to customers.

Institutionalizing Change.    The choice of words here is telling and specific. The wording is deliberately not "Institutionalizing the Change" because that would imply re-rigidifying the organization. Institutionalizing change suggests that management plans to create the kind of organization that will respond to ongoing change and that adaptive behavior will be organic, not mechanistic.[21] In terms of our earlier discussion, state **B** must be able to produce ongoing learning and change, or it will trigger similar problems at a later date. Our conception of an externally oriented organization is one that senses its environment in this way, although there are times when it may be desirable to initiate change, instead of merely reacting to market forces.[22]

## The Strategic Challenge for Human Resource Management

Increased intensity of competition has wrought tremendous change in the structure and processes of companies around the world. The need for quick response and market focus led to the creation of strategic business units (SBUs), bringing about significant decentralization and the consequential need for general managers in firm after firm. The need for low cost has encouraged outsourcing and led to flatter organizations with broader spans of control. A stronger focus on business processes that cuts across functional lines often accompanies these changes. Industry consolidation has married corporate cultures, often of erstwhile competitors, at the same time that concern with core businesses has led to dispositions. The need to innovate more speedily and effectively, and to integrate the entire resources of a business around a market opportunity, has caused significant increases in the use of teams. This is probably the biggest set of challenges to a firm's human resources management that has ever existed. How well are managers meeting these challenges?

The answer in many cases is poorly, though with some signs of improvement. The reasons are multiple. Historically, the human resource function has received little respect in companies, particularly in the United States. In a chicken-and-egg irony, this has made the problem worse. There have been at least two knock-on effects. One is that talented management students who might otherwise have focused on the area are choosing to avoid it. Indeed, one of our colleagues, a noted human resources expert, always advised students interested in the area to major in something else and to pursue their HR interests after earning their spurs in another field. The attitude of business managers seems to pervade the business school student population. Few show any interest in courses dealing with organization or human resources because the subjects seem irrelevant to their future managerial careers.

To be fair, these attitudes did not arise without reason. In more placid times, HR departments were preoccupied with writing procedures manuals, rewriting job descriptions, administering bureaucratic pay structures, and dealing with labor relations. Important though these tasks may be, they do not rank with the issues of change on the scale being discussed here. The rise of consulting practices dealing with change management and business process reengineering is tangible evidence that the help firms need is not forthcoming from their HR departments. These departments frequently have been politicized and staffed with individuals whose skills are scarcely commensurate with the challenges facing companies today.

## Human Resource Management and Marketing Strategy

What should a chief executive be looking for from human resource managers? First, the CEO should recruit individuals for the department whose background and skills are sufficiently well rounded that they can understand and contribute to strategy development. The problems discussed in this chapter arise from the rapid changes in strategy and structure that occurred in the 1980s and the 1990s. An HR department can add enormous value if it is attuned to the firm's goals and strategies. Likewise, one that is not so attuned may constitute a severe impediment. Second, executives must recognize that while the HR department should have a positive influence on the actions of managers in the firm, it cannot be responsible for managing. An HR department is effective primarily through its influence on the way that managers do their job. Third, senior HR managers must have the capability to develop long-range strategic plans for their function. Contrary to the opinion of some, people are not instantly hirable or productively deployable. To work productively requires not only the requisite skills, but in many cases knowledge of an industry or of specific technologies. To change the competence base of a company requires some lead time, and at today's pace of change, managers can only achieve this by planning in advance. The adequacy of the strategic human resources plan will be a key determinant of the future competitiveness of the firm. This is not just a "field of dreams." In forward-looking operations, HR departments can and do work like this.

## CUSTOMER SATISFACTION AS AN HRM ISSUE?

Lesley Colyer is Vice-President-Personnel at Avis Europe, and she talks compellingly about "synergizing customer and employees to create competitive advantage."* Avis Europe has achieved remarkable success in differentiating itself in the European auto rental market on the basis of superior customer service and continuous service innovation, enshrined in the "We Try Harder" vision inherited from Avis in the United States. At one level, this involves managing symbols—ads placed in employee wage packets ahead of publication, wall posters detailing corporate beliefs and values, lapel badges about continuous improvement, and senior executives regularly working shifts at rental depots to "hear the tills ringing" and to wash autos when necessary.

But underpinning these symbols are large investments in systems to continuously track and match customer and employee satisfaction, and to manage these issues in parallel because they are directly related to each other. Behind this, the processes and structures of the company are designed and operated around the key marketing strategy. It is a flat, decentralized structure (with only a few management levels between the chief executive and the employee washing cars). Management processes are built explicitly around customer retention and employee empowerment (Avis used the word "empowerment" long before it became a cliché). There is management socialization between senior executives and employees at all levels. Recruitment, selection, and development are driven by the business strategy to an almost brutal extent (it is unwise to aspire to be an Avis headquarters worker unless you are prepared to wash an auto every so often). Avis Europe is a great illustration of how the integration of human resources management with marketing strategy can be an incredibly powerful source of leverage on performance. The amount of time that Colyer now spends talking to other companies about how they can achieve similar results underlines how unusual the Avis approach still remains.

*Personal conversations with author, and case notes in N. F. Piercy, *Market-Led Strategic Change: A Guide to Transforming the Process of Going to Market* (Oxford, England: Butterworth-Heinemann, 2002), 130–147.

## Human Resource Management and Marketing Competencies

The human resource function carries a special responsibility for the organization's needs in marketing skills. Increased competitiveness will demand ever-greater marketing competence. The general direction of change is reasonably clear, even though the specifics are not.

The role of marketing as a philosophy and a process as well as the design of Total Integrated Marketing will require the recruiting of marketers who not only have outstanding marketing skills and knowledge, but can also work effectively across the boundaries of traditional functions in the organization. Marketers have often had to rely on their persuasion and leadership abilities to encourage others to invest resources in what they believed to be the right strategies for the future of the business. Traditionally, they have rarely possessed positional authority commensurate with their responsibility. In the knowledge-based economy, it will become even more important to convince those around them to make tough resource allocation decisions. They must appreciate and understand the role of other functions, and cannot afford the arrogance with which many traditional marketers have approached interfunctional relations. They must be ready to work in business teams, as opposed to following the "Be a general manager and have your own bottom line" philosophy, which HR has traditionally used to recruit brand managers.

To attain competitive advantage will demand a high order of intellect as well as creativity in marketing positions. As we have argued elsewhere,[23] marketers will have to demonstrate deeper insight into their target markets, for the obvious sources of advantage will already have been exploited and it will be necessary to find and create new ones. To compete globally will require an end to xenophobia and ability to empathize with and understand other cultures. The challenge will be particularly acute in the search for global account managers, charged with managing relationships with major customers on a worldwide basis. Multilingual skills will become ever more desirable, as will previous experience interacting directly with customers.

Marketers have often been charged with significant short-term responsibilities, but with the changes that are taking place in the sales function (Chapter 8), many companies are emphasizing the strategic aspect of the marketing job. Management of brands and brand equity, innovation, and growth are higher on the new priority list than looking after this month's market share. A close friend of one of the authors experienced this metamorphosis. He was appointed a Global Category Development Manager and told that he could only work on projects with longer than a three-year horizon—any shorter-term projects would be the responsibility of others. When we met a few months later, he was miserable despite his promotion, confessing that he really missed the action of his previous marketing job— visiting stores, working with the sales force, meeting with the advertising agency, and so on. This consummate marketer was ill suited to his new responsibilities, which revolved largely around an esoteric planning and strategy task having little to do with today's "real world." Just as change outdated the need for physical strength and stamina in the steel mill (because of automation), so change has begun to challenge the skill base that companies have traditionally sought in their marketing jobs.

Equally, the competitive intensity stressed throughout this book demands that those working in nonmarketing functions also become better equipped to deal with the stringent demands of customers in the fast-moving and aggressive competitive landscape. These changes will affect every facet of human resources activity—recruitment, selection, training and development, retention, recognition, and reward. Human resource managers that link their activities to support emergent business and market strategies can contribute exceptional value to the firm.

## OPERATIONAL CONSIDERATIONS

To support strategy operationally, HR managers must work with appropriate tools. The classic organizational model suggests that we should always consider systemic linkages among three key elements: Environment à Strategy à Structure. However, modern management thinking demands that we recognize that organization means much more than the mechanistic paradigms that people think of when they hear terms like "organization structure." A holistic model is required to develop the full implications of the changes in the human resources function. Several alternatives are available, including the 7S model (strategy, structure, systems, staff, style, skills, and superordinate goals),[24] the congruence model,[25] and our own version, shown in Figure 11.1, to which we return in our concluding chapter. These models all try to demonstrate the holistic challenges in strengthening the customer focus of organizations.

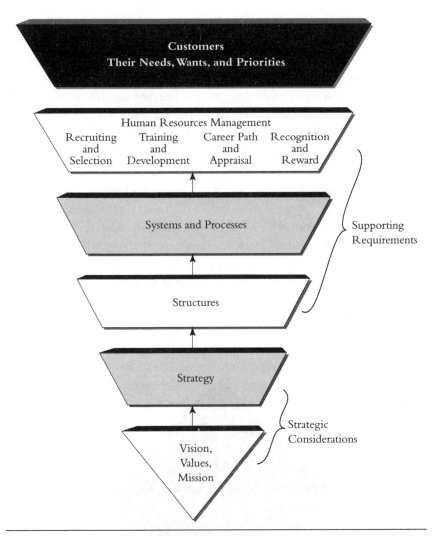

Figure 11.1 A MODEL FOR ACHIEVING TOTAL INTEGRATED MARKETING.
*Source:* Reproduced by permission from J. M. Hulbert and L. F. Pitt, "Exit Left Center Stage? The Future of Functional Marketing," *European Management Journal,* 14 (February 1996), 47–60.

The basic idea underpinning these models is that the change process has to be holistic, even if it is not organization-wide. Changing only one element in such a system is bound to have repercussions for the other parts. Further, unless the other elements are reengineered at the same time, their inertia almost certainly will defeat any significant change in that single element. Any major change should initiate a comprehensive reconsideration of the implications of the desired strategy for all the elements of the organization system and can help assure a good fit. Figure 11.1 also emphasizes that while many change efforts focus on strategic issues like creating new visions, missions, and strategies, the supporting infrastructure (here shown inverted) often defeats such efforts, because it reflects the old organizational culture. The challenge is to identify the real degree of "organizational stretch" that will be required for implementing a strategy, not just to assume it away.[26]

The congruence model is displayed differently (Figure 11.2), but it also stresses the importance of fit, both internally (among the elements in the model's system) and externally (to the strategy and the environment). It

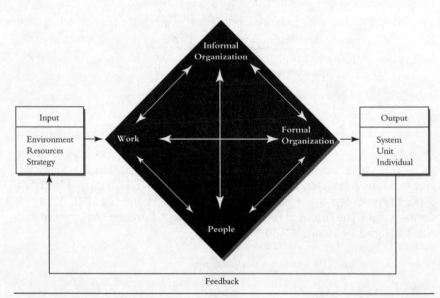

Figure 11.2 THE CONGRUENCE MODEL. *Source:* Reproduced by permission from D. A. Nadler and M. Tushman, *Competing by Design* (New York: Oxford University Press, 1997).

emphasizes the critical role for HR in selection, job design, formal organizational design (including structure, reporting relationships, processes), and in building architecture for the informal organization (culture) of the firm.

Whether managers use the 7S's, or other models, they cannot avoid the implications of the environmental changes discussed in Chapter 2. Consequently, HR professionals may expect to be faced with systemic challenges requiring such tools much more frequently than in the past. Successful managers will become critical partners with senior management. Those who fail to meet the challenge will undoubtedly fall by the wayside. It is not only traditional marketing departments that appear vulnerable in the new order.

The following subsections describe some specific and straightforward initiatives that can help align the company's human resources with marketing processes.

## Customer Contact and Competitiveness

In a competitive environment, nowhere is the role of the human resources more important than in the quest for competitive advantage through increased customer and market orientation. Research at the Marketing Science Institute has established that direct customer contact is one of the best ways to advance this process. Further, today's flatter, leaner organization structures will bring individuals closer to the customer than in the past. This implies new criteria for recruitment, selection, training and development, recognition, and reward.

Imaginative new approaches to these traditional HR tasks can advance the cause. We have grown weary of participating in company training programs about customer and market orientation, in which a real customer never appears. Not only should customers (and ex-customers from whom we might learn why they are ex-customers) participate in such activities, their appearances need not be restricted to cameos. In some companies (e.g., Ford Motor Company and UNISYS), customers routinely participate alongside executives in company training and development programs because this is the best way to learn about customer priorities.

More typical, it must be said, was one author's experience of making an after-dinner speech for a top management team from a division of a prestigious multinational company. The participants took fully four hours of unexpected discussion after the speech to prove conclusively (to themselves) that it was inappropriate for senior managers to meet customers. They were very pleased with the compelling logic they developed. The division was subsequently sold and was later closed by its new owner.

Going far beyond training exercises are action-learning assignments.[27] One of the authors has worked as a consultant with a company where one of the supplier's salespersons went to work in the customer's receiving department, while a customer's buyer went to work in the supplier's customer service department. This same company was actually awarded a contract to run a customer's department for a period of time to demonstrate whether their ideas would produce an increase in category profitability. These true learning experiences can create insight and empathy for both parties.

Some companies are becoming more imaginative. A supplier that needed to select a new key account rep for Kmart whittled the applicants down to a short list of three, sent the résumés to the Kmart buyer, and asked him to interview and select the new appointee. Not only did this open up the organizational boundary to embrace the customer, the seller also thought that a representative selected by the customer just might have a selling edge, albeit infinitesimally small.[28] IBM used a similar process to select a key account manager for Coca-Cola. [29]

More and more companies are also incorporating customer satisfaction measures into their measurement and reward systems. These measures not only are used to evaluate the efforts of sales or customer service and provide incentives, but also are being driven farther into the organization, in some cases even being incorporated in managerial incentive schemes. The results can be spectacular.

## GETTING THE ACT TOGETHER BY WORKING WITH PEOPLE

At Ford Cellular Systems (then a unit of Ford Motor Company, but subsequently purchased by its management team), Chief Executive Nigel Bunter faced a seemingly massive problem in maintaining satisfactory customer service levels in the tough mobile phone business. His solution was both novel and effective.

First, he introduced clear quality level measures summarized in a single service level metric, which is updated continuously and displayed on electronic boards in front of customer service operatives and managers. Second, he linked companywide bonuses to performance against the service level metric.

Chronic "insoluble" problems began to disappear. Finance found they could stagger invoicing after all (to avoid all customer queries coming in on the same two days every month and swamping customer service), although previously they had resisted this change as unworkable. Dispatch found they could stay later to ensure all the day's orders got to the courier for next-day delivery, even though this meant adjusting working hours for employees. Marketing found that they actually did need to liaise with customer service to match service staffing levels and stocks of products with sales promotions.

The company went on to win several major industry customer service awards. Bunter may have understood Total Integrated Marketing ahead of the game. Solving customer service problems may not require rocket science, but simply matching rewards and evaluation focuses everyone's attention on the things that matter most.

## Teamwork and Strategic Success

Effective human resource management should also have a major impact on critical processes of strategy development and implementation. Total Integrated Marketing demands a high level of cooperation among the traditional functions. The benefits of teamwork go considerably further, and the appropriate use of team resources dramatically improves the quality of strategies that are developed. Further, collaboration and commitment are vital to the successful implementation of strategy. Of the central implementation skills identified by Bonoma and Crittenden,[30] three involve a high level of interpersonal competence. Likewise, Jon Katzenbach of McKinsey, another great believer in the power of teamwork, emphasizes the importance of managing teams and team dynamics in the quest for strategic success.[31]

The remarkable turnaround of the U.K. division of CIGNA, from a run-down insurance company to a market leader in providing health care benefits for corporate employees, depended in large part on the power of teams. That power was so dramatic that the CIGNA operation in Scotland became a reference site for other CIGNA divisions and many customer organizations. Douglas Cowieson, the manager of the turnaround, replaced functional structures with multifunctional teams, largely staffed by people with no experience in the financial services industry. In response to industry criticisms of this policy, he responded "Professionals built the *Titanic* . . . amateurs built Noah's Ark." His somewhat lighthearted response is underpinned by taking his business unit from substantial losses into healthy profitability. He gave junior employees on customer service teams the power and responsibility for managing the customer relationship, as well as for allocating performance bonuses within the team and even replacing team leaders. Then he stood back to see his teams provide a single point of problem-solving contact for each customer.

## TOTAL INTEGRATED MARKETING DEPENDS ON EFFECTIVE HUMAN RESOURCE MANAGEMENT

We have emphasized the centrality of the human resource to competitive success. As we move into the information age, knowledge and knowledge management will become crucial to company prospects. Managing this intellectual capital is much more an issue of people management than it is of information technology. We have identified some major implications of these issues for human resource management, indicating both its limitations and its unique potential contributions. In inward-oriented firms, the HR department is typically reactive; it merely fills slots and responds, often in an overtly political manner, to the requests of senior management. Departments of this kind will not play a significant role in twenty-first-century organizations. Those operations can be routinized and easily subsumed within management roles in new organizational forms, or even outsourced. By contrast, in outward oriented firms, HR will develop strategic plans linked with the company's business and marketing strategies, and become a key contributor to the ultimate success of those plans. These HR departments are worthy partners in Total Integrated Marketing. The difference is between HR professionals who are active, contributing partners in managing change processes, and those who cling to policing the bureaucracy and rigidity of the organization—and who will become as irrelevant to the future as the bureaucracies they protect. The challenge is there for all managers concerned with building superior marketing processes and capabilities: Share the task with HR and see what the partnership can achieve.

Finally, we have emphasized the power of teamwork in generating better strategy and excellence in execution. Only by achieving the highest standard of human resource management skills can a company receive these benefits and realize the promise of Total Integrated Marketing. Achieving these goals will be an enormous challenge for HR departments. As new managers are wont to announce, new challenges mean new opportunities, and if one accepts this premise, HR has a rosy future.

# MAKING TOTAL INTEGRATED MARKETING THE WAY OF LIFE IN YOUR COMPANY

In our journey through a world in which Total Integrated Marketing is the priority, we first focused on the real meaning of marketing. We looked at how companies have tried to develop their marketing capabilities by establishing marketing departments. We argued that this approach represents a fundamental misunderstanding of the original concept of marketing. Moreover, clinging to this approach will lead to escalating difficulties in surviving the fiercely competitive world of the twenty-first century.

As executives maneuver for competitive advantage amid the complexities of downsizing, restructuring, disintermediation, management gurus, and new forms of virtual organization, it is easy to lose sight of the basics that drive a business. In this final chapter, we review those basics and examine some of the key issues involved in implementing the only genuine expression of the marketing concept—Total Integrated Marketing.

## HOW CAN FIRMS ACHIEVE TOTAL INTEGRATED MARKETING?

It is self-evident that customer choice creates customer power. We are living in a world where customers' choices are growing at a fast rate. As a result, the pressures to practice Total Integrated Marketing will surely increase. The inverted pyramid model[1] (Figure 12.1) builds on the approach taken by such firms as SAS and Nordstrom's to transform their organizations. It places customers at the top, as the most important among

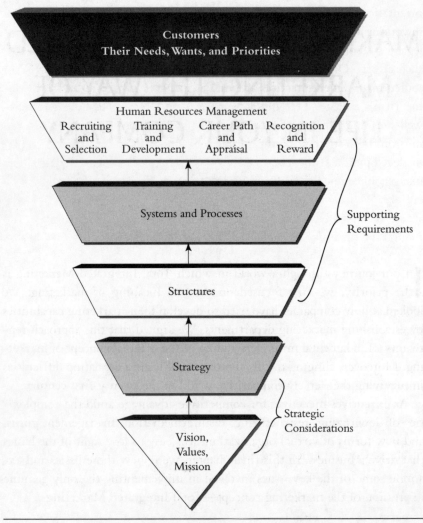

Figure 12.1   A MODEL FOR ACHIEVING TOTAL INTEGRATED MARKETING.
*Source:* Reproduced by permission from J. M. Hulbert and L. F. Pitt, "Exit Left Center Stage? The Future of Functional Marketing," *European Management Journal,* 14 (February 1996), 47–60.

multiple stakeholders, and then provides a comprehensive view of the elements that contribute to marketing becoming a true capability instead of just a function.

For organizational transformation to succeed, all elements in the model must reflect and reinforce a commitment to the external (customer) orientation. Many transformation programs have focused on developing (or reworking) statements of vision, values, missions, and strategy, but the legacy systems of the organizational infrastructure have usually defeated such efforts. Organization structure, systems and processes, and human resource management practices are vital elements that both reflect and shape the firm's culture. Left untouched, they will inevitably undermine any well-meaning attempts to accomplish change by restating vision, values, and mission. Both strategic considerations and supporting requirements are vital in developing a truly integrated yet externally focused organization. For many companies, the challenge is no less than changing the organization's culture. We have no patience with academic theorists who whine that such a task is impossible. You can change the culture of any organization, although the road may be rough and the costs substantial.

## STRATEGIC ISSUES

The most critical role for a general manager or CEO is to set direction for the business as a whole. Vision, values, and mission are best viewed as tools that assist in executing this responsibility. Many important issues underlie the choices the CEO must make, and their resolution frequently involves important marketing considerations. Each of these choices can support a commitment to Total Integrated Marketing.

### Strategic Considerations—Vision

A company's vision is a description of the ideal state it desires—a picture of what the future should be. Total Integrated Marketing requires the customer to be the central focus of any vision statement. This said, no vision statement should be excessively restrictive, because employees should find in it something to inspire them personally.[2] In addition, since the statement should be aspirational, visions should not be too easily achievable; they should beckon for the longer run.[3]

The following examples do not make customer commitment explicit enough to meet our requirements:

- CEO Lou Gerstner provided this vision statement for IBM: "To lead big companies into the brave new networked world, IBM will devise their technology strategies, build and run their systems, and ultimately become the architect and repository for corporate computing, tying together not just companies but entire industries."[4]

- In 1999, Microsoft changed its vision from "A computer on every desk and in every home" to "Giving people the power to do what they want, where and when they want, on any device."[5]

In contrast, some of the world's leading proponents of customer focus made the following statements:

- In his 1999 Annual Report, Jeff Bezos recounts his response to a shareholder's question about what she actually "owned" with her 100 Amazon.com shares. He said, "You own a piece of the leading e-commerce platform," but explained further, "The Amazon.com platform is comprised of brand, customers, technology, distribution capability, deep e-commerce expertise, and a great team with a passion for innovation and a passion for serving customers well. . . . Our vision is to use this platform to build Earth's most customer-centric company, a place where people can come to find and discover anything and everything they might want to buy online. . . . We'll listen to customers, invent on their behalf, and personalize the store for each of them, all while working to earn their trust.[6]

- A similar vision about customers is found in Michael Dell's mission statement at his computer company. It reads, "Dell's mission is to be the most successful computer company in the world at delivering the best customer experience in markets we serve. In doing so, Dell will meet customer expectations of: highest quality, leading technology, competitive pricing, individual and company accountability, best-in-class service and support, flexible customization capability, superior corporate citizenship, financial stability.[7]

- At the global computer services company UNISYS (the company that coined the word "customerize" to describe integrating customer responsiveness into all its systems and processes), CEO Lawrence Weinbach commits to the vision statement, "Unisys helps clients apply technology to address the challenges and opportunities of the Internet economy. Our knowledge of the business processes of seven vertical markets is key to helping clients become more successful."[8]

CEO mandates may not change peoples' behavior overnight, but at least it is a start. How often do people not do what their superiors want, largely because no one bothered to tell them what is "right"?[9] For a company committed to Total Integrated Marketing, marketing concepts must play a key role in the vision statement. However, hard-won experience indicates the absolute necessity of not creating excessive or unrealistic expectations among customers. One CEO we know publicly announced the firm's vision of becoming the most preferred supplier across all of their customers' purchasing categories. This statement raised customer expectations way ahead of changing the company's performance, creating significant customer dissatisfaction. It did not do a great deal that was positive for employee perceptions either.

As mentioned, British Airways (BA) had similar problems. The airline had made a public commitment to customer service as part of its vision and strategy. Later, however, its dogged pursuit of cost cutting and outsourcing so alienated its staff that a strike ensued, stranding and inconveniencing tens of thousands of customers. Months later, traffic levels were still running behind the previous year despite traffic boom times for the industry.

The vision statement can provide an important vehicle for managing the shift to an external yet integrated perspective. The aspirations it embodies can powerfully reflect the principles developed in Total Integrated Marketing. At the very least, the vision should be consistent with the concept of an external orientation and, whenever possible, reflect its ideals.

For people throughout the organization to actively embrace a vision, they must own it. Things often go wrong when senior executives or consultants construct visions in isolation and then foist them on the organization. Although extensive involvement may slow the development process, participation not only evolves and improves the vision, the broader commitment enables other process realignments to occur more smoothly. At ARAMARK, a large services company based in Philadelphia, over 8,500 employees participated directly in the development of a new vision statement.

Part of the problem is that CEOs sometimes delude themselves that employees always obey their leader's every word. Consider what happened at Oracle, the software company. In 1995, after examining Netscape Navigator and chatting with Steve Jobs (founder of Apple computer), Oracle CEO Larry Ellison mandated the conversion of all enterprise software to work as Internet applications. He also ordered that development of client-server products cease and that the sales force should advise customers of product phaseout by 2000. Several months later, Ellison discovered that not only was product development not proceeding as planned, the sales force was assuring long-standing customers that client-server products would **not** be withdrawn![10]

## Strategic Considerations—Values

Vision is linked to values—a common set of beliefs to guide the behavior of organizational members. Organizational values are often integral to company success but, with some notable exceptions, they have tended to be implicit. Environmental pressures are leading executives to rethink corporate values and to make them far more explicit. Values can be thought of as "hard" (profitability, market share) and "soft" (integrity, trust, respect for others, and preeminence of customers).

As with vision, values statements are only worthwhile if they are embraced throughout the organization. The extent of members' participation in the development of values typically influences their buy-in. Developing a values statement gives the firm an opportunity to enshrine the concepts of Total Integrated Marketing. It also can provide the "cultural glue"[11] that enables a firm to overcome market turbulence, when others struggle to survive.

The key issue is, What does the company have to be good at, and how do all employees have to behave, to make Total Integrated Marketing a reality for customers? Far too often, management actions contradict the statement of values, and management hypocrisy has a significant negative effect on employees' morale. In contrast, Johnson & Johnson (J&J) is an excellent example of a company whose famous values statement epitomizes external orientation and drives executive behavior. Its credo (Table 12.1) was put to the test some years ago in the Tylenol cyanide scare. Faced with a product contamination incident, J&J immediately withdrew the product to protect customers from even the smallest chance that other capsules might be tainted.

## Strategic Considerations-Mission

Vision and values statements embrace lofty ideals of how the enterprise will function, but the role of mission is more humble. By defining the

We believe our first responsibility is to the doctors, nurses and patients,
to mothers and all others who use our products and services,
in meeting their needs everything we do must be high quality.
We must constantly strive to reduce our costs
in order to maintain reasonable prices.
Customers' orders must be serviced promptly and accurately.
Our suppliers and distributors must have an opportunity
to make a fair profit.

We are responsible to our employees,
the men and women who work with us throughout the world.
Everyone must be considered as an individual.
We must respect their dignity and recognize their merit.
They must have a sense of security in their jobs.
Compensation must be fair and adequate,
and working conditions clean, orderly and safe.
Employees must feel free to make suggestions and complaints.
There must be equal opportunity for employment, development
and advancement for those qualified.
We must provide competent management,
and their actions must be just and ethical.

We are responsible to the communities in which we live and work
and to the world community as well.
We must be good citizens—support good works and charities
and bear our fair share of taxes.
We must encourage civic improvements and better health and education.
We must maintain in good order
the property we are privileged to use,
protecting the environment and natural resources.

Our final responsibility is to our stockholders.
Business must make a sound profit.
We must experiment with new ideas.
Research must be carried on, innovative programs developed
and mistakes paid for.
New equipment must be purchased, new facilities provided
and new products launched.
Reserves must be created to provide for adverse times.
When we operate according to these principles,
the stockholders should realize a fair return.

Table 12.1   THE JOHNSON & JOHNSON CREDO

company's business, mission statements constrain and guide the firm's search for opportunity and delineate the competitive set. The usefulness of a mission statement rests on the notion that organizations can leverage their capabilities best by focusing on limited areas, instead of dispersing energy in many directions. Ideally, the mission codifies management's judgment about where the firm can expect to yield generous shareholder returns. For firms comprising several businesses, individual business units may also develop missions that are encompassed by the corporate mission.[12]

Our research shows that few firms proactively manage mission evolution,[13] and many handle the process badly. Changes in mission usually occur as a reaction to major problems instead of as a spur to new opportunities. Capital market pressures also play a role in reviewing missions, even when managers claim that synergies exist. In the late 1990s, Du Pont comprised three types of business—chemicals, oil, and life sciences—with 1997 sales (operating income) figures respectively of $20 billion ($2 billion), $20 billion ($1 billion) and $2 billion (almost $1 billion loss). Analysts believed that Du Pont should split into three firms to "release value," and it later spun off the oil operations.[14]

Focusing only on what the firm does well implies a strong internal focus, but choice of mission should also subsume an informed view of market opportunities. The Finnish company Nokia provides a dramatic example of such a change. In the early 1980s, Nokia made rubber, cables, and paper. In the late 1990s, sales were increasing at 25 percent per annum; it enjoyed about 25 percent global market share in mobile telephones, and its stock market valuation reached almost $110 billion.[15]

As with statements of vision and values, mission statements present another opportunity to drive an external perspective into a business, and to build the shared sense of commitment required for Total Integrated Marketing. The current core competency vogue poses the danger that the essential externally focused perspective will get lost in a backward and inward-looking exercise to the neglect of customers, competitors, and market opportunity.

Some mission statements reflect an excellent customer perspective:

- Otis Elevator's mission is "To provide any customer a means of moving people and things up, down, and sideways over short distances with higher reliability than any similar enterprise in the world."

■ Courtyard by Marriott's mission is to provide economy and quality-minded frequent business travelers with a premier lodging facility, which is consistently perceived as clean, comfortable, well maintained, and attractive, and is staffed by friendly, attentive, and efficient people.

Executives do not always recognize the importance of marketing considerations in mission statement design. Even worse, some executives ignore their businesses' missions and act at will, leaving underlings to dismiss the mission statement as a mere exercise in wordsmithing. Like vision and values, however, the mission is another opportunity to publicly communicate the essential message: The requirement is Total Integrated Marketing.

## Strategic Considerations—Strategy

The role of strategy was discussed at length in Chapter 5, so a brief statement will suffice here. A strategic approach to markets and market segments is an essential precondition to Total Integrated Marketing. Many companies develop business and market strategies that lack any substantial insight into either their customers or their competitors.

In this competitive world, firms must use every available means to secure insight into customer problems by identifying latent, as well as expressed, needs and wants. Furthermore, although some firms have developed serviceable systems for understanding the changing requirements of target customers, fewer have developed the infrastructure to gain accurate insights into their competitors. Such insights are essential to successful Total Integrated Marketing, which is but a means to an end: delivering seamless strategies into the marketplace, thereby achieving superior performance.

## Strategic Considerations—Conclusions

Vision, values, mission, and strategy are all about ideas, but these ideas cannot influence behavior without effective communication. If the shift from where the firm is now, to where it needs to be is substantial, then *internal marketing* may be the critical, tangible requirement for the new start. Internal marketing involves comparing external strategies with the internal characteristics of the company. This examination will identify the degree and types of change needed to realign those internal issues with the requirements of the strategy. It exposes the practical internal barriers to implementing Total Integrated Marketing and helps build action programs to overcome them. It provides a formal basis for creating cross-functional, cross-boundary, and multilevel teams of executives with a commitment to embedding new and better ways of doing things in the organization. Figure 12.2 suggests considering internal marketing programs as parallels to external marketing, and as part of the essential iteration between market strategy and planning and action programs. At the very least, the model challenges executives to match their external marketing strategies with some of the realities in their companies.

## SUPPORTING REQUIREMENTS FOR ACHIEVING TOTAL INTEGRATED MARKETING

Statements of vision, values, mission, and strategy represent excellent opportunities to reinforce the message about the central position of customers in determining the company's success and the consequent need for an external orientation. Internal marketing also can give a big boost

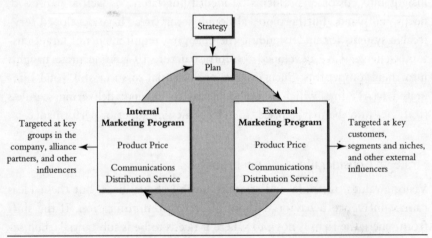

**Figure 12.2   A STRUCTURE FOR INTERNAL MARKETING**

to adoption. Nonetheless, our experience with large-scale organizational change convinces us that deep-seated characteristics of the firm often defeat a change program, even when it is well marketed. As a human resources executive put it: "A lot of people [view] the Vision, Values and Strategy stuff as being just a lot of words."[16]

Embedded in the infrastructure are the patterns of the "old way," and these implicit but always deeply entrenched elements are the silent enemies of change. We focus on three of the most crucial elements: organization structure, systems and processes, and human resource management.

## Organization Structure

Organization structure should facilitate development of an integrated approach to marketing. In reality, it more often impedes the process. Because of large manufacturers' historical origins in controlling and transforming resources into products, most of them organized their operations around products and technologies. Quite simply, this means the organizational form for marketing is distinctly non–customer-oriented; the mind-set is predisposed to see the factory floor, not customers, as the source of profit and growth.

Structure alone is not responsible for the problems companies face in attempting to implement Total Integrated Marketing. Nor can structural change alone resolve those problems. Yet structure is not just about formal task allocations—it also mirrors organizational culture, affects the distribution of power and influence, and determines the way the members of the organization perceive the outside world.

Slowly, as customer power has increased, market-based organizations have gained in importance. Further, the emergence of competitors organized around customer-focused supply chains underlines the urgency of breaking free from product- and technology-based structures. Examples of the stunning success of these new organizational forms include Dell and Toyota.

You might imagine that product-driven structures and attitudes are prevalent only among the dinosaurs of traditional heavy industry and that fast-moving consumer goods firms would be immune. Sadly, you would be disappointed. The so-called best-practice marketers suffer from similar problems in at least two respects.

The first problem lies in their traditional neglect of the intermediary customer, typically the retailer. In their quest for market power, packaged goods manufacturers have traditionally focused on the consumer, not the trade. Yet, as trade concentration has increased and trade customers become increasingly powerful, there has been a belated response from the manufacturers. This has often reflected pressure from the sales force, not an imaginative effort from the marketers. As a result, the 1990s saw the mighty Procter & Gamble moving away from its much-imitated organization for sales and marketing, to a Customer Business Development structure—mainly to implement cooperative relationships with retailers in the Efficient Consumer Response program (i.e., a supply chain collaboration).

The second problem in consumer marketing is branding. As noted in Chapter 4, brands play important roles for the brand owner and the consumer—some obvious, others more subtle. Brands also are an obvious means to an end: The goal is maintaining profitable long-term relationships with target customers. But if this is so obvious, why do brand managers in prestigious consumer goods companies act as though the brand was the end instead of the means, losing sight of their customers in the process?

Despite a widespread management preference for viewing the world through brand, product, or technology spectacles, the marketing concept demands assigning more importance to the customer's spectacles. They are much less prone to inducing corporate myopia. Although structure alone cannot make companies more customer-oriented, it can have significant impact. It can either create better enabling conditions or provide barriers to implementing Total Integrated Marketing.

All large firms have to manage complex dimensions. These include not only customer and market, but also technology, product, brand, geography (now often global), business unit, and process. Formal structure can typically help with only one or two of these dimensions. Effective management will always require the ability to reach out across the boundaries that inevitably arise in any organization, large or small. It was exactly for this reason that an IBM executive once famously remarked in a fit of frustration, "There is no best way to organize, there is only the least worst!" Certainly, if asked how they would organize if they only had one customer in the world, most executives would have little difficulty in concluding it would be prudent to organize around that customer. When customers are plentiful, however, perceptions and attitudes seem to change. Just as scarcity is key to the perception of value inherent in many luxury goods, the same seems to be true with customers.

In the following sections, we describe the transition from organizing marketing as a traditional specialized activity to managing the boundary between the company and its customers in broader ways that will feed back into the whole company. The end point will undoubtedly be the emergence of new types of company organization structure that now we can only guess at. Still, it is well worth considering some of the pros and cons of different organizational approaches, both traditional and novel, at the departmental and organization-wide level.[17]

## Traditional Marketing Organization

*The functional organization.* This is an early-stage marketing organization in which such activities as marketing research, advertising, customer service, and new product development are typically separated from the sales force. If viewed as simply supporting the sales effort, they may also report to the sales VP. More commonly, because of their different focuses and time horizons, they report to a separate marketing executive at an organizational level similar to that of the sales VP. A major problem with this structure is that only the firm's senior executives can resolve conflicts between long-term (marketing) and short-term (sales force) perspectives. A structure in which both sales and marketing VPs report to a single executive with responsibility for all customer-related functions usually enables better integration of sales and marketing, although there is an ever-present danger that short-term pressures will drive out long-term strategic activities. Purely functional organizations tend to work best with homogeneous markets and product lines, but as these become more complex, specialization is usually necessary. Product/brand management and market segment structures developed to solve this problem.

*Product/brand management organization.* The product management organization, originally developed at Procter & Gamble, has ruled the marketing roost at fast-moving consumer goods (FMCG) companies for eons. Sales and marketing activities are overlaid with a product management system in which managers are responsible for individual products and brands.[18] These managers develop marketing plans for their products/brands and work within the organization to ensure plan implementation. In successful systems, improved financial performance has historically more than offset the cost (mainly in duplicated efforts) of focusing on individual products.

Although widely adopted in both consumer and industrial products companies, product management systems have had their problems. First, although product/brand managers have responsibility, they typically do not have commensurate authority and rely heavily on persuasion. Second, internal competition for resources (e.g., sales-force time or advertising dollars) among brand managers may defeat a coherent strategy for the product group as a whole.[19] Third, frequent brand manager turnover may lead to truncated short-term strategies in developing brands. Defective performance measurement systems can produce the same result, as noted in Chapter 4.

*Category management.* Partly as a response to problems generated by internal competition, Procter & Gamble and many other companies have subordinated the brand management system to category management. The original motive was to avoid "friendly fire" casualties among company brands and brand managers. By assuring complementary, rather than competitive, brand positioning, shareholder value presumably would increase.

However, the rise of retailer power in the packaged goods industry has given a whole new meaning to category management. Sophisticated retailers now have at their disposal significant data analysis capabilities that enable them to determine profitability category by category, broken down by region, state, city, and even individual store. These retailers add products and brands only if they help achieve goals set for the category. The brand manager, on the other hand, is typically only too happy to see a rival's shelf space reduced or even disappear! Nowadays, manufacturers hoping to extend a product line or launch a new brand are increasingly required to demonstrate that their addition will increase profits and/or sales for the entire category. Even then, they may be asked to pay a "slotting fee."

*Market segment organization.* Another organizational logic divides management responsibility by individual market segments; business-to-business marketers particularly favor geography and industry/end-use organizations. For example, one computer company's business sector managers are responsible, respectively, for manufacturing, banking and financial services, transportation, and retailing. This system overlays the other marketing and sales functions. The benefit of this system is that it aligns the firm more closely with its target customers and reduces the potential for interproduct conflict.

*Combined product/brand management and market segment organizations.* The problem with both the previous systems is that each omits a crucial dimension. In the product/brand management system, no one is specifically responsible for market segments; in the market segment organization, no one is specifically responsible for individual products. Some firms have incorporated both organizations. Du Pont Textile Fibers combined these areas, with segment managers for end-use markets (household textiles, men's apparel, women's apparel, industrial rubber goods) and product managers for the individual product lines (different types of polyester, nylon, and other fibers).

## Alternative Approaches to Marketing Organization

*Inclusion organizations.* Pillsbury described how, long ago, it grouped virtually all organizational activities under marketing in its early attempts to become "marketing-oriented."[20] It was a "brute-force" approach to developing an external perspective, that Pillsbury subsequently found unsatisfactory. Under Colin Marshall, however, this approach to organization was helpful for British Airways (BA). Recognizing that operations controlled two of customers' most important requirements, safety and schedule reliability, BA restructured to have operations report to marketing. As a result, 80 percent of employees were responsible to marketing, and BA then came close to McKenna's dictum: "Marketing is everything and everything is Marketing."[21]

*Organizing by business processes.* The attempt by some companies to organize around business processes is an outgrowth of the reengineering movement.[22] The firm retains a classic functional structure but much organizational output results from cross-functional process teams. A British-based Unilever subsidiary reorganized on this basis (Figure 12.3). The most interesting aspect of this example is that operational marketing activities are removed from marketing and given to sales. The marketers focus on innovation and brand development, exclusively strategic responsibilities.

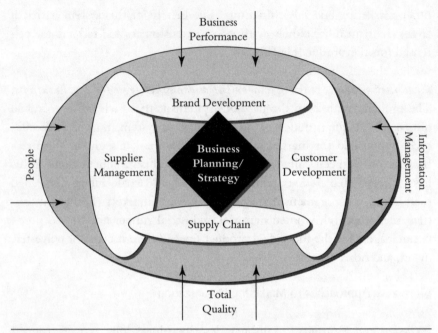

Figure 12.3 A UNILEVER SUBSIDIARY'S PROCESS-BASED ORGANIZATION. Developed from J. M. Hulbert and L. F. Pitt, "Exit Left Center Stage? The Future of Functional Marketing," *European Management Journal,* 14 (February 1996), 47–60.

Since many functional marketing departments have concentrated on operational aspects to the virtual exclusion of their strategic role, the motive for this particular change is evident. A potential problem with this reorganization concerns recognition and reward, for evaluation of performance remains a tricky issue, at least in the short term.

Customer Management Organizations.   Whereas many business-to-business companies and services firms can identify their customers by name, historically, most consumer goods firms selling through distribution systems could not. Since supplier-to-customer links have become a fundamental part of traditional direct and Internet marketing, these practices as well as the customer loyalty cards used in supermarkets are providing similar information to some retailers and manufacturers.[23] The enhanced ability to identify purchasers raises the possibility of organizing around end customers, even at the consumer level, instead of around products or brands.

Although few businesses serve "once-only" clientele, only recently have firms recognized the value of treating customers in relational rather than transactional terms.[24] Business-to-business and service firms are usually further ahead in building long-term customer relationships because of customer knowledge, particularly in industries with both high fixed costs and high customer acquisition costs. In the mid-1990s, IBM scrapped its geographic regional structure for one based on industry lines (manufacturing, financial services, retail), each headed by an industry director. Within each industry organization, global account managers are responsible for IBM relationships with major global clients; local salespeople in each country report through the industry organization.[25] A geographic structure remains for government relations, corporate advertising, and "care and feeding" of locally employed personnel, but country managers no longer have budgetary responsibility.[26]

There is little doubt that the pressures for change will have a dramatic impact on both marketing and brand and product management. One likely shift is that larger elements of the supplier organization will be focused around the customer. Technology now permits firms to identify customers individually, whether they are consumers or intermediary customers. Airlines, direct marketers such as L.L.Bean and Lands' End, and leading retailers like Tesco in Great Britain are already heavily committed to such strategies. Furthermore, as the Internet businesses have demonstrated, this capability now exists irrespective of industry, product/service, or size of firm. Organizing and managing on a customer basis instead of a product basis may seem revolutionary at first sight, but many professionals believe, "Organizations need a structure that can evolve from brand management into a more practical and forward looking format."[27]

For FMCG manufacturers also, loyal customers typically represent substantial cash flow over time. As the pace of new product introduction quickens, consumer-driven cash flows may be more stable than those associated with the firm's fast-changing product lines. Furthermore, a focus on the customer, across brands and products, should reveal significantly greater customer insight. Managers would assume responsibility and authority for a customer "portfolio" of some size and value.[28] Wachovia Bank, one of the most successful superregionals in the United States, has long managed its retail customers in this manner.[29]

Under customer management, the product/brand management organization is turned on its side (see Figure 12.4).[30] Whereas, previously, the products or brands ($B_1 \ldots B_4 \ldots B_n$) were the pillars of the firm and all other functional activities served the brands, in the customer-based structure, brand management is almost a staff function. The product/brand

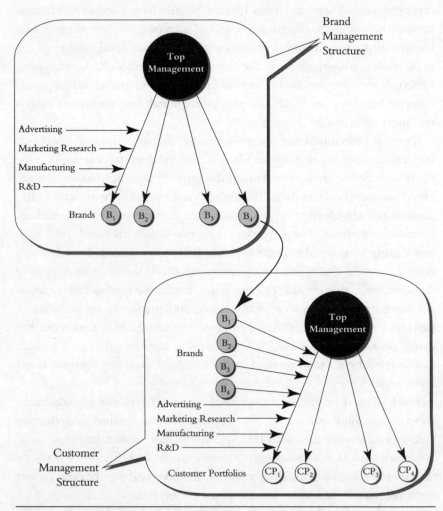

Figure 12.4   TRANSITION FROM BRAND MANAGEMENT TO CUSTOMER MANAGEMENT. From P. Berthon, J. M. Hulbert, and L. F. Pitt, "Brand Management Prognostications," *Sloan Management Review*, 40 (Winter 1999), 53–65.

manager becomes the product/brand expert, managing the brand asset and supporting customer portfolio managers in developing/providing products and/or brands to increase customer lifetime value. Customer portfolios ($CP_1 \ldots CP_4 \ldots CP_n$) then become the organizational pillars, served by the other functions and brands.

Neither brand managers nor firms typically think of customers in this novel way—holistically and empathetically. Historically, companies have not selected brand managers for these traits, nor have they included these capabilities in developing, training, evaluating, or rewarding them. Moving to managing customers instead of keeping brands and products as the primary focus requires an enormous shift in corporate thinking. To begin with the customer, instead of with products, brands, or geography changes the firm's entire marketing structure, but potentially it can alter much more.

In a customer management structure, the brand or product managers will cease selling the brand to as many customers as possible and will serve as product or brand experts. They will support the firm's customer portfolio managers in developing and providing the products and brands they need to increase lifetime values of their customers. It may also mean realizing that they will not sell particular brands or products to certain customer portfolios, based on a computation of the impact on the net present value of the portfolio. Managing relationships with the customers in a portfolio will become the critical challenge. No longer will brand managers research markets to identify what a reasonably large segment of "average" customers want. More and more, the focus will be on the individual customer.

Many business-to-business companies already have key account managers, responsible for the firm's relationship with a customer at its many locations, not only in individual countries but also around the globe. Wherever a company has a direct relationship with customers, it is moving to organize around them. Firms that lack such a relationship should be using the tools of information technology to try to create one, lest they become the mere handmaidens of powerful intermediaries that have such knowledge.

This reinvention of the boundary between company and customer will have a potentially bigger impact than just reshuffling personnel in marketing departments. Customer-based marketing structures may ultimately be the vehicle for building customer-based companies. Instead of just preaching customer focus and marketing orientation, customer management structures may provide the leverage for Total Integrated Marketing to link all the functions, product groups, strategic business units, teams, and process managers in the company.[31]

Significant organizational change is required to implement this paradigm shift.[32] It has serious implications for recruiting, selecting, developing, training, evaluating, rewarding, and retaining the individuals who will populate the organization. Yet the possibilities for true customer insight multiply as empathetic managers are immersed in continuous and ongoing customer interaction. Product and brand blunders should diminish,[33] although contact between customers and "their" manager is an experience that must be carefully engineered.[34]

The changes in organizational structure and philosophy required to focus around the customer will be profound, for they imply quantum shifts in thinking and conceptualization for many companies. Structural change may not be the whole answer, but it is likely an important element in implementing Total Integrated Marketing.

New Corporate Organizational Forms.   The mandate for taking the organizational issue seriously in managing marketing processes is driven also by the development of new organizational forms that are already transforming competitive realities in some industries.[35] New-style competitors do not carry the baggage of the past and can organize to build their operations around customers from the start. Their structures are likely to be flatter and supported through networks of partners instead of internal functions. Because customer-focused processes drive these firms, they are more flexible and responsive. They will use untraditional business models and will be formidable competitors.

## WHAT WILL OUR NEW COMPETITORS LOOK LIKE?

IKEA, the Swedish furniture retailer, built a global sourcing network of 2,300 suppliers in 67 countries, to place about 10,000 products on its shelves at prices 30 percent lower than those of traditional rivals.* The company's flat and unconventional organization is highly customer focused in its niche market. Its advertising is frequently offensive to those outside that market—one ad playfully suggested that one good reason for splitting with a spouse or partner is that the reader would get to choose a pile of new furnishings at IKEA! It has been difficult for traditional competitors to combat IKEA's strategy.

*"Furnishing the World," *The Economist* (November 19, 1994), 101.

The implication is that driving a customer focus across and throughout a business operation has massive power. In whatever sector you work, you will have to survive competitors who have never had traditional structures, and who build their companies around customer targets from the start. You will need to find ways of achieving the same company-wide focus on customers, not just move people around in the marketing and customer service organization. For many companies, the time left for talking about these issues is fast running out.

Final Organizational Issues for Total Integrated Marketing.  It is a management axiom that structure should follow strategy and that strategy should derive from environmental realities. Regardless of how a firm is organized, specialization breeds differentiation; thus conflicts and problems inevitably arise among organizational units.[36] This is why some have turned the axiom on its head to suggest that, in the short term at least, there is a danger that structure drives strategy; for example, the product-based organization is likely to develop product-focused strategies.[37] This is a trap that managers have to avoid or escape to make Total Integrated Marketing a reality. Furthermore, whereas organization structure can facilitate strategy and operations, structure alone is never a solution to all problems.

It is because of these issues that General Electric's then-CEO, Jack Welch, described his vision of the boundaryless corporation. In today's competitive environment, effective managers must be proficient in spanning boundaries to get things done, whether those boundaries are internal to the firm (between different organization units) or across the organizational interface with external constituencies such as customers, shareholders, alliance partners, or government. Because of the division of responsibility and authority, these skills are particularly important for managers working within traditional structures.

## Supporting Requirements for Achieving Total Integrated Marketing: Management Processes and Systems

In building the case for Total Integrated Marketing, we have stressed the thinking side of marketing. Understanding the nuances of customer behavior, predicting competitive actions, and designing winning strategies in the face of a fast-changing, competitive world pose intriguing and difficult challenges even for the most able. But the most creative strategies and tactics come to nothing unless managers and employees can implement them. There is an all-important doing side to marketing, just as there is an intellectual aspect to marketing implementation. Ask any managers of a major new product launch (especially if they have been with the project from its early days), and they will confirm that it constitutes a task of great complexity. We may intellectually grasp the need to integrate the marketing mix and other functional supports, but making it happen correctly and on time is still demanding. The unavoidable truth is that strategies and tactics are implemented with and through people, and the manager who is unable to motivate others will probably be unsuccessful.

*Processes.* As noted, in the traditional functionally organized company, marketing was charged with considerable responsibility, but did not receive commensurate authority. The whole ethos of Total Integrated Marketing is that managers need to coordinate not only the marketing mix, but also all the other support functions that underpin the strategy's success. However, marketing managers in most companies are not, and arguably never will be, able to control most of the activities that impact on customer value. How then can they be successful?

This is why we call for Total Integrated Marketing. The way to put this into effect is not to create a post of "Marketing Integrator," devise a new functional department for coordination, or set up committees. Instead of yet more formal bureaucracy, firms need to shape the entire organization around the principles embedded in the marketing concept.

Although it will not automatically solve all the practical problems that are bound to occur in implementation, resolving the inevitable conflicts over resource allocation priorities will be much easier if this philosophy is credible and shared. It is not necessary to do everything perfectly, but just significantly better than competitors do. Most important of all is to recognize the need for good planning processes and good process skills.

In our consulting work with companies and executives, we see far too many otherwise capable, even outstanding, managers fail because they lack these skills.

*Planning processes.* As noted, we have spent an inordinate amount of time in our academic careers studying the ways in which companies plan. We have no hesitancy in saying that most of them do it poorly. A good planning process is open and creative; it commences with an attempt to develop the best possible understanding of the market conditions under which the firm expects to be doing business. This effort should embrace an in-depth analysis of the market and its present and prospective competitive structure, as well the existing and emergent wants and needs of customers. Only such an externally driven planning process allows executives to develop winning strategies and tactics from which they can derive realistic forecasts and budgets. This is emphatically not the way that most companies plan. Typically, planning is a financially driven, glorified budgeting process, imposed on line managers who have little or no sense of ownership. Furthermore, all the evidence indicates that such planning fails to produce any measurable result.[38] We are firm advocates of team-based approaches to the development of strategy. Not only does such a process improve the quality of output, the sense of ownership that emerges from a well-run group process can be truly remarkable.

Instead of looking at planning as a boring, bureaucratic task that must be done (and then largely ignored, if possible), actively managing the planning process can provide a practical tool for moving closer to Total Integrated Marketing.[39] Our observations of innovative practices in companies suggest that managers can use the following approaches to change planning from mundane bureaucracy into an exciting, external, strategizing process:

- Actively manage the planning process as a team-based, cross-functional vehicle for change, even if it means wresting control away from staff planners—they can play as well, if they want, but important decision-making processes as belong to line management, not staffers!
- Provide line managers with the analytical tools for the planning task, without making them think it is a programmed exercise in computation.

- Creatively manage participation in planning. Develop teams representing "thinking" and "doing" capabilities to represent and provide feedback from those throughout the firm who will have to implement the changes that enhance customer value. Include those committed to change as well as those who carry the culture of the organization.
- Reconfigure the planning process to focus on priorities for radical change, not incremental change from the past. Start with line managers' feedback from the market; work back from that to a strategy and test it against market insights.[40]
- Demand[41] that implementation and ownership are the key outcomes of the planning process, not just a written plan.[42]

You may remark that this hardly seems like rocket science. You would be dead right. So, why should managers tolerate planning being anything less than an externally focused strategic process that builds Total Integrated Marketing? Apart from anything else, planning should be one of the most exciting things a manager ever does, not boringly bureaucratic. Few managers in fewer companies achieve these simple goals. The same logic applies to other critical decision-making processes. Why has the development of appropriate spending to support marketing strategies become a political war inside companies? Logically, it should just be a way of allocating resources to achieve the things that need to happen with customers.[43]

*Managerial processes.* For a company to operate an open, externally oriented, and strategy-driven planning process, managers have to develop their own interpersonal skills. Although not everyone is equally sensitive in their dealings with other people, all executives can learn effective interpersonal techniques. The reaction of many managers to this statement is simple: "Okay, how, when, and where?"

The typical business school curriculum does a less than adequate job in this area for several reasons. First, academics are predisposed to seek intellectual solutions for all problems. Consequently, interest in skill-building is typically low. In addition, the reward structures in academic institutions favor intellectual pursuits, so that the availability of suitable faculty is limited. Finally, skill development is a labor-intensive teaching task, and thus senior administrator positions in schools of business tend not to favor it. Business schools generally place little emphasis on interpersonal skills in their degree programs; such classes are more common in nondegree executive education offerings.

This book is not meant to be a primer for developing skills to get ahead in business, but we urge managers to take on their own shoulders a commitment to acquire essential interpersonal skills. Without always having formal authority, executives must be able to cajole, induce, or persuade people to cooperate in the design and implementation of market strategy. Senior managers will inevitably require these skills to manage the many interfaces that will affect their success.

Systems.    All organizations incorporate systems for organizational output. These systems may be arrayed along a continuum, from solely computer-based (hard systems), such as automatic teller machines (ATMs), to almost exclusively manual (soft systems), such as retail customer service desks. In the middle are combination systems, such as those for securing telephone numbers.

When used creatively, the technological power of computer-based systems can contribute enormously to making firms more externally focused, improving marketing effectiveness, and securing competitive advantage. In many firms, these systems are mostly used to improve operational efficiency and reduce costs instead of being designed to increase strategic effectiveness and add value for customers and shareholders. Systems can contribute to marketing effectiveness in several ways.

First, by making customer information generally available throughout the firm, systems can help employees understand important problems and develop an external perspective.[44]

Second, because user-friendly, computer-based systems reduce customers' time, effort, and risk in making purchases, they also enable firms to get closer to their customers.

Third, by providing records of purchase history and other interactions, they allow companies with large numbers of customers to attack the soulless anonymity of transaction-based markets. Large firms may emulate the high-personal-service strategies of small firms (e.g., neighborhood grocers used to know their customers by name and built their businesses on a one-to-one basis). Many firms seem to be ignoring these goals, which are central to the strategic role of customer relationship management (CRM) systems (Chapter 10).

Airlines have established customer loyalty programs and credit card companies have emulated them, for example, the Discover card and Apple Computer's Visa card. These programs have also infiltrated retailers such as Ukrop's and Dominick's in the United States and Tesco, Boots, and Sainsbury's in Great Britain.[45] These programs, however, are primarily about customer information and insight, not customer loyalty. Those who missed this point (e.g., Sainsbury and Safeway in the British supermarket arena) are already dropping their schemes. Those who understood are using their superior insights into customers to power their strategic development.

Fourth, systems are at the core of supply chain management, offering better supply/demand matching, reduced inventory, and new ways of achieving superior customer value. Pioneered by American Hospital Supply[46] and practiced by such firms as Unilever and Procter & Gamble, computer-based vendor-managed inventory systems offer significant advantages to both buyer and supplier.

Fifth, database systems allow firms to be more responsive to customer needs and support so-called segment-of-one marketing.[47] At Dell's Web site, customers can configure a computer purchase to meet their individual requirements, place an order, and pay. The company builds the product to order and delivers it promptly. By 2002, Dell was receiving over 750 million page requests per quarter on 80 country-specific Web sites in 20 languages and 40 currencies, and approximately half of all sales came through this channel. Competitors—Apple, IBM, and Compaq—have all modified their production and ordering systems in vain attempts to emulate Dell.

Finally, in companies at the forefront of such systems changes, personnel throughout the company experience directly the crucial importance of firm-customer relationships. The industry-leading best practice example in insurance is USAA—its superior systems are an essential ingredient in its success. Not only do computer screens provide a full client record, they prompt the service associate to inquire about other services (e.g., a call about homeowners insurance for a new home triggers a change of address for auto insurance).

## Supporting Requirements for Achieving Total Integrated Marketing: Human Resource Management

The traditional tools of human resource management (HRM)—recruitment and selection, formal training, work processes and career paths, and recognition and reward systems—offer many obvious opportunities to support developing Total Integrated Marketing. It is less obvious, but equally true, that these processes may provide a fundamental barrier to Total Integrated Marketing. Many companies see HRM as a staff function, instead of a key component of strategic change. Because of this, they fail to benefit from the enthusiasm of HRM professionals who want to make a strategic impact in their companies instead of being relegated to the "health and welfare" role of the past.

Recruitment and Selection.    It is self-evident that hiring personnel with the appropriate skills and experience can have a major impact on developing Total Integrated Marketing. It is equally likely that standing by while the company recruits personnel with the skills and experience relevant to the company of the past will create a self-perpetuating barrier to Total Integrated Marketing. Linking recruitment to strategic change is a powerful source of leverage.

### LINKING RECRUITMENT TO STRATEGIC CHANGE

Many large firms that were internally oriented have made dramatic use of recruitment to build strategic change:

- Citibank's hiring of experienced marketing professionals from such well-known marketing companies as Procter & Gamble and General Mills had a major effect on its external perspective. Other financial services firms, such as Prudential, have more recently employed this model.
- The U.S. Postal Service hired marketing professionals from consumer goods and financial services companies.

In each of these cases, senior management was seeking a more external perspective; carefully seeding the organization with marketing professionals helped achieve this goal.

On the other hand, the ingrained reluctance of the great British retail firm, Marks & Spencer, to make executive appointments outside its own culture in the late 1990s partly explained the difficulties management faced in turning that struggling business around. As we earlier noted, only in the early 2000s, with an externally appointed chairman and the removal of many traditional M&S managers from middle management, are there signs of a beginning corporate turnaround.

More generally, careful shaping of recruitment and selection criteria can aid a firm's progress toward Total Integrated Marketing. Firms as diverse as Hyatt, Singapore Airlines, Wal-Mart, L.L.Bean, and Nordstrom's go to considerable lengths to select customer-responsive employees. Southwest Airlines makes loyal customers (frequent fliers) part of the selection team that interviews prospective customer-contact employees, and as indicated earlier, some business-to-business marketers with key account programs allow customers the final choice of key account manager among several qualified candidates. Some companies regularly recruit employees from their customers to secure greater insight into customer needs and spread these insights through the new company.

Although many firms accept that customer-responsive employees are critical for customer contact positions, these attitudes and values must penetrate the firm as a whole to achieve Total Integrated Marketing. Because many firms interpret customer contact so narrowly, they fail to achieve a required level of external orientation nor does it extend widely enough throughout their companies. Credit departments are often notorious for their rudeness and fail to retain profitable customers instead of helping to find and keep them. Operations personnel also interface directly and indirectly with customers, and sometimes have the same negative impact as a bad credit department. The competitive conditions of the twenty-first century demand ubiquitous customer sensitivity throughout the firm. A vigorous and continual review of recruitment and selection criteria and policies against the goals of external orientation can play a significant role in achieving Total Integrated Marketing.

Training and Development.    The areas of training and development present outstanding opportunities for attitude change, as well as knowledge and skill acquisition. These activities can help fill the gap between the knowledge, skills, and abilities required to do any particular job, and the quality of the current set of human resources. If the firm is attempting to shift toward Total Integrated Marketing, this gap is likely to be significant at many levels and employee education facilitates effective change.

Since the change in orientation must start at the top, in-depth marketing education for the full cadre of senior and middle management can be exceptionally beneficial. Not only can off-site education sensitize managers in many different functions to the value of an external perspective and help them learn new behaviors, team building is a valuable secondary benefit. The signal sent by educational efforts focused high in an organization is highly visible to employees elsewhere in the business.

Training at just the senior and middle management levels may be insufficient for many firms, especially in service industries where many employees interact with customers. Faced with word-of-mouth research data suggesting a 1:7 positive-to-negative ratio, Jan Carlzon, CEO of SAS, introduced extensive education for *all* employees on how to treat customers; British Airways implemented a similar program during its initial turnaround. Both airlines received critical acclaim on employee/customer interaction performance; subsequently, market share and profits improved.

Many companies are modifying their training courses to include greater customer participation, both as speakers and, in some cases, as participants and facilitators in the learning process. State-of-the-art companies are using old-style action learning[48] to break down traditional barriers both between learning and action, and between firm and customer.[49]

Work Processes and Career Paths. The functional specialization found in most organizations means that managers responsible for critically important customer-based decisions may sit in organizational ivory towers, far removed from the market. Firms can reduce this distance by ensuring that management in many functions, and at many levels, has consistent and regular contact with customers. For example, bankers may spend half a day per month as tellers; insurance company executives can answer policyholders' inquiries; shipping personnel may need to spend time at the customer's receiving dock; executives should regularly schedule lunches with customers. Managers should not underestimate the impact of executive/customer interaction. The introduction of lunches between senior Norwegian Telecom management and customers led to greater awareness of significant service shortfalls. A series of actions was designed to bring about greater customer awareness throughout the organization.

In addition to formal training, periods of customer contact can be built into all career paths, preferably early in the employee's experience, as a prerequisite for advancement. Avis, Disney, Hyatt, and many other service companies require that managers have periodic reexposure to customers. Going beyond the basics, some companies are especially creative in seeking insight into customers' lives, and they are careful to involve more than just the marketing department. In some Unilever companies, cross-functional teams receive extensive exposure to customer input. Gessy-Lever of Brazil has experimented with ethnographic market research in which employees from multiple functions live for several weeks in the favellas of Rio de Janeiro.

**Recognition and Reward Systems.**   The firm truly committed to Total Integrated Marketing can put real teeth into these efforts by basing recognition and reward on customer-focused measures and extending these far beyond the marketing and sales areas in which they are more usual.

Managers are often skeptical about basing take-home pay on the results from survey instruments. Yet many firms report excellent results from basing managerial incentives in part on both hard and soft customer satisfaction measures. If the firm does a good job in survey instrument design, rigorously tests the items, and secures the services of a competent, reputable, and independent research company, these methods will likely secure internal acceptance. When Du Pont faced the challenge of improving its marketing competence, it not only trained more than 20,000 (marketing and nonmarketing) employees, it instituted a marketing excellence evaluation that deliberately included extrafunctional considerations such as demonstrating excellence both within and between business units. When using traditional measures, regardless of the performance metric(s) selected, it is particularly important to require an attainable performance level. In recent years, several major companies have had to deal with severe problems because of unethical (and possibly illegal) actions of executives faced with excessively high performance targets.

## IMPOSSIBLE TARGET

In the late 1980s and early 1990s, the compensation package for Dun and Bradstreet (D&B) salespeople selling business credit reports was heavily weighted in favor of incentive compensation. Salespeople were paid a fairly low base salary but could earn significant amounts if sales were high. However, the incentive compensation package only took effect when sales exceeded the previous year plus 15 percent! In many sales territories, exceeding previous year's sales plus 15 percent was virtually impossible, let alone increasing sales sufficiently to earn reasonable compensation. The result: Many customers received D&B reports they had never ordered. When this practice came to light, D&B paid significant amounts to several customers including six-figure amounts to AT&T and IBM. According to one senior D&B executive, "We were a cesspool."*

* *Business Week* (November 27, 1989).

## MAINTAINING THE COMMITMENT

It is an awesome challenge for an internally focused organization to grow into a Total Integrated Marketer. To maintain this perspective on an ongoing basis provides an even bigger challenge. If the firm's alignment to the environment leads to marketplace success, competitors will likely emulate its actions. Kaizen—continuous improvement—is therefore an absolute requirement of a competitive marketplace. Yet the very success that results from a successful change process often sows the seeds of complacency. Likewise, the pressure of a competitive marketplace and demanding shareholders can produce a negative result.

The transformation of British Airways (BA) from the dead hand of government ownership into a dynamic, high-performing totally integrated marketer was one of the success stories of the late twentieth century. Moving into the CEO position in 1996, Robert Ayling correctly recognized that the competitive airline industry was globalizing, and that BA would require a much lower cost base. He also realized that the business traveler segment was less price oriented and should respond to a higher level of service. Although these were sound strategic conclusions, he proceeded to try to implement them with a combination of insensitivity and clumsiness almost without parallel in a major corporation. Within a few short years, BA had alienated huge numbers of customers (losing about 50 percent of its executive club members) and its own staff, and suffered significant operating losses. Ayling was sacked in March 2000 by a board of directors who belatedly recognized their responsibility to shareholders, customers, and employees. That the situation was permitted to continue so long provides ample evidence to support the critics of current corporate governance!

The best way to avoid the danger of corporate recidivism is to identify mechanisms that keep the firm externally oriented and ensure it becomes a learning organization. Learning and responsiveness are described in different ways by organization theorists, for example, as adhocracy (developing an adaptive response to change), as information-based organizations,[50] and as intelligent enterprises.[51] The choice of words suggests that many firms fail to use knowledge and expertise appropriately. These newer models of flatter organizations pose a threat to tradition in most large firms that thrive on hierarchy and formalism. Deference to knowledge and expertise is threatening to traditional managers who look to positional authority for their legitimacy.

In these new types of organization, management exercises less control external to the individual; instead control is an internal exercise of the employee. This is a sharp break with tradition, but with appropriate values and incentive systems, it is arguably a more efficient and effective option for the modern organization.[52]

Finally, the philosophy that drives Total Integrated Marketing will not endure long unless the CEO (or general manager) is wholeheartedly committed to its implementation. Senior managers provide the focal point around which to rally the firm, and their actions signal what is important. Jan Carlzon, who turned around ailing SAS by a single-minded devotion to serving the business customer and James Burke of Johnson & Johnson, who demonstrated his company's dedication to its customers at the height of the Tylenol crisis provide vivid examples of externally focused leadership in action.

## FINAL THOUGHTS

The challenge is not just knowing what Total Integrated Marketing means. If the truth be known, there is nothing dramatically new in Total Integrated Marketing—it is what marketing set out to be in the first place, but generally failed to achieve. The real challenge is implementation. The strategic considerations (vision, values, mission, strategy) on which change efforts usually concentrate may assist in the effort, but they will seldom be sufficient on their own—even when managers pay considerable attention to internal marketing. The change program must also embrace the underlying infrastructure of the organization (organizational structure, systems and processes, and human resource management). These elements comprise an integrated whole. Without this holistic approach, the effort is almost certain to fail.

To be successful, managers must create, nurture, and re-create very different types of organization from the ones that sufficed in the twentieth century. Firms that adopt the philosophy of Total Integrated Marketing must juggle paradoxical demands. They must be responsive yet show initiative, learn new behaviors but not forget important lessons, understand human resources yet demand high performance, be customer-sensitive but remain competitive, create shareholder value yet not be shortsighted. To reconcile these pressures demands a high caliber of creativity and leadership. Executives must provide this leadership in economies dominated by information technology, and in markets that not only change quickly, but in unpredictable ways. Whereas the key principles of effective marketing do not change, the milieu and manner in which they are practiced will be as different as the organizations that employ them. Welcome to the world of twenty-first-century competition!

# NOTES

## PREFACE

1. Note that the term "Integrated Marketing" has sometimes been used to describe the use of integrated marketing communications. Our view is much more encompassing, another reason for adding the adjective "Total."

## CHAPTER 1

1. See, for example, "Shadowing Industry Trends, Morgan Stanley Creates Two Big Divisions," *The New York Times* (January 17, 1997); or "P&G, Seeing Shoppers Were Being Confused, Overhauls Marketing," *The Wall Street Journal* (January 15, 1997).
2. Concerns over the ability of managers to direct very large enterprises, increasing competition leading to greater organizational focus, and the inability of investors fully to understand highly diversified businesses has led to a questioning of the value of size and growth per se. As a result, an increasing number of large corporations are being broken-up into more manageable units (e.g., AT&T, Tyco U.S.; Hanson Trust, U.K.).
3. Sometimes it is necessary to sell all, or part of, the firm to secure capital and managerial talent to allow it to function at all.
4. This conflict is one manifestation of the so-called principal/agent problem in economics.
5. If this job is performed poorly, the firm's survival is at risk. A dramatic example of this occurred in the U.S. in the 1980s and early 1990s. Of the 500 firms in the Fortune 500 in 1981, only 271 remained as independent entities in 1992. Most of the missing 229 were merged out of existence. The definition of the "500" was changed in the mid-nineties, but the attrition rate of about 50 percent every ten years was a characteristic of the late twentieth century.
6. P. F. Drucker, *The Practice of Management* (New York: Harper & Row, 1954), 37–38.

7. J. M. Hulbert and L. F. Pitt, "Exit Left Center Stage? The Future of Functional Marketing," *European Management Journal,* 14 (February 1996), 47–60.
8. Interestingly, something very similar happened at the beginning of the quality movement in the United States, when senior executives typically hired someone to "do" quality. These attempts failed for the same reasons that marketing is in crisis today, namely a failure to recognize that to fully implement the principles of quality management required a profound and thoroughgoing transformation of the company.
9. See note 7.
10. R. Dennis, Managing Director, McLaren International, quoted in *The Economist* (March 7, 1998), 46.
11. R. Boehm and C. Phipps, "Flatness Forays," *McKinsey Quarterly,* 3 (1996), 134–135.
12. Ibid, 135.

## CHAPTER 2

1. By which we mean close to zero. The possible reversal of the cost/value relationship posited may apply when the advice comes from consultants paid fees to be pundits.
2. P. Drucker, "A Turnaround Primer," *The Wall Street Journal* (February 2, 1993).
3. See P. Berthon, J. M. Hulbert, and L. F. Pitt, "To Serve or to Create? Strategic Orientations toward Customers and Innovation," *California Management Review,* 42 (Fall 1999), 37–58; and N. F. Piercy, *Market-Led Strategic Change* (Oxford, England: Butterworth-Heinemann, 1997), 148–168.
4. See N. F. Piercy, *Market-Led Strategic Change: A Guide to Transforming the Process of Going to Market* (Oxford, England: Butterworth-Heinemann, 2001), 82–117.
5. The U.S. health care industry has been particularly prone to this activity. See, for example, the consolidation of Baxter Travenol and American Hospital Supply to create Baxter Healthcare, and the acquisition of pharmaceutical distribution companies by Eli Lilly and Merck. Such mergers generally fail to create shareholder value, and Merck has announced the divestment of Medco, its distribution arm.
6. M. E. Porter, *Competitive Strategy: Techniques for Analyzing Industries and Competitors* (New York: Free Press, 1980).

7. We are indebted to Professors Pierre Berthon and Leyland Pitt for the new "five forces" formulation. This framework was also used in N. Capon and J. M. Hulbert, *Marketing Management in the 21st Century* (Upper Saddle River, NJ: Prentice Hall, 2001).

8. MIPS is an acronym for "million instructions per second."

9. Similar thinking suggests that if you owe the bank $1,000, you are in debt, but if you owe the bank $1 million, then you are in partnership.

10. Kelly has pointed out that Metcalfe's Law was based on telephone or fax networks where connections are point-to-point. On the Internet, because many connections can be made simultaneously, the potential value of the network is $n^n$, where n is the number of people connected.

11. Economists have shown great interest in this change, describing network economics as those of increasing returns, as opposed to the traditional assumptions of economics, which postulate that eventually diminishing returns to scale must set in. See W. Brian Arthur, "Increasing Returns and the New World of Business," *Harvard Business Review,* 74 (July/August 1996), 100–109.

12. R. H. Coase, "The Nature of the Firm," *Economica,* 4 (1937), 386–405.

13. See, for example, "Increasing R&D Expenditures Drive Opportunities for Contract Research Organizations," *Frost and Sullivan Report,* 5865-52 (August 1999).

14. *The Wall Street Journal* (December 31, 1999).

15. See, "The Accidental Superhighway," *The Economist* (July 1, 1995), special supplement.

16. An interesting thought is how many CEOs deserve to have a white patch fixed to the seat of their pants, given their desperation to run with the herd rather than to develop new strategies, with the inevitable consequence that their lemming-like behavior leads to all firms in the industry with the same strategy.

17. BBC News (March 8, 2002).

18. E. Platt, "The Revolution Starts Here," *The Business* (February 17, 2001).

19. "Apple Reverses a Move to Raise Some Prices," *The New York Times* (October 16, 1999).

20. See note 15.

21. It is telling also that it took the combined might of the FBI, the Canadian Mounties, the British police, and a team of computer experts to track him down.

22. Prior to September 11, 2001, both Expedia and Travelocity were reported to be operating profitably by the business press.

23. See, for example, S. Ghoshi, "Making Business Sense of the Internet," *Harvard Business Review,* 76 (March/April 1998), 125–135.

24. There is a compelling argument that only when times are simple can companies afford the luxury of complex strategies, and as times have become more complex, the need is for simple strategies that are well-understood. K. M. Eisenhardt and D. L. Sull, "Strategy As Simple Rules," *Harvard Business Review,* 79 (January 2001), 107–116. Indeed, toward the end of his tenure as General Electric's CEO, Jack Welch exhorted General Electric's top management to <destroyyourbusiness.com>.

25. M. E. Porter, "Strategy and the Internet," *Harvard Business Review,* 79 (March 2001), 63–78.

26. P. Evans and T. S. Wurster, *Blown to Bits: How the New Economics of Information Transforms Strategy* (Boston: Harvard Business School Press, 2000). See also, R. D'Aveni, *Hypercompetition* (New York: Free Press, 1994).

27. F. Cairncross, *The Death of Distance: How the Communications Revolution Will Change Our Lives* (London: Orion Business Books), 1997.

28. See L. Pitt, P. Berthon, and R. Watson, "Just When You Thought Service Marketing Was More Difficult: Cyberservice!" *Business Horizons,* 42 (January/February 1999), 11–18.

29. N. Capon, *Key Account Management and Planning* (New York: Free Press, 2001).

30. See, for example, B. Schmitt, *Experiential Marketing: How to Get Customers to Sense, Feel, Think, Act and Relate to Your Company and Brands* (New York: Free Press, 1999); and J. B. Pine II and J. H. Gilmore, *The Experience Economy: Work Is Theatre and Every Business a Stage* (Boston: Harvard Business School Press, 1999).

31. See note 4, 198–200.

32. Ibid.

33. Ibid, 177–179.

34. *Business Week* (October 25, 1999), 106.

35. H. Courtney, J. Kirkland, and P. Viguerie "Strategy under Uncertainty," *Harvard Business Review,* 75 (November/December 1997), 67–79.

36. We are not the only ones to believe this; see note 26, D'Aveni.

37. For more on the dissolution of traditional boundaries, see J. M. Hulbert and P. Berthon, "Morphing Marketing: Dissolving Divisions" in *The Many Facets of Leadership,* ed. M. Goldsmith, B. L. Kaye, V. Govindarajan, and A. Vicere (Upper Saddle River, NJ: Prentice-Hall, 2002).

38. Many believe that decisions by U.S. chains to allow Nielsen and IRI to become scanner intermediaries is a major contributor to their poor margins,

rendering them vulnerable to suitors. (At time of writing, 25 percent of the U.S. supermarket industry is foreign-owned; many industry experts expect the proportion to rise to 50 percent.)

39. See, for example, F. Gouillart and F. Sturdivant, "Spend a Day in the Life of Your Customers," *Harvard Business Review,* 72 (January/February 1994), 116–125.

40. J. Willman, "Elida Returns to its Youth to Find Success," the *Financial Times* (November 5, 1999).

41. V. P. Barabba and G. Zaltman, *Hearing the Voice of the Market* (Boston: Harvard Business School Press, 1991).

42. See, for example, D. W. Cravens, N. F. Piercy, and S. H. Shipp, "New Organizational Forms for Competing in Highly Dynamic Environments," *British Journal of Management,* 7 (September 1996), 203–218.

## CHAPTER 3

1. Readers who seek more in-depth coverage and detail of these issues are referred to N. Capon and J. M. Hulbert, *Marketing Management in the 21st Century* (Upper Saddle River, NJ: Prentice Hall, 2001).

2. Opportunities can derive from many sources, for example, customers. In winter 1947, Kaye Draper, whose cat's sandbox had frozen, asked neighbor Edward Lowe for some sawdust from his father's sawdust business. On an inspiration he offered her some kiln-dried (highly absorbent) granulated clay his father was selling to mop up grease spills. A few days later she came back for more and, thinking he might be onto something, filled some bags with 5 pounds of material, marked them "Kitty Litter" and had a local pet shop offer them at 65 cents per bag (sand was one penny per pound). A business was born (*The New York Times,* early 1996, Obituaries).

3. C. Christensen addresses this issue head-on in *The Innovator's Dilemma* (Boston: Harvard Business School Press, 1997).

4. While the politics of allocation decisions create problems for the larger firm, smaller companies' difficulties often derive from their dependency on one or a few market segments. Their lack of diversity exposes them to greater risks in a downturn, and their lower volume may produce cost disadvantages. As the target market segment grows and becomes more attractive to other players, they may ultimately be doomed by scale-driven cost inefficiencies, or become acquisition targets.

5. For example, research in Europe has found that grandparents are major purchasers of the latest rock music CDs. While parents are enthusiastic to keep

such noise out of their houses, it appears that grandparents exact revenge by buying their grandchildren the loudest music available.

6. Both these examples provide marketing illustrations of what Liddell Hart terms an "indirect" strategic approach. That is, neither McDonald's nor FedEx took the obvious choice of customer target. See B. H. Liddell Hart, *Strategy: The Indirect Approach* (New York: Praeger, 1954).

7. The acronym by which the marketing mix is often known is the "four Ps"—product, place, promotion and price nowadays typically enhanced by the addition of service.

8. This is a vitally important point, clearly understood by the likes of companies such as Nike or Adidas, but one that escapes far too many company executives who see only the expenses involved in marketing communications.

9. For example see N. F. Piercy and N. A. Morgan, "Internal Marketing—The Missing Half of the Marketing Program," *Long Range Planning,* 24 (April 1991), 82–93.

10. J. M. Hulbert and L. F. Pitt, "Exit Left Center Stage? The Future of Functional Marketing," *European Management Journal,* 14 (February 1996), 47–60.

11. M. A. Devanna and N. M. Tichy, "Creating the Competitive Organization of the 21st Century," *Human Resource Management,* 29 (Winter 1990), 455–472.

12. J. N. Sheth and R. J. Sisodia, "Feeling the Heat," *Marketing Management,* 4 (Fall 1995), 8–23.

13. We discuss some alternative measures when we discuss brand health checks in Chapter 4.

14. Other dimensions of selectivity include levels in the distribution system; focus on nonusers, current customers, competitors' customers, or influencers of the buying process; and product portfolio choices.

15. For example, see N. F. Piercy and N. A. Morgan, "Strategic and Operational Market Segmentation: A Managerial Analysis," *Journal of Strategic Marketing,* 1 (March 1993), 123–140.

16. This may sometimes lead to longer-term competitive vulnerability, as Christensen has pointed out. See note 4.

17. For further discussion on these ideas see G. S. Carpenter, R. Glazer, and K. Nakamoto, *Readings on Market-Driving Strategies: Toward a New Theory of Competitive Advantage* (Reading, MA: Addison-Wesley, 1997); and P. Berthon, J. M. Hulbert, and L. F. Pitt, "To Serve or to Create? Strategic Orientations toward Customers and Innovation," *California Management Review,* 42 (fall 1999), 37–58.

18. See, for example, A. Slywotsky, *Value Migration* (Boston: Harvard Business School Press, 1996).
19. H. Simon, *Hidden Champions: Lessons from 500 of the World's Best Unknown Companies* (Boston: Harvard Business School Press, 1996).
20. See, for example, D. W. Cravens, N. F. Piercy, and G. S. Low, "The Innovation Challenges of Proactive Cannibalization and Discontinuous Technology," *European Business Review,* 14(4) (2002), 257–267.
21. See R. Foster, *The Attacker's Advantage* (New York: Summit Books, 1986).

CHAPTER 4

1. See, for example, P. Doyle, *Value-Based Marketing* (Chichester, England: Wiley, 2000).
2. No, let's be honest—they DO say . . .
3. These tasks and principles were outlined in the last chapter.
4. Returns to shareholders are a combination of dividends and capital gains from increases in share price.
5. Sometimes significant unrest occurs even when shareholder value has increased significantly. For example, toward the end of 1997, TIAA, a large institutional shareholder in Disney, openly argued for significant change in Disney's board membership. TIAA argued that too many outside board members were close personal acquaintances of CEO, Michael Eisner.
6. *The New York Times* (March 25, 1998).
7. A. Rappaport, *Creating Shareholder Value: The New Standard for Business Performance* (New York: Free Press, 1986), 3; see also, A. Rappaport, *Creating Shareholder Value: A Guide for Managers and Investors* (New York: Free Press, 1997).
8. Of course, many forms of organization exist in addition to state and publicly held corporations, including sole proprietorships, private corporations and partnerships. In most cases the goal of these organizations is to create wealth for the owners. However, for mutual organizations, typically owned by depositors (banking) or policyholders (insurance), ownership diffusion often means that the major wealth gainer is senior management. This may partly explain why countries like the United Kingdom have seen a wave of demutualization of such organizations, unlocking value for their members, now shareholders.
9. Cost of capital is a combination of the firm's cost of equity and cost of debt. Note that if the firm is operating multiple businesses, then appropriate risk adjustments may result in different target rates of return for each business,

see J. C. Van Horne, *Financial Management and Policy* (Upper Saddle River, NJ: Prentice Hall, 1995), Chapter 8.

10. More precisely, EVA is operating net income on a cash basis (or operating net income excluding the amortization of goodwill and certain intangibles) less an explicit charge for capital. See G. B. Stewart III, "EVA™, Fact, and Fantasy," *Journal of Applied Corporate Finance,* 7 (summer 1994), 72–84. Simply speaking, there are three ways to increase EVA: increase profit without increasing capital, invest in projects expected to earn more than the cost of capital and withdraw from projects earning unattractive returns.

11. See note 7.

12. See B. T. Gale, *Managing Customer Value* (New York: Free Press, 1994), 9, Exhibit 1–1.

13. See note 12, Chapter 14, pp. 342–362.

14. The Standard & Poor's (S&P) 500 firm index is a broader measure of stock-market performances than the Dow Jones average, which is based on only 30 firms.

15. *Business Week* (March 16, 1998).

16. R. S. Kaplan and D. P. Norton, *The Balanced Scorecard* (Boston: Harvard Business School Press, 1996).

17. See note 1.

18. D. A. Aaker, *Managing Brand Equity* (New York: Free Press, 1991), 15. See, also, other books on branding by the same author: *Building Strong Brands* (New York: Free Press, 1995); and *Brand Leadership* with E. Joachimsthaler (New York: Free Press, 2000).

19. Awareness is the *sine qua non* for brand equity; however, the cost to develop awareness can be staggering. For example, in 1996, Lucent Technologies, formerly a part of AT&T (including Bell Laboratories), spent $50 million to create awareness for the new company, *The New York Times* (June 3, 1996).

20. What we are calling organizational brand equity is sometimes termed "brand value."

21. In consumer package goods, a proximate measure of brand equity relates to the difference in price over a store brand. Of course, some store brands have considerable equity in their own right; for example, Bloomingdale's, Macy's, and Marks & Spencer.

22. Of course, for accurate assessment, this method relies on an efficient market value for the brand. A recent study casts doubt on market efficiency. Thus, M. J. Cooper, O. Dimitrov, and P. Raghavendra, "A Rose.com by Any Other Name," www.mgmt.purdue.edu/mcooper/newpapers/dotcom.pdf,

May 1999, showed that on average the value of companies that changed their names to include a web-orientation (".com," ".net" or "Internet") increased in value 125 percent more than comparable companies! Of course, by 2001 the opposite effect was occurring, confirming to the doubting yet again that Keynes' view of market irrationality was more than justified.

23. This approach compares the revenues (price*volume) earned by the brand in a product category with the revenues (price*volume) earned (or estimated) by a generic product in the same category.

24. The problem of accounting for "goodwill" (the excess of acquisition price over net tangible assets) is that, in some countries, companies are penalized for "good acquisitions" by having to take significant amortization charges against income or by writing off the amount against reserves.

25. We are indebted to our colleague Tim Ambler of London Business School for this insight.

26. For a discussion of some of the issues surrounding the brand management system, see P. Berthon, J. M. Hulbert, and L. F. Pitt, "Brand Management Prognostications," *Sloan Management Review,* 40 (winter 1999), 53–65.

27. Customer brand equity is closely related to Blattberg and Deighton's concept of customer equity. See R. C. Blattberg and J. Deighton, "Manage Marketing by the Customer Equity Test," *Harvard Business Review,* 74 (July/August 1996), 136–144).

28. Some observers explain the loss in market share of fast moving consumer goods brands to store brands to loss in brand equity due to excessive price promotions.

29. F. F. Reichheld, *The Loyalty Effect* (Boston: Harvard Business School Press, 1996).

30. Ibid.

31. One reason for the success of Internet bookseller Amazon.com is its negative working capital: It maintains little inventory (turnover 26 times p.a.), receives cash from sales charged to customer's credit cards within one day yet pays suppliers on average in 46 days, *The New York Times* (July 19, 1998). Wal-Mart uses suppliers' cash in a similar manner.

32. Cost savings may be highly significant. For example, in the mid-1990s, AT&T (now Lucent technologies) claimed the Pentagon would save $1.5 billion by outsourcing the building of a new telephone system rather than developing it in house.

33. R. Peisch, "When Outsourcing Goes Awry," *Harvard Business Review,* 73 (May/June 1995), 24–37.

34. In some cases, outsourcing has moved into more strategic functions. For example, in spring 1996, Computer Software Associates, a major software developer, made an agreement for then Digital Equipment's 22,000 computer-services engineers to support its products.
35. Based on K. Ohmae, *The Mind of the Strategist* (New York: McGraw-Hill, 1982).

## CHAPTER 5

1. We use the term market strategy rather than marketing strategy to emphasize that the efforts of many functional areas, not just marketing, are required to help develop and implement the strategy.
2. See, for example, H. Mintzberg, *The Rise and Fall of Strategic Planning* (New York: Free Press, 1994). See also N. Capon, "Review of *The Rise and Fall of Strategic Planning*" in *Academy of Management Review,* 21 (January 1996), 298–301.
3. For interesting perspectives on competitive advantage, see J. R. Williams, "How Sustainable Is Your Competitive Advantage," *California Management Review* 34 (spring 1992), 29–52; P. Ghemawat, "Sustainable Advantage," *Harvard Business Review,* 64 (September/October 1986), 53–94; and M. E. Porter and V. E. Millar, "How Information Gives You Competitive Advantage," *Harvard Business Review,* 63 (July/August 1985), 149–159.
4. As volume increases, the implicit fixed cost per unit is reduced.
5. Although the notion of positioning strategy is typically more familiar to consumer marketers than industrial marketers, the same basic principles apply, especially the three Cs concept.
6. Many organizations confuse performance objectives and mission. Mission is a broad statement of where the firm will seek business; by contrast, performance objectives are statements of the results the firm seeks to achieve.
7. For more details on this project, a multicompany ongoing empirical study of business performance, see R. D. Buzzell and B. T. Gale, *The PIMS Principles: Linking Strategy to Performance* (New York: Free Press, 1987).
8. We should note that it is important to distinguish shareholder value creation from blind conformance to a budget that may have, but too often has not, taken into consideration the true interests of shareholders.
9. The acronym SMART is often used to describe well-formulated objectives: **S**pecific, **M**easurable, **A**chievable, **R**ealistic, **T**imely.

10. For an example of how some leading firms are dealing with this issue, see the discussion of "brand health" checks in Chapter 4.

11. There are other ways to build such chains. For example, we could expand the revenue and/or reduce the cost components that comprise profit. As with Figure 5.1, for each of these broad pathways, a variety of more specific actions (tactics) could be used to implement a particular focus.

12. See Chapter 10 for more discussion of customer relationship management.

13. *The New York Times* (January 31, 1999).

14. This approach, masterminded by John Sculley and involving offering large bottles of soft drinks, was used by Pepsi to take away Coca Cola's advantage with its "hour glass" bottle in supermarket business. See, J. Sculley with J. A. Byrne, *Odyssey: Pepsi to Apple . . . A Journey of Adventure, Ideas and the Future* (New York: Harper & Row, 1987).

15. This approach, traditionally used by automobile manufacturers, diminishes the value of already purchased products. It has become central to the strategies of many software companies that periodically introduce product upgrades.

16. Perhaps the chief exemplar of this strategy is Church and Dwight, whose Arm and Hammer baking soda product has found its way into end uses as diverse as cat litter, toothpaste, detergent, and cattle feed.

17. Price promotions have been a major feature of supermarket products and automobile marketing in recent years. Unfortunately, these tactics often do little more than shift purchases forward in time without securing an enduring increase in usage. As a result, they often create havoc in the supply chain and destroy shareholder value. Price incentives to purchase are often unproductive unless linked to actions that increase usage.

18. In certain businesses, the nature of the product or service, typically those that involve a direct relationship such as financial services, leads to firms having significant data on their customers; this data can be used to make specific offers. In other areas, especially for many consumer goods, a variety of marketing tactics may require that the firm specifically identify its customers.

19. See Chapter 10 for more detailed commentary on this issue.

20. These ideas were developed further in Chapter 4.

21. In this discussion, the customer may be either an individual or family, or a formal organization.

22. It is interesting that in 2000, Avon Cosmetics, after 115 years of selling direct to the consumer, took its products into department stores and shopping malls for the first time. Changing social patterns and competitive channels forced a new distribution strategy to emerge.

23. College Savings Bank (A) and (B) in N. Capon, *The Marketing of Financial Services: A Book of Cases* (Upper Saddle River, NJ: Prentice Hall, 1992).

24. One of the greatest thinkers about military strategy similarly advocates what he terms "the indirect approach." See B. H. Liddell Hart, *Strategy: The Indirect Approach* (New York: Praeger, 1954).

25. Note that the McDonald's child is also value-responsive; value is represented by the contents of the Happy Meal!

26. In addition to McDonald's, we could add breakfast cereal, snowboarding equipment, teenage fashion, and many more categories.

27. Such approaches are not without risks, however. British Airways is struggling to hold its share of European business travelers with its frequent-flier cards and lounges, while no-frills operators EasyJet and Ryanair are growing rapidly by offering corporate buyers massively lower fares.

28. In the argot of industrial marketing, this targeting is known as the "specification sell"; the goal is to specify the attributes of the product/service so that the purchasing agent is left with little or no choice of supplier.

29. For more detail on the "value proposition," see "Achieving Market Focus," Chapter 7 in F. J. Gouillart and J. N. Kelly, *Transforming the Organization* (New York: McGraw-Hill, 1996).

30. A. Ries and J. Trout, *Positioning: The Battle for Your Mind* (New York: McGraw-Hill, 1993).

31. Developed by Robert Christian, formerly of the Impact Planning Group, Stamford, Connecticut.

32. Of course, product quality has many dimensions, but they need not be explored for the purpose of this example.

33. The Japanese heavy-equipment manufacturer Komatsu ran into this problem when it first entered the U.S. market.

34. L. Mazur, "Booking Skills for the Future," *Marketing Business* (October 2000), 4.

## CHAPTER 6

1. A British term for an untrustworthy individual.

2. "Marketers—Not 'Soft' Enough," *Marketing Business* (November 1998), 10.

3. S. Baker, "What Non-Marketers Think about You," *Marketing Business* (September 2000), v–vii.

4. R. Fazio Maruca, "Getting Marketing's Voice Heard," *Harvard Business Review,* 1 (January/February 1998), 10–11.

5. R. Howell, "Time for Business to Value the Brand," *The Financial Times* (February 18, 2000).

6. R. Wachman, "BT Finance Chief May Go in Shuffle," *Sunday Business* (March 5, 2000).

7. L. Buckingham, "Bosses Fall in W. H. Smith Cull," *Financial Mail on Sunday* (June 4, 2000), 1.

8. T. Ambler, *Marketing and the Bottom Line* (London: Financial Times/Prentice Hall, 2000), 1.

9. *Fortune* (March 19, 2001), 135–138. Jeffrey Immelt, Welch's successor at General Electric, now has to deal with much greater scrutiny over this issue.

10. This was discussed in Chapter 4.

11. For some readable and interesting perspectives on these subjects from the accountants themselves, see A. Rappaport, *Creating Shareholder Value: The New Standard for Business Performance* (New York: Free Press, 1986), especially Chapter 2; and H. Thomas Johnson and R. S. Kaplan, *Relevance Lost: The Rise and Fall of Management Accounting* (Boston: Harvard Business School Press, 1991). The flurry of Congressional hearings in the wake of the Enron scandal has added weight to many of these criticisms.

12. See, for example, D. B. Hertz, "Risk Analysis in Capital Investment," *Harvard Business Review,* 42 (January/February, 1964), 95–106.

13. See, for example, H. Courtney, J. Kirkland, and P. Viguerie, "Strategy under Uncertainty," *Harvard Business Review,* 75 (November/December 1997), 67–79.

14. However, nothing is sacrosanct in the modern world—since 1977 the Swedish bank Svenska Handelsbanken has been managed without budgets, achieving outstanding performance results, and European drinks company, Diageo, has redesigned its strategic planning to focus on "value drivers" instead of "budgets." See, T. Lester, "Cutting the Planning Ties that Bind," *The Financial Times* (May 9, 2000).

15. See C. F. Mela, S. Gupta, and D. R. Lehmann, "The Long-Term Impact of Advertising and Promotion on Consumer Brand Choice," *Journal of Marketing Research,* 35 (May 1997), 248–261; and C. F. Mela, S. Gupta, and K. Jedidi, "Assessing Long-Term Promotional Influences on Market Structure," *International Journal of Research in Marketing,* 15 (February 1998), 89–107.

16. For a fuller exposition of these concepts, see G.S. Carpenter, R. Glazer and K. Nakamoto *Readings on Market-Driving Strategies: Toward a New Theory of Competitive Advantage* (Reading, MA: Addison-Wesley, 1997).

17. R. G. Cooper, "Dimensions of Industrial New Product Success and Failure," *Journal of Marketing,* 43 (Summer 1979), 93–103.

18. J. N. Sheth and R.J. Sisodia, "Feeling the Heat," *Marketing Management,* 4 (Fall 1995), 8–23.

19. Over 40 years ago, a major pricing study found the same result. See A. D. H. Kaplan, J. B. Dirlam, and R. F. Lanzillotti, *Pricing in Big Business* (Washington, DC: Brookings Institution, 1958).

20. B. T. Gale, *Managing Customer Value* (New York: Free Press, 1994).

21. R.S. Kaplan and D.P. Norton, "Putting the Balanced Scorecard to Work," *Harvard Business Review,* 71 (September/October 1993), 134–142.

22. N. Capon, *Key Account Management and Planning* (New York: Free Press, 2001).

## CHAPTER 7

1. We use the term operations broadly, to include logistics under a total supply chain conception.

2. For example, see N. F. Piercy, "The Power and Politics of Sales Forecasting: Uncertainty Absorption and the Power of the Marketing Department," *Journal of the Academy of Marketing Science,* 17 (Winter 1989), 109–121.

3. *The Daily Telegraph* (January 27, 2000).

4. S. Buckby, "Consumer Choices Fox Marketers," *The Financial Times* (November 11, 1998).

5. The development of flow-based models appears to offer promise in the new product area. See, for example, G. L. Urban, J. R. Hauser, and J. H. Roberts, "Prelaunch Forecasting of New Automobiles," *Management Science,* 36 (April 1990), 401–421.

6. For this reason, some senior managers have been attending seminars on chaos theory!

7. See Chapter 2.

8. For a more complete discussion of these changes, see P. Berthon, M. B. Holbrook, and J. M. Hulbert "Beyond Market Orientation: A Conceptualization of Market Evolution," *Journal of Interactive Marketing,* 14 (Summer 2000), 50–66.

9. Superior efficiency in the use of capital turns out to be one of the U.S.'s major competitive advantages over Germany and Japan. See R. Agrawal, S. Findley, S. Greene, K. Huang, A. Jeddy, W. H. Lewis, and M. Petry, "Why the U.S. leads and why it matters," *McKinsey Quarterly,* 3 (1996), 38–55.

10. See, for example, W. A. Shewhart, *Statistical Method from the Point of View of Quality Control* (New York: Dover, 1986).

11. For discussion of the evolution of the quality movement, see B. T. Gale, *Managing Customer Value* (New York: Free Press, 1994).

12. K. B. Kahn and J. T. Mentzner, "Marketing's Integration with Other Functions," *Journal of Business Research,* 42 (May 1998), 53–62.
13. J. R. Hauser and D. Clausing, "The House of Quality," *Harvard Business Review,* 66 (May/June 1988), 63–73.
14. J. P. Womack and D. T. Jones, *Lean Thinking: Banish Waste and Create Wealth in your Corporation* (New York: Simon & Schuster, 1996); J. P. Womack and D. T. Jones, "From Lean Production to the Lean Enterprise," *Harvard Business Review,* 72 (March/April, 1994), 93–103; and J. P. Womack and D. T. Jones, "Beyond Toyota: How to Root out Waste and Pursue Perfection," *Harvard Business Review,* 74 (September/October 1996), 140–158.
15. D. R. Towill, "The Seamless Supply Chain: The Predator's Strategic Advantage," *International Journal of Technology Management,* 13 (1997), 37–56.
16. M. Christopher, *Marketing Logistics* (Oxford, England: Butterworth-Heinemann, 1997).
17. See, for example, N. F. Piercy, "Marketing Implementation: The Implications of Marketing Paradigm Weakness for the Strategy Execution Process," *Journal of the Academy of Marketing Science,* 26 (Summer 1998), 222–236; N. F. Piercy and N. A. Morgan, "The Impact of Lean Thinking and the Lean Enterprise on Marketing: Threat or Synergy?" *Journal of Marketing Management,* 13 (January 1997), 679–693.
18. Ibid, Piercy and Morgan.
19. See A. J. Slywotsky, *Value Migration: How to Think Several Moves Ahead of the Competition* (Boston: Harvard Business School Press, 1996).
20. M. Christopher, "The Agile Supply Chain," *Industrial Marketing Management,* 29 (January 2000), 37–44.
21. J. B. Taylor, M. M. Naim, and D. Berry, "Leagility: Interfacing the Lean and Agile Manufacturing Paradigm in the Total Supply Chain," *International Journal of Production Economics,* 62 (May 1999), 107–118.
22. See, for example, M. Christopher and D. R. Towill, "Supply Chain Migration From Lean to Functional to Agile and Customized," *Supply Chain Management,* 5 (2000), 206–221; B. Evans and M. Powell, "Synergistic Thinking: A Pragmatic view of 'Lean' and 'Agile'," *Logistics and Transport Focus,* 2 (December 2000); and M. Whitehead, "Flexible: Friend or Foe," *Supply Management* (January 6, 2000), 24–27.

## CHAPTER 8

1. The H.R. Challey Group, *The Customer Selected World Class Sales Executive Report* (Dayton, OH: Chally, 1996.

2. R. C. Blattberg and J. Deighton, "Manage Marketing by the Customer Equity Test," *Harvard Business Review,* 74 (July/August 1996), 136–144.

3. According to *Business Week,* November 2, 2001, 85 percent of OEM's expected to increase outsourcing during the year, and would eventually outsource some 70 percent or more of their manufacturing functions.

4. For the factors driving the growth of key account management and a deeper discussion of many of these issues, see N. Capon, *Key Account Management and Planning* (New York: Free Press, 2001).

5. Indeed, an interesting side issue that managers have only recently started to take seriously in even the most street-wise companies is—what are the costs of getting out of this close buyer-seller relationship, if we want to? It is sad but true that many marriages end in divorce. We may need to think about corporate "prenuptial agreements" in the future, about who pays for what if things don't work out. We may also need to think about the vulnerability and risk to which we are exposed by the dependence inherent in partnering strategies.

6. For IBM, this strategic thrust was a belated recognition of the concept that motivated Ross Perot's founding of Electronic Data Systems (EDS).

7. See M. B. Holbrook and J. M. Hulbert, "Elegy on the Death of Marketing: Never Send to Know Why We Have Come to Bury Marketing but Ask What You Can Do for Your Country Churchyard," *European Journal of Marketing,* 36 (June, 2002), 706–732.

8. See P. Berthon, J. M. Hulbert, and L. F. Pitt, "Brand Management Prognostications," *Sloan Management Review,* 40 (Winter 1999), 53–65. See also, note 4.

9. In reality, many firms pay salespeople on some combination of salary and incentive compensation.

10. D. W. Cravens, "The Changing Role of the Salesforce," *Marketing Management,* 4 (Fall 1995), 48–58.

11. For the cynical reader we emphasize that forging is a metaphor from the metals industry and does not imply counterfeiting.

## CHAPTER 9

1. M. Christen, "Mastering Marketing—Does It Pay to Be a Pioneer?" *The Financial Times* (October 19, 1998).

2. See, for example, D. W. Cravens, N. F. Piercy, and G. S. Low, "The Innovation Challenges of Proactive Cannibalization and Discontinuous Technology," *European Business Review,* 14(4) (2002), 257–267. D. W.

Cravens, N. F. Piercy, and A. Prentice, "Developing Market-Driven Product Strategies," *Journal of Product and Brand Management,* 9 (2000), 369–388.

3. See, for example, R. J. Fisher, E. Maltz, and B. J. Jaworski, "Enhancing Communication between Marketing and Engineering: The Moderating Influence of Relative Functional Identification," *Journal of Marketing,* 67 (July 1997), 54–70; A. K. Gupta, S. P. Raj, and D. Wilemon, "A Model for Studying the R&D Marketing Interface in the New Product Development Process," *Journal of Marketing,* 60 (January 1996), 7–17.

4. C. Cookson, "R&D Proving to Be the Engine of Growth," *The Financial Times* (September 15, 2000).

5. Quoted in R. Murray-West, "Can Drug Firms Kick the R&D Habit," *Daily Telegraph* (January 6, 2001).

6. P. Marsh, "The Need to Harvest Home-Grown Creativity," *The Financial Times* (March 22, 2001).

7. N. Capon and R. Glazer, "Marketing and Technology: A Strategic Co-Alignment," *Journal of Marketing,* 51 (July 1987), 1–14.

8. B. Donath, "Marketers of Technology Make Promises They Can't Keep," *Marketing News* (October 13, 1997), 5.

9. C. M. Christensen, *The Innovator's Dilemma: When New Technologies Cause Great Firms to Fail* (Boston: Harvard Business School Press, 1997).

10. M. L. Tushman and C. A. O'Reilly, "Ambidextrous Organizations: Managing Evolutionary and Revolutionary Change," *California Management Review,* 38 (Summer 1996), 8–30.

11. See, for example, P. Berthon, J. M. Hulbert, and L. F. Pitt, "To Serve or to Create? Strategic Orientations toward Customers and Innovation," *California Management Review,* 42 (Fall 1999), 37–58.

12. This particular typology was first introduced by H. I. Ansoff and J. M. Stewart, "Strategies for a Technologically-Based Business," *Harvard Business Review,* 45 (November/December 1967), 71–83; and further developed by N. Capon and J. Hulbert, *Marketing Management in the 21st Century* (Upper Saddle River, NJ: Prentice Hall, 2001).

13. To succeed, these companies must "shape" the structure of demand. For this reason we originally labeled them as "shapers." See note 11.

14. In some circles, the received wisdom holds that R&D spending is critical for success in developing new products. However, in many cases of successful new products, for example, color television, required market development spending outstripped R&D.

15. There is extensive literature on this subject in strategy and marketing.

16. See note 13.

17. A recent estimate in the R&D-intensive pharmaceuticals industry was that patents are typically invented around within four years, at 65 percent of the innovator's cost. See note 13.

18. See, for example, G. L. Lilien and A. Rangaswamy, *Marketing Engineering* (Reading, MA: Addison Wesley, 1998).

19. An oxymoron is a self-contradictory phrase. The classic example is the term "bitter-sweet." Other examples may include: "airline service" and "fast food."

20. For a fascinating discussion of the capital market implications of this change, see R. N. Foster and S. Kaplan, *Creative Destruction* (New York: Currency, 2001).

21. D. J. Teece, "Profiting from Technological Innovation: Implications for Integration, Collaboration, Licensing and Public Policy," *Research Policy*, 15 (December 1986), 285–306; H. W. Chesbrough and D. J. Teece, "When Is Virtual Virtuous? Organizing for Innovation," *Harvard Business Review*, 74 (January/February 1996), 65–73.

22. R. N. Foster, *Innovation: The Attacker's Advantage* (New York: Summit Books, 1986).

23. H. Drnec, *The Independent* (August 2, 1992).

24. J. Wind, P. E. Green, D. Shifflet, and M. Scarborough, "Courtyard by Marriott: Designing a Hotel Facility with Consumer-Based Marketing Models," Copyright—The Institute of Management Sciences, in C. H. Lovelock *Managing Services: Marketing, Operations and Human Resources* (Upper Saddle River, NJ: Prentice-Hall, 1992), 119–137.

25. M. R. Millson and D. Wilemon, "Strategic Partnering for Developing New Products," *Research-Technology Management*, 39 (1996), 41–49.

26. P. Zagnoli and C. Cardini, "Patterns of R&D Cooperation for New Product Development: The Olivetti Multimedia Product," *R&D Management*, 24 (January 1994), 3–15 of p. 14.

27. N. Tzokas, M. Saren, and D. Brownlie, "Generating Marketing Resources by Means of R&D Activities in High Technology Firms," *Industrial Marketing Management*, 26 (July 1997), 331–340.

28. N. Capon, J. U. Farley, and J. M. Hulbert, *Corporate Strategic Planning* (New York: Columbia University Press, 1988).

29. R. G. Cooper and E. J. Kleinschmidt, "An Investigation into the New Product Process: Steps, Deficiencies and Impact," *Journal of Product Innovation Management*, 3 (June 1986), 71–85.

30. Raymond C. Odioso, "An R&D Executive Looks at Marketing," *Research Management*, 30 (September/October, 1987), 20–25.

31. Ibid, 20.
32. J. Deschamps, "Managing the Marketing/R&D Interface," *Prism* (Fourth Quarter 1994), 5–19.
33. Ibid., 16.
34. Ibid., 19.

CHAPTER 10

1. S. Brown, "Torment Your Customers (They'll Love You for It)," *Harvard Business Review,* 79 (October 2001), 83–88.
2. K. Albrecht, "Truths of Service," *Executive Excellence* (Homewood, IL: Dow Jones-Irwin, 1985), 11.
3. Ibid.
4. T. O. Jones and W. E. Sasser Jr., "Why Satisfied Customers Defect," *Harvard Business Review,* 73 (November/December 1995), 88–99.
5. See, for example, A. Parasuraman, V. A. Zeithaml, and L. L. Berry, "A Conceptual Model of Service Quality and Its Implications for Future Research," *Journal of Marketing,* 49 (Fall 1985), 41–50.
6. See, for example, W. H. Davidow and B. Uttal, *Total Customer Service* (New York: Harper & Row, 1989); C. Lovelock and L. Wright, *Principles of Service Marketing and Management* (Upper Saddle River, NJ: Prentice Hall, 2001); and L. L. Berry and A. Parasuraman, *Marketing Services: Competing Through Quality* (New York: Free Press, 1991).
7. Perhaps the best known of these efforts is the SERVQUAL model. See note 5.
8. By which, dear reader, we do not actually mean offending customers, but taking the initiative.
9. Personal discussion with Professor David Ulrich, author of *Human Resource Champions* (Boston: Harvard Business School Press, 1997).
10. Reported at April 1997 meetings of the Marketing Science Institute.
11. K. Horner, "Customer Relationship Management: The Business Challenge," *Marketing Business* (May 2001), xi–xiii.
12. G. S. Day, "Tying in an Asset," in *Understanding CRM* (London: Financial Times, 2000).
13. C. Field, "Loyalty Cards Are Unlikely to Carry All the Answers," *The Financial Times* (May 3, 2000); and M. McDonald, "On the Right Track," *Marketing Business* (April 2000), 28–31.
14. M. Treacy and F. Wiersema, "Customer Intimacy and other Value Disciplines," *Harvard Business Review,* 71 (January/February 1993), 84–93.
15. See note 6, Davidow and Uttal.

16. The benighted and ultimately rejected government of John Major in Great Britain attempted to introduce a citizen's charter to decree limits to bureaucratic inertia, but it was a poorly marketed initiative by a failing government. Although some improvements resulted, most voters remained in ignorance of the effort.

17. P. Martin, "Dangerous Gifts," *The Financial Times* (December 12, 1998).

18. J. Carlzon, *Moments of Truth* (Cambridge, MA: Ballinger, 1987).

19. Since this company employs not a few of our students, and is now under new management, we have omitted its name. It is worth noting, however, that although we had an horrendous service experience, this company was noted and, indeed, written up in the major business magazines, for its service excellence!

20. See F. F. Reichheld, "Learning from Customers Defections," *Harvard Business Review,* 74 (March/April 1996), 57–69, for an instructive discussion of analyzing service failures.

21. There are interesting similarities to the reputed comment of the British film actor, Noel Coward, when he was asked about his experiences in the First World War—"Oh, my dear, the noise . . . the people . . ."

22. Part of the folklore surrounding the British automobile company Rolls Royce is that in its early days the firm positively vetted all prospective customers to assure itself they had the financial means for appropriate upkeep of the automobile.

23. *The New York Times* (June 10, 1997). In a game between the New York Mets and the Cincinnati Reds, a fan behind home plate called out the catcher's instructions to the Met's pitcher. Despite his efforts, the Reds' batters were unable to take advantage and the Mets won 4–2.

24. P. Berthon, J. M. Hulbert, and M. B. Holbrook, "Beyond Market Orientation: A Conceptualization of Market Evolution," *Journal of Interactive Marketing,* 14 (Summer 2000), 50–66.

## CHAPTER II

1. M. Skapinker, "A Higher Status for the People Person," *The Financial Times* (January 29, 2002).

2. B. J. Pine II and J. H. Gilmore, *Every Business a Stage: Why Customers Now Want Experiences* (Boston: Harvard Business School Press, 1999); and B. J. Pine II and J. H. Gilmore, "Welcome to the Experience Economy," *Harvard Business Review,* 76 (July/August 1998), 97–105.

3. S. Ghoshal and C. A. Bartlett, "Play the Right Card to Get the Aces in the Pack," *The Financial Times* (July 28, 1998).

4. J. Ridderstrale and K. Nordstrom, *Funky Business* (Hemel Hempstead: Prentice-Hall, 2000).

5. M. Skapinker, "The Competition for Talent," *The Financial Times* (January 15, 2001).

6. K. Brown, "Skills Shortage Leads List of Business Concerns," *The Financial Times* (January 17, 2001); S. Hoare, "Allies on the Home Front," *Sunday Business* (February 4, 2001); and R. McClure, "Central Perks," *Sunday Business* (February 4, 2001).

7. A. Maitland, " 'It's Tough at the Top' Say Leading Companies' CEOs," *The Financial Times* (June 10, 1999).

8. Glassman, M. and B. McAfee, "Integrating the Personnel and Marketing Functions: The Challenge of the 1990s," *Business Horizons,* 35 (1999), 52–59.

9. J. B. Quinn, Intelligent Enterprise (New York: Free Press, 1992).

10. For example, Chemical Bank used to have a 2000 page branch manual; six pages were allotted to opening the front door!

11. One of our colleagues, Don Hambrick, has convincingly demonstrated the influence of the CEO background on his decisions, S. Finkelstein and D. C. Hambrick, *Strategy and Leadership: Top Executives and Their Effects on Organizations* (St. Paul, MN: West, 1996).

12. Reputedly developed by Mahatma Gandhi and hung in his law office in South Africa.

13. J. G. March and H.A. Simon, *Organizations* (New York: Wiley, 1958).

14. N. Tichy and M.A. Devanna, *The Transformational Leader* (New York: Wiley, 1990).

15. P. Senge, *The Fifth Discipline: The Art and Practice of the Learning Organization* (New York: Doubleday, 1990).

16. N. F. Piercy and D. W. Cravens, "The Imperatives of Value-Driven Strategy," *Journal of Change Management,* 1 (July 2000).

17. N. Capon and J. M. Hulbert, *Managing Marketing in the 21st Century* (Upper Saddle River, NJ: Prentice Hall, 2001).

18. See note 14.

19. For more discussion of these issues see C. Christensen, *The Innovator's Dilemma: When New Technologies Cause Great Firms to Fail* (Boston: Harvard Business School Press, 1997).

20. N. F. Piercy and N. Lane, "Marketing Implementation: Building and Sustaining a Real Market Understanding," *Journal of Marketing Practice: Applied Marketing Science,* 2 (1996), 15–28.

21. Cf. the original use of these terms in T. Burns and G. M. Stalker, *The Management of Innovation* (Oxford, England: Oxford University Press, 1994, rev. ed.).

22. P. Berthon, J. M. Hulbert, and L. F. Pitt "To Serve or to Create? Strategic Orientations toward Customers and Innovation," *California Management Review,* 42 (Fall 1999), 37–58.

23. P. Berthon, J. M. Hulbert, and L. Pitt, "Brand Management Prognostications," *Sloan Management Review,* 40 (Winter 1999), 53–65.

24. For more detail, see R. T. Pascale and A. G. Athos, *The Art of Japanese Management* (London: Allen Lane, 1981).

25. D. A. Nadler and M. Tushman, *Competing by Design* (New York: Oxford University Press, 1997).

26. See, for example, the discussion of organizational stretch in implementation strategy in Nigel F. Piercy, *Market-Led Strategic Change: A Guide to Transforming the Process of Going to Market* (Oxford, England: Butterworth-Heinemann, 2002, 3rd ed.), 689–692.

27. R. W. Revens, *The ABC of Action Learning* (London: Lemos and Crane, 1998, 3rd ed.).

28. Professor David Ulrich, personal conversation. Interested readers may want to look at his latest book, *Human Resource Champions: The Next Agenda for Adding Value and Delivering Results* (Boston: Harvard Business School Press, 1997).

29. N. Capon, *Key Account Management and Planning* (New York: Free Press, 2001).

30. T. V. Bonoma and V. Crittenden, "Managing Marketing Implementation," *Sloan Management Review,* 29 (Winter 1988), 7–15.

31. J. R. Katzenbach and D. K. Smith, *The Wisdom of Teams* (Boston: Harvard Business School Press, 1993).

## CHAPTER 12

1. First briefly discussed in Chapter 11.

2. See J. C. Collins and J. I. Porras, "Building Your Company's Vision," *Harvard Business Review,* 74 (September/October 1996), 65–77.

3. Although he does not call it a vision statement, Jan Carlzon describes exactly this problem in his book on the turnaround of SAS, *Moments of Truth* (New York: Harper & Row, 1989).

4. *Fortune* (April 14, 1997). Note that Gerstner did not immediately attempt to articulate a vision, but waited until he understood his new business better.

5. *Business Week* (May 17, 1999). Microsoft's new vision was accompanied by a shift to a customer focused organization, see later in the chapter.

6. Extracted from Amazon.com's online 1999 Annual Report to Shareholders.

7. Extracted from Dell's online investor information page, March 31, 2002. Note, however, that we use the term "mission" differently from Dell.

8. Extracted from Unisys' online investor information page, March 31, 2002.

9. Poor quality of direction is one of the main killers of successful strategy implementation. See M. Beer and R. A. Eisenstat, "The Silent Killers of Strategy Implementation and Learning," *Sloan Management Review,* 41 (Summer 2000), 29–40.

10. *Fortune* (May 24, 1999).

11. We attribute this term to Professor Lester Thomas, founder and director of the Industrial Performance Center, MIT.

12. Business missions may serve the function of determining organizational boundaries for the various businesses as a means of avoiding resource waste caused by multiple business units addressing the same market. Alternatively, business missions may be written more loosely under the philosophy that internal competition has positive value in ensuring that market opportunities are addressed.

13. See, for example, N. F. Piercy and N. A. Morgan, "Mission Analysis: An Operational Approach," *Journal of General Management,* 19 (Spring 1994), 1–20; and N. Capon, J. U. Farley, and J. M. Hulbert, *Corporate Strategic Planning* (New York: Columbia University Press, 1988).

14. These analysts cited rising stock prices from chemical companies shedding mature product divisions; for example, in 1998, Monsanto's stock price was over 40 times anticipated earnings, the *New York Times* (March 3, 1998).

15. As a result of the early 2000s, Nokia's valuation has dropped, but it retains its strong market share position.

16. M. Beer, R. A. Eisenstat, and B. Spector, *The Critical Path to Corporate Renewal* (Boston: Harvard Business School Press, 1990), 29.

17. This section draws heavily on ideas developed in P. Berthon, J. M. Hulbert, and L. F. Pitt, "Brand Management Prognostications," *Sloan Management Review,* 40 (Winter 1999), 53–65.

18. This is often described as a matrix organization inasmuch as individuals charged with marketing activities, for example, individual salespeople, "work for" the various brand managers yet report to their own sales organizations.

19. This is one of the reasons for the increased importance of category management.

20. R. J. Keith, "The Marketing Revolution," *Journal of Marketing,* 24 (January 1960), 35–38.

21. R. McKenna, "Marketing is Everything," *Harvard Business Review,* 69 (January/February 1991), 65–79.

22. M. Hammer and J. Champy, *Reengineering the Corporation: A Manifesto for Business Revolution* (New York: Nicholas Brealy, 1993).

23. R. C. Blattberg and J. Deighton, "Interactive Marketing: Exploiting the Age of Addressability," *Sloan Management Review,* 33 (Fall 1991), 5–14;

Inc., 1995; D. Peppers and M. Rogers, *The One-to-One Future: Building Relationships One Customer at a Time* (New York: Century Doubleday, 1993).

24. F. F. Reichheld, *The Loyalty Effect* (Boston: Harvard Business School Press, 1996).

25. This organization is matrixed with a brand management organization focused on the various types of IBM products.

26. N. Capon, *Key Account Management and Planning* (New York: Free Press, 2001).

27. D. Schultz, "A Better Way to Organize," *Marketing News* (March 27, 1995), 15.

28. Our thinking in this regard has been influenced by the terminology of Peppers and Rogers and, to a considerable extent, by Blattberg and Deighton. See note 23.

29. N. Capon, "Wachovia Bank and Trust Company," *The Marketing of Financial Services* (Upper Saddle River, NJ: Prentice Hall, 1992).

30. This approach is sympathetic to Tom Peters suggestion of turning the organization on its head, T. Peters, *Thriving on Chaos* (New York: Bantam Books, 1987).

31. Interestingly, this challenge has recently been described as one of "creating a company for customers"—M. McDonald, M. Christopher, S. Knox, and A. Payne, *Creating a Company for Customers: How to Build and Lead a Market-Driven Organization* (London: Financial Times/Prentice-Hall, 2001).

32. See note 23, Peppers and Rogers.

33. J. K. Johanson and I. Nonaka, "Market Research the Japanese Way," *Harvard Business Review,* 65 (May/June 1987), 29–32.

34. For further reading, see L. P. Carbone and S. H. Haeckel, "Engineering Customer Experiences," *Marketing Management,* 3 (Winter 1994), 8–19; G. A. Churchill, R. H. Collins, and W. A. Strang, "Should Retail Salespersons be Similar to Their Customers," *Journal of Retailing,* 51 (Fall 1975), 29–42; and A. G. Woodside and W. J. Davenport, "The Effect of Salesman Similarity and Expertise on Consumer Purchasing Behavior," *Journal of Marketing,* 11 (May 1974), 198–202.

35. See, for example, N. F. Piercy and D. W. Cravens, "Marketing Organization and Management" in *IEBM Encyclopedia of Marketing,* ed. M. J. Baker (London: International Thomson Business Press, 1999).

36. P. R. Lawrence and J. Lorsch, *Organization and Environment: Managing Differentiation and Integration* (Cambridge, MA: Harvard University Press, 1967).

37. See note 35.

38. See note 13, Capon, Farley, and Hulbert.

39. See, for example, N. F. Piercy and N. A. Morgan, "The Marketing Planning Process: Behavioral Problems Compared to Analytical Techniques in Explaining Marketing Planning Credibility," *Journal of Business Research,* 29 (March 1994), 167–178.

40. See, for example, N. F. Piercy and W. D. Giles, "The Logic of Being Illogical in Strategic Marketing Planning," *Journal of Services Marketing,* 29 (Summer 1990), 167–178.

41. Incidentally, there are nice ways of "demanding"—in one company we advised this simply meant a company policy that any plan going to the CEO had to start with a signed-off statement identifying the executives determined to make the plan "happen."

42. More detailed coverage of these approaches to energizing planning process can be found in N. F. Piercy, *Market-Led Strategic Change: A Guide to Transforming the Process of Going to Market* (Oxford, England: Butterworth-Heinemann, 2002).

43. See, for example, N. F. Piercy, "The Marketing Budgeting Process: Marketing Management Implications," *Journal of Marketing,* 52 (1988), 45–59.

44. V. P. Barabba and G. Zaltman, *Hearing the Voice of the Market* (Boston: Harvard Business School Press, 1991).

45. See note 24.

46. Now Baxter Healthcare.

47. See note 23, Peppers and Rogers.

48. R. W. Revans, *Developing Effective Managers: A New Approach to Business Education* (New York: Praeger, 1971).

49. See, for example, L. Fortini-Campbell, *Hitting the Sweet Spot* (Chicago: The Copy Workshop, 1992); and F. J. Gouillart and F. D. Sturdivant, "A Day in the Life of Your Customers," *Harvard Business Review,* 72 (January/February 1994), 116–125.

50. P. F. Drucker, "The Coming of the New Organization," *Harvard Business Review,* 76 (January/February 1998), 45–53.

51. J. B. Quinn, *Intelligent Enterprise* (New York: Free Press, 1992).

52. This observation is supported by implementation of Total Quality Management in many firms.

# PERMISSIONS

The authors gratefully acknowledge permission from the following sources to reprint material in their control:

"The Congruence Model" from *Competing by Design: The Power of Organizational Architecture* by David Nadler and Michael Tushman, copyright © 1997, Oxford University Press, Inc.

"A Model for Achieving Total Integrated Marketing" adapted from *European Management Journal,* Vol. 14, No. 1, 54.

"General Characteristics of Internal and External Orientations" adapted from *Planning Review,* May/June 1995, 11.

# INDEX